The food companions

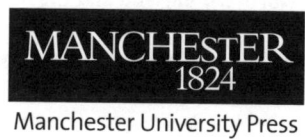

MANCHESTER
1824

Manchester University Press

STUDIES IN POPULAR CULTURE

General editor: Professor Jeffrey Richards

Already published in this series

The food companions
Cinema and consumption
in wartime Britain, 1939–45

RICHARD FARMER

Manchester University Press

Manchester and New York

distributed exclusively in the USA by Palgrave Macmillan

Published by Manchester University Press
Oxford Road, Manchester M13 9NR, UK
and Room 400, 175 Fifth Avenue, New York, NY 10010, USA
www.manchesteruniversitypress.co.uk

Distributed exclusively in the USA by
Palgrave Macmillan, 175 Fifth Avenue, New York,
NY 10010, USA

Distributed exclusively in Canada by
UBC Press, University of British Columbia, 2029 West Mall,
Vancouver, BC, Canada V6T 1Z2

British Library Cataloguing-in-Publication Data
A catalogue record for this book is available from the British Library

Library of Congress Cataloging-in-Publication Data applied for

ISBN 978 0 7190 8313 6 *hardback*

First published 2011

The publisher has no responsibility for the persistence or accuracy of URLs for any external or third-party internet websites referred to in this book, and does not guarantee that any content on such websites is, or will remain, accurate or appropriate.

Typeset in Adobe Garamond with Gill Sans display by
Koinonia, Manchester
Printed and bound by
CPI Group (UK) Ltd, Croydon, CR0 4YY

STUDIES IN
POPULAR
CULTURE

There has in recent years been an explosion of interest in culture and cultural studies. The impetus has come from two directions and out of two different traditions. On the one hand, cultural history has grown out of social history to become a distinct and identifiable school of historical investigation. On the other hand, cultural studies has grown out of English literature and has concerned itself to a large extent with contemporary issues. Nevertheless, there is a shared project, its aim, to elucidate the meanings and values implicit and explicit in the art, literature, learning, institutions and everyday behaviour within a given society. Both the cultural historian and the cultural studies scholar seek to explore the ways in which a culture is imagined, represented and received; how it interacts with social processes; how it contributes to individual and collective identities and world views, to stability and change, to social, political and economic activities and programmes. This series aims to provide an arena for the cross-fertilisation of the discipline, so that the work of the cultural historian can take advantage of the most useful and illuminating of the theoretical developments and the cultural studies scholars can extend the purely historical underpinnings of their investigations. The ultimate objective of the series is to provide a range of books which will explain in a readable and accessible way where we are now socially and culturally and how we got to where we are. This should enable people to be better informed, promote an interdisciplinary approach to cultural issues and encourage deeper thought about the issues, attitudes and institutions of popular culture.

Jeffrey Richards

For Olivia and Isaac

Contents

List of illustrations

Acknowledgements

This book began life as a PhD thesis and I would like to begin by thanking the three members of my supervisory team at the University of East Anglia: Charles Barr, Andrew Higson and Lawrence Napper. Each was a pleasure to work with, and each has in their different way offered inspiration and advice that has shaped the content and tone of this work. I must also express my gratitude to the Arts and Humanities Research Council for the doctoral award that made this project possible.

I would also like to thank the many people employed at the various libraries and archives that I have visited over the course of my research. Special mention should go to the British Film Institute where the staff of the library, the National Film Archive and the Special Collections department responded enthusiastically to what must have often seemed like most unusual requests, and to all at the History of Advertising Trust in Raveningham, Norfolk, who also granted me permission to quote from the *Official History of the Publicity Club of London*. The British Library (both the reading room at St Pancras and at the newspaper archive at Colindale) and the National Archives have proved invaluable to my research and provided me with stimulating environments in which to work. I have also made use of films and materials held by the Imperial War Museum, and would like to thank the staff there for their patience in answering my questions. The Woolton Papers are held at the Bodleian Library in Oxford, and I am grateful to the current Lord Woolton for permission to quote from them. Thanks are also due to BECTU for permission to access and use material contained in the Esther Harris interview. Parts of Chapter 3 were published, in different form, as 'Food fight! The cinema of consumption in wartime Britain', in *University of Sussex Journal of Contemporary History*, 12 (2008). Thanks are due to the editors for permission to reprint.

Images in the book are reproduced by permission of the Imperial War

Museum, Solo Syndication/Associated Newspapers Ltd., the British Cartoon Archive at the University of Kent, Paramount, Cambridge University Library, BFI Stills, ITV Studios Global Entertainment and Canal+ Image UK. They were funded in part by a grant from the Faculty of Arts and Humanities Dean's Fund at University College London.

It is important that I express my gratitude to my family, my colleagues and my friends. It hardly seems like a fair exchange that all they got in return for their kindness was a constant stream of references to Potato Pete and the Radio Doctor. I hope that acknowledging my debt to them goes some way to repaying it. I'm prepared to forget the balance if they are.

Finally, I would like to express my love and thanks to Olivia and Isaac, who inspired me when I needed motivating, but were even better at holding my attention when I needed distracting. This book is dedicated to them.

Note on sources

Ministry of Food press publicity, such as the Food Facts newspaper columns and other print advertising, are referred to throughout the book by number and date, for instance Food Facts No. 59, week of 15 September 1941, or MoF advertisement P. 28, week of 1 March 1943. Where no reference number exists in the original source document, the most significant line of text has been used, for example 'MoF advertisement "Reasons for Rationing", week of 8 January 1940'.

List of abbreviations

BBC   British Broadcasting Corporation
BFI   British Film Institute
BoT   Board of Trade
CEA   Cinematograph Exhibitors' Association
M-O   Mass-Observation
MoF   Ministry of Food
MoI   Ministry of Information
NCSS   National Council of Social Service
NSS   National Screen Service Ltd
PRD   Public Relations Division, Ministry of Food
TNA   The National Archives (formerly the Public Records Office)
USAAF United States Army Air Force

General editor's foreword

It was Napoleon Bonaparte who stressed the importance of food in wartime when he famously remarked: 'An army marches on its stomach.' But, as Richard Farmer demonstrates in this fascinating, ground-breaking book, the Home Front also marches on its stomach and food is a major factor in the maintenance of national morale. There remains a faint folk memory of ration books, snoek, Woolton Pie and 'Dig for Victory' campaigns, reinforced by endless television re-runs of series like *Dad's Army*. Farmer expertly establishes the context in which rationing was accepted by the majority of the British population as a necessary evil and the Ministry of Food, particularly under its popular minister, Lord Woolton, successfully promoted the policy. The Ministry used newspapers, posters, radio and cinema to disseminate information, its Food Facts newspaper advertisements, *Kitchen Front* radio broadcasts and *Food Flash* cinema shorts being notable successes. Woolton, himself, mastered the art of broadcasting, speaking directly, sincerely and confidentially in person to the public, persuading them of the truthfulness of the Ministry's wartime motto: 'We don't just cope. We care.'

The Ministry's communications strategy consisted of disseminating facts about rationing and food provision and messages aimed at changing behaviour, promoting the importance of a balanced, healthy diet and the benefits of particular foodstuffs and underlining the contribution of ordinary consumers to the war effort. Cinema, as 'the essential social habit of the age', was a primary means of achieving these objectives.

Farmer analyses the way in which the Ministry deployed popular comic performers to get their messages over. Elsie and Doris Waters, in their cockney characters Gert and Daisy, starred in a series of radio broadcasts *Feed the Brute*, Mabel Constanduros, the lovably cantankerous 'Grandma Buggins', on radio, stage and film, featured in the *Kitchen Front* broadcasts, and Tommy Trinder promoted the attractions of the newly established subsidised canteens known as 'British Restaurants' in the Ministry of Information short *Eating Out With Tommy Trinder*.

After examining the Ministry's policies and practices in detail, Farmer takes up three themes and pursues them through close readings of key films. He looks at the role of food and eating in reinforcing the wartime ethic of communal identity and community solidarity in the war effort, particularly in the prominence accorded to the role of canteens and messes in films like *Millions Like Us* and *Listen to Britain*. This is contrasted with the escapism of conspicuous consumption in past eras, in the Gainsborough melodramas such as *Madonna of the Seven Moons* and *The Wicked Lady* which provided a release from austerity in the latter part of the war.

He gives a systematic account of the depiction of the black market in a succession of low-budget films, *Gert and Daisy Clean Up*, *Old Mother Riley, Detective* and *Up With the Lark* (with Ethel Revnell and Gracie West), in which working-class female protagonists are given the task of catching the black marketeers whose activities are depicted as an offence against basic British fairness as well as against the law. Finally, Farmer explores the symbolism of tea and tea drinking as a symbol of national identity and an expression of allied solidarity, with the Americans (*The Way to the Stars*) and the Russians (*The Demi-Paradise*). Abundantly illustrated with advertisements, cartoons and film stills, *The Food Companions* is an engaging, intriguing and consistently readable exploration of a neglected aspect of wartime propaganda.

Jeffrey Richards

Introduction:
this is a film about food!

In 2001, a family of twenty-first-century Britons were asked by the producers of *The 1940s House*, a televised recreation of life in the Second World War, to survive on the restricted diet allowed by rationing. The family stuck to the task with some reluctance and achieved it only with considerable difficulty. That this particular aspect of the historical reconstruction proved so problematic for a modern family is testament not only to the varied, cheap and plentiful foodstuffs available in the United Kingdom at the start of this century, but also to the challenges faced by British consumers during the war – challenges which ensured that food became a vital element of British wartime life and culture.

The documentary *World of Plenty* (1943) is forthright in its recognition that consumption is an issue of essential importance within the human experience, insisting that 'without food men die, even if all the banks are filled with gold'. We might equally say that without food individuals or nations cannot fight. Between 1939 and 1945, the British public was encouraged to recognise the connection that existed between food and the war, and one radio broadcast by Lord Woolton, Minister of Food between April 1940 and November 1943, described food as bringing 'the *reek of battle* into your kitchens'.[1]

A direct link was forged between the Ministry of Food (MoF), the food it distributed, British consumers and the war effort. Indeed, so central was the Ministry's work that one MP could insist that 'Next to the Fighting Forces the Ministry of Food will play the most important part in the war.'[2] Food was militarised for the duration: British-grown vegetables became the 'home-guards of health' (and were shown, anthropomorphised, with rifles and steel helmets); cake was 'put into battledress'; and cooks and shoppers became the army of the Kitchen Front – a fighting force as crucial to the nation's prospects as the men in uniform.[3] This army was encouraged to acknowledge its contribution and obligations to the war so that food might be 'conserved as ammunition is in a beleaguered city'.[4] Such martial terminology encouraged consumers to understand food in the context of the conflict, as a vital component of Britain's fight, as, in the words of the a long-running slogan, 'a munition of war'.[5]

Indeed, at the height of the 'Phoney War', rationing, which was introduced in January 1940, was one of the few signs that the country was actually at war. As Mass-Observation (M-O) diarist Olivia Cockett noted, the war had not been 'the ever-present horror which in the past I dreaded having to face'. It had, though, been the cause of numerous 'slight discomforts', one of which was increased concern about food.[6] Later, in parts of the country that had not been subjected to the Blitz, food brought consumers into contact with the war. One land girl wrote that in Dorset 'we should certainly not know there was a war on if it was not for the fact that we have our butter on separate dishes with our names stuck on with stamp paper and our jam in jars likewise'.[7]

Food was of critical physical and psychological importance, and would remain so 'for the duration'. Food has an absolute physical utility that can be understood in terms of its nutritional value and its ability to sustain the body. The relationship between food-as-physical-product and morale – especially in terms of the maintenance of social order – has been discussed elsewhere, most notably in works by Ina Zweiniger-Bargielowska and Robert Mackay.[8] However, food also has an ideological or psychological value which, though much harder to identify and quantify, is no less important. While we might understand this in terms of the faith that the maintenance of a regularised food supply allowed the British population to have in the government, it extends beyond that.

As Mary Douglas and Baron Isherwood suggest in *The World of Goods*, consumption choices make 'visible statements about the hierarchy of values to which their chooser subscribes. Goods can be cherished or judged inappropriate, discarded, and replaced.' Products do not exist in a solely physical sense, but are associated with particular ideas and concerns that are inextricably linked to conceptions of an individual's relationship to other individuals, and also to their position within society. Attitudes about consumption therefore become a 'vital source of the culture of the moment'.[9] But, we might add, *specifically* of that moment, whenever that might be, for the meanings ascribed to goods, products and services are temporally specific, transformed by the transition between one historical instant and the next.

Anthropologists often point to the role that food plays in the construction of self, at both a personal and national level, pointing out that consumption is very closely associated with the different senses of identity that assist in the formulation of both the individual and the group. In an influential article, Claude Fischler observed, 'The way a human group eats helps it assert its diversity, hierarchy and organisation, and at the same time, both its oneness and the otherness of whoever eats differently.' He continued:

> [Ideas about food] are part of the fundamental bond between the self and the world, the individual and society, microcosm and macrocosm. It is clear ... that culinary systems play a part in giving a meaning to man and the universe, by structuring them in relation to each other in an overall continuity and contiguity.[10]

As our bodies are constructed by the food we ingest, so are our identities constructed by the ideas we hold about the foods we consume; we are, both literally and figuratively, what we eat.

Following the introduction of rationing, ideas concerning food, nutrition and taste were mediated by the government. Although predominantly intended to ensure equal distribution of limited foodstuffs, food control also bound the nation together through shared experience. Diet became a function of the state, an integral element of the national experience of the war that had recognisable impacts at a personal and a familial level. One consequence of such a regimented gastronomic situation was that Britons came to construct their identity in part through reference to the link that existed between the individual-as-consumer and the state-as-provider: eating the rationed diet made one British, and one could demonstrate one's Britishness by living according to the sumptuary laws established by rationing. The mythical common diet became the basis for a secular communion, a gastronomic expression of the nation's coherence and identity.

Rationing therefore helped to establish Britain as a 'food-based community', a national group defined in part by its shared consumption patterns and rituals. Robert Boothby, Parliamentary Secretary to the Ministry of Food, described his hope that during the war 'comradeship in matters of food – a sort of community of "food companions" might grow'.[11] Boothby's phrase, which he used on more than one occasion, plays on the title of J. B. Priestley's *The Good Companions* – popular as a novel, a stage play and in 1933 as a feature film – and so situates his own food companions in the cultural mainstream.[12] By producing a uniform diet at the national level, by publicising such a diet in the mass media and by promoting the use of factory canteens and state-administered British Restaurants, the government established a communalist gastronomic paradigm, which used food's association with mutuality, collectivity and consensus to integrate the private individual into the public body-corporate. The government's decision to construct and address wartime consumers in this communal manner was not entirely unproblematic, however. For not only did comprehensive state control on occasion attract criticism during a fight against totalitarian regimes, it also risked alienating individuals who agreed with the general objectives of the state but disagreed with particularly harsh restrictions.

Food policy and food-related propaganda were part of a much wider public discourse concerning the wartime experience and the nature of the relationship between the individual and the state in a period of national crisis. Indeed, fear of the public's reaction to bad news about food led politicians to tread carefully when it came to making announcements that they thought might be unpopular. In early 1941, for example, Woolton was, according to *The Economist*, nearly 'indicted in some quarters for [spreading] "alarm and despondency"'. His crime was to tell the House of Lords that he was 'deeply concerned' about the food situation.[13] Winston Churchill was adamant that such statements, and others like them, were 'much to be deprecated', especially because of the effect that they would have on the morale of British consumers 'when repeated, as they no doubt will be, upon the enemy radio'.[14]

The British public, however, was also acutely sensitive to the implications of food information issued by domestic broadcasters. Not long before rationing was introduced, the promotion of vegetables on the BBC prompted one listener to turn to his parents and say: 'I don't like to suggest it, but it looks as if the Government's scared ... They think we won't be able to get enough food across with all these boats sunk.'[15] It is clear, then, that the ways in which food information was presented to the public was of paramount importance as the British nation attempted to understand the war. It is also clear that the government could not always control the way in which the information it issued was interpreted by the public.

Representations of food in wartime culture in general, and in film, the main concern of this book, in particular, need to be understood as products of a 'food-conscious' country in an especially food-conscious period.[16] Rationing, food control, shortages, coupons, points, queues and the much-maligned snoek (and other gastronomic novelties) combined to make food, always materially important, culturally and psychologically paramount. Images of consumption are not inert; food in wartime cinema is never simply a passive element of the *mise-en-scène*. Rather, its presence – and, sometimes as interestingly, its absence – is vital, alive, linked to a complex web of meanings and ideas concerning consumptional realities at the time of production and reception. Rationing was a cultural as well as a material phenomenon; the MoF's ubiquity in British popular culture – on the radio, in newspapers and magazines, in the cinemas

– made it one of Britain's most prominent propagandists during the war, and patrons' experiences as consumers of particular films were conditioned by their changing perceptions as consumers of food within a tightly regulated social environment.

Consequently, the bold declamation heard at the start of *World of Plenty*, 'This is a film about food', is also true, to a degree, of many films made in wartime Britain, for all films released in Britain during the war were not only products of, but were also screened in, Woolton's food-conscious nation. Although *World of Plenty* was unusual in adopting food as a dominant theme, it was not alone in using food – such an integral and intimate part of the individual's understanding of the war – to explore a very particular set of economic, material, social and historical realities.

To borrow the courage of *World of Plenty*'s convictions, I can state my own intentions in a similarly bold and simple way: this is a book about film and food. Or, to elaborate slightly, a book that looks at some of the different ways in which food was used in both propaganda and commercial films – and, where appropriate, other media – to explore, construct and contest the national and individual experience of the war. Despite continued interest in the war, an expanding catalogue of work dealing with British cinema history and the increased interest in food demonstrated by certain sections of British society in recent years, little work has been produced which investigates how the crucially significant issue of food in wartime was treated in the films of the period.

Filmmakers certainly recognised the cultural importance of food, understanding its ability to represent a consensual, communal national identity as well as its capacity to explore the illicit, sensual appeal of self-indulgence arising from the tensions generated by rationing and regulated consumption. It is evident that food had no single 'meaning' in wartime cinema, and that different films mobilised different aspects of food control and different attitudes to rationing to promote different agendas. Rather than undermine claims about the importance of consumption in wartime culture, the diversity of approaches to food adopted by wartime filmmakers reflects contemporary recognition of the complexity and vitality of the issues surrounding the position of the MoF, and of food more generally, in wartime Britain.

The Ministry of Food

The MoF, initially under the control of William S. Morrison, came into being on 8 September 1939, five days after the declaration of war.[17] Months of planning meant that the administrative machinery required to run the Ministry was already in place. Such pre-planning resulted from the knowledge that Britain's dependence on imported food would make its diet vulnerable to U-boat attack. The idea that international conflict might bring starvation resulted in the public welcoming government initiatives: in 1918, food control had only been introduced as a response to severe shortages. However, even if they were unable to sink enough merchant ships to starve Britain into surrender, there were concerns that the German submarines might provoke social unrest if they succeeded in restricting trade in basic foodstuffs.

By November 1939, the amount of food imported into the country had fallen by a third, and as the war progressed this figure declined yet further.[18] Under such circumstances, the government was keen to stress that the hardships of war would be borne equally by all sections of British society. Morrison, speaking in November 1939, made this quite explicit: '[The purpose of rationing] is to secure that if we should have to go short of any particular article of food for a time, everyone in the island will get an equal share of what is available, rich and poor alike.'[19] While it would be misleading to suggest that rationing succeeded in ensuring absolute equality in terms of access to foodstuffs, the system, through its insistence on uniformity and impartiality, allowed the *idea* of a common diet to gain cultural currency.

The MoF became solely responsible for the purchase and importation of food, as well as the regulation of prices and the distribution of foodstuffs within the United Kingdom. Although it had the power to compel, in the early months of the war, the MoF asked Britons to voluntarily reduce their consumption of imported foodstuffs such as sugar. When such appeals failed to produce the desired effect, and with food shortages a very real possibility, formal rationing was implemented. In January 1940 the government announced that bacon, butter and sugar were to be rationed, with each British citizen guaranteed a specific amount per person, per week, redeemable against coupons in their ration book. To be included in this 'basic' system, a product had to be considered 'essential ... to maintain the life of the country'.[20] Meat, cheese and tea were soon added to the list of rationed foods. Fish, vegetables and bread were never rationed; they were considered such staples that regulating sales might be taken as an admission of failure by the MoF. Alcohol, too, escaped inclusion in the system, much to the annoyance of temperance campaigners.

Although rationing was intended to promote uniformity, communality and shared sacrifice, the MoF was concerned that too great a restriction of individuality might be counterproductive and hand a propaganda victory to the Germans.[21] It was decided that a system was needed which allowed for equality of access to foodstuffs while preserving an element of choice, which was seen as crucial in a democracy. Woolton would later write:

> We are a nation of individualists, and our strength lies in persistent determina-tion not to sacrifice that individuality. Taste, individual taste, is worth preserving and cultivating; it adds to the joy of living and flavours existence.[22]

Personal choice was one of the freedoms considered important enough to enshrine within the rationing system, allowing British consumers to maintain a sense of individuality, and ensuring that food remained, theoretically at least, something that consumers might take pleasure in. In an interview with J. B. Priestley, Woolton outlined the Ministry's position:

> After all, this food question is not simply a matter of eating what will sustain us. There are psychological factors. We want to *enjoy* our food. And that enjoyment – by way of more variety – is what I'm aiming at now.[23]

The result of all this concern for the individual, and of the MoF's realisation that food had both a material and an ideological power, was points rationing. Introduced in December 1941, the system allowed Britons to spend a personal allocation of points on whichever of the goods included in the scheme they chose. It was, as far as any rationing system could be, a popular scheme. Part of its appeal lay in the variety it afforded consumers; part in the renewed sense of individuality it permitted shoppers. M-O diarist Pam Ashford concurred:

> If all the psychologists in the Kingdom had been given the job of devising a way of keeping the women folk from worrying about the war, they could never have devised anything that would do so more effectively than Lord Woolton and his points.[24]

Such phrases should also make clear the fact that food was understood in gender-specific terms: cooking and shopping – the most important and time-consuming elements of the domestic food routine – were understood to be important elements of a woman's life. Men, for their part, needed food in order to work or fight. Woolton believed that the element of choice that the points system reintroduced 'gave [women] a little pleasure in their harassed lives and an exercise in their natural skill'.[25]

Food preparation was such an integral element of contemporary construc-tions of femininity that much of the MoF's propaganda adopted a gendered address. However, during the war ideas of what terms such as 'feminine' and 'masculine' might mean underwent real, rapid and, to some, uncomfortable changes. The Ministry's propaganda therefore needed to carefully negotiate the shifting minefields of cultural, sexual and gastronomic politics. On the whole, the MoF continued to assume that those who would be most interested in the propaganda it issued would be women. It did, though, make a number of concessions to the realities of wartime life. Most important among these were the recognition that an increased number of women were working outside as well as inside the home, that the certainties of pre-war domestic life were liable to be upset by wartime change, and, in a few instances, that men were learning to feed themselves. While much MoF propaganda continued to understand the role of women through reference to the work that they did in the domestic sphere, the importance of food in wartime culture and life meant that this propaganda also worked to integrate women into the national struggle, as active participants in the war.

Economy measures resulted in the disappearance of many of the basic luxuries of peacetime living. Shortages of sugar led iced cakes to be banned – an action which led to many a couple being photographed preparing to cut a cardboard wedding cake – and only twenty of the 350 varieties of biscuit available to British consumers in September 1939 were permitted to remain in production.[26] However, further reductions in sugar consumption proved necessary: Personal Points were introduced in July 1942 in order to ration chocolate and confectionery, while ice-cream manufacture was prohibited in September 1942. Both regulations can be understood to have been of special concern to the managers and patrons of British cinemas.

The Ministry was, however, careful not to overextend its reach:

> There are those who attach so much importance to equitable distribution that they advocate a large extension of the list of commodities now rationed. [The MoF does] not share this view. Rationing is a rigid, arithmetical and somewhat inhuman way of allocating the food of individuals. It takes no account of individual tastes.[27]

Woolton was loath to get into arguments with Parliament over the niceties of rationing. Regarding himself as a businessman and his department as a non-political organisation, he attempted to keep the legislature at arm's length, protecting the MoF's reputation by refusing to propose the restriction of commodities such as alcohol, which he knew that Parliament would never agree to ration.[28]

Rationing was accepted by the majority of the British public as a necessary evil. In February 1942, a survey found nobody willing to admit to a government pollster any dissatisfaction with the principles on which the system was founded, while in late 1943 rationing still enjoyed a 90 per cent approval rating.[29] However, it should be remembered that the black market, although perhaps not as well-developed as in other countries, was a significant enough threat to the principle of rationing for the government to come down hard on offenders. Even so, some Britons were prepared to enter into what in *World of Plenty* Woolton described as 'black bargains' – proof that adherence to rationing had its limits, especially in the latter years of the war.

Woolton and his immediate successor, John 'J. J.' Llewellin (in office between November 1943 and July 1945) were members of a coalition government facing down a very real external threat and, as such, were not obliged to tailor their policies to the vicissitudes of the ballot box. In contrast, the post-war Labour Ministers of Food, Ben Smith (August 1945–May 1946), John Strachey (May 1946–February 1950) and Maurice Webb (February 1950–October 1951), and their Conservative successor Gwilym Lloyd George (October 1951–October 1954), had to deal not only with popular discontent but also with more frequent political attacks.

A near-bankrupt Britain could not afford finally to halt rationing until 1954, and the post-war continuation of parts of the system drew frequent criticism, especially after the return of party politics and the election of the Attlee government. The MoF recognised these changes: 'with [the wartime] coalition Government … there was no political focus for discontent. Public opinion was not influenced by politically inspired attacks on controls.'[30] As attitudes to rationing soured in the post-war Age of Austerity, the MoF came under increasing pressure to justify its continued role as food administrator.

The cinema in wartime Britain

The importance placed on food publicity meant that, during the war, the MoF was keen to embrace cinema, an institution that A. J. P. Taylor has described as 'the essential social habit of the age'.[31] Although Taylor's writing on the cinema is brief, it is important in that it recognises the medium's position at the heart of British leisure culture. Following a gradual increase in the years before the war, cinema attendance rose by some 60 per cent between 1939 and 1945, eventually peaking in 1946 when more than 1.6 billion tickets were sold, the equivalent of approximately 30 million paid admissions each week.[32] By the late 1930s, box-office receipts accounted for some five-eighths of Britain's total leisure expenditure,[33] a figure surely related to the sheer number of venues showing films: in 1937 there were very nearly 5,000 cinemas in Britain, with the equivalent of one cinema seat for every twelve Britons.[34]

Although the degree of influence the cinema was able to exert can be disputed, and although such influence was not always viewed positively (especially in regard to the popularity of American films), the government was, nonetheless, keen to use film's communicative power to publicise its aims and its work. Having invested in the commercially successful feature *49th Parallel* (1941), the Ministry of Information (MoI) was discouraged by Parliament from direct investment in further commercial film ventures, meaning that for the remainder of the war the state's most frequent filmic contributions were the thousands of short publicity and documentary films commissioned by the MoI and other government departments such as the MoF.[35] Taken as a whole, government-sponsored short films advocated the benefits of consensus, community, stoicism, and recognition and acceptance of the state's right to intervene in everyday life. The state was also involved in the production of longer documentaries such as *Desert Victory* (1943) and *Fires Were Started* (1943), a select few of which were released commercially, with varying degrees of success.

While the government remained involved in the production of documentaries of varying lengths, it came to view commercial feature films as an ideal medium for the dissemination of political, cultural or ideological material:

> The film being a popular medium must be good entertainment if it is to be good propaganda. A film which induces boredom antagonises the audience to the cause which it advocates. For this reason an amusing American film with a few hits at the Nazi regime is probably better propaganda than any number of documentaries showing the making of bullets, etc.[36]

The government's ability and/or desire to interfere with the work of commercial filmmakers is still a matter of some debate. The furore surrounding the (not entirely positive) representations of the British military in *The Life and Death of Colonel Blimp* (1943) – 'the film that Churchill tried to ban' – is notable because it was so unusual.[37] On the one hand, the government's involvement in such a potentially damaging row, combined with the Board of Trade's control of film stock and the submission of scripts to the MoI, would suggest that the state was a willing participant when it came to determining the content of British feature films during the war. On the other hand, the state's eventual capitulation in allowing *Blimp* to be released and, after a short delay, distributed overseas, demonstrates the limitations of its powers and also its desire not to be perceived as acting in an authoritarian manner. While the paucity of other causes célèbres in the field of wartime film censorship might be viewed as arising from either the timidity of an industry unwilling to challenge the power of the state or the effectiveness of censorship procedures enforced during pre-production, it seems most likely that there was broad agreement between filmmakers and the government on the matter of what were considered suitable or desirable themes, meaning that most films would have contained little to arouse the censors' ire.

Indeed, a good number of films contained only nominal or oblique references to the war, or used the conflict as a topical backdrop for otherwise generic plots. Others attempted to ignore the conflict altogether. After an uncertain start to the war marred by financial uncertainty and the requisition of several studios, British producers and directors began to find bigger audiences for their films, often on the back of an increasingly positive critical reception. The increased prominence of the documentary movement in government-sponsored shorts 'played a part in creating [a] taste for films of fact', which, in turn, influenced some commercial producers and prompted talk of the development of a distinctly British style which infused commercial cinema with documentary techniques.[38] Films made in this 'documentary realist' style tended to favour restrained emotional portrayals and often focused, in Andrew Higson's phrase, on 'the melodrama of everyday life'.[39]

For all the critical praise heaped on the documentary realists' 'authentic' representations of wartime Britain by certain sections of the media – praise which sometimes (although by no means always) translated into ticket sales – the majority of films produced in Britain between 1939 and 1945 fall outside this cinematic tradition. British cinema during the war was far from monolithic, but instead drew on a variety of generic and cultural sources to produce an industry composed of sometimes complementary, sometimes competing, commercial and aesthetic strands.

However, the critical elite was apt to decry unashamedly commercial features as derivative, trivial and lurid. Dilys Powell of the *Sunday Times* dismissed such films as 'inferior' and declared them to be 'undeserving of the popular success they have won'.[40] It is evident, then, that critical discourse concerning British cinema was often out of step with the attitudes of British cinema-goers. A small canon of 'quality' films privileged ideas of authenticity, restraint and sobriety, but these were not necessarily the films that patrons paid to see.[41] The box-office success of George Formby's comedies, Gainsborough's melodramas and the numerous thrillers and musicals screened each year point to the diversity of entertainment styles available to, and enjoyed by, British cinema-goers.[42] Furthermore, Hollywood films continued to be extraordinarily popular.

The momentous societal, political, economic and artistic developments which occurred in Britain during the war make the period fertile academic ground. In terms of cinematic propaganda, perhaps the most comprehensive account of the relationship between cinema and the state is contained in James Chapman's *The British at War*, which analyses the work of the MoI's Films Division and acknowledges an able and enthusiastic cinematic publicist.[43] This element of the MoI's work had been left unrecognised by Ian McLaine's earlier *Ministry of Morale*.[44] However, the interest in the MoI, understandable though it is, has left other government departments somewhat in the shade. For while the MoI was undoubtedly the most significant government propagandist, other ministries were also eager to use the mass media to communicate with the British public. The National Savings Committee, for example, spent vast sums attempting to persuade Britons to invest in government bonds. Its work remains under-researched. Similarly, the MoF has received scant attention for the work it commissioned and issued, despite the Ministry's official historian calling in 1951 for a 'specialist monograph' to be prepared on MoF propaganda: 'its importance would be difficult to overstate'.[45]

Indeed, although the Ministry of Food has been the focus of work by many scholars, most have adopted a purely economic or administrative standpoint, investigating the mechanics of the rationing system while marginalising the publicity the Ministry issued to promote food control. R. J. Hammond's official history, published in three volumes between 1951 and 1962, focuses in the main on the administrative function of the MoF. This meticulously researched account acknowledges the scope of the Ministry's public relations campaign, but explores it only in passing.[46] More recently, Ina Zweiniger-Bargielowska has furthered our understanding of both rationing policy and public attitudes towards food control, especially in terms of the extent and limits of consumer approval, but devotes little space to the details of the MoF's publicity campaigns. Instead, she concentrates on public attitudes towards rationing, paying less attention to the extensive publicity campaigns orchestrated by the MoF that did so much to shape and mediate such attitudes.[47]

Much of the work focusing on food in film revolves around commercial features that adopt food as a dominant narrative concern and a recognisable aesthetic feature: *Babette's Feast* (1987), *Eat Drink Man Woman* (1994), *Like Water for Chocolate* (1992), *The Cook, the Thief, his Wife and her Lover* (1989) and *Big Night* (1996) have all received attention. Such films, sometimes grouped together as 'food porn', often focus on the sensual elements of consumption by presenting food in a highly stylised way, with lengthy and beautifully-lit sequences of food preparation, or carefully composed shots of plates of food or dining tables. In August 1998, the National Film Theatre in London screened a season of what it called 'foodie films'. The title of this season, 'A Feast for the Eyes', points to the dominance of the alimentary aesthetic within these films and suggests the important role that visual gastronomic motifs play in our understanding and enjoyment of them.[48] However, it would be short-sighted to suggest that only those films that deploy food in so obvious a manner are worthy of our attention. Because food operates in different ways, to understand how films take advantage of this multiplicity of meanings it is vital to look both at and beyond the image.

Recent work by Jane F. Ferry and an edited collection by Anne L. Bower,[49] and more general accounts by Gaye Poole and Steve Zimmerman and Ken Weiss, suggest that interest in this field is growing.[50] Although these works, and others like them, adopt a variety of approaches and look at films from a wide range of different cultures and eras, they tend to start from an understanding that very rarely is food *just* food: so important a role does it play in the construction of identity, for recently arrived migrants and established communities, for individuals in periods of personal or social upheaval, that it can be used as a signifier within a number of cultural, sexual, political and historical frameworks.[51] As such, this work also makes clear that context is crucial if we are to understand the ways in which food operates within different texts. The meanings that consumers apply to specific foods are culturally and historically contingent; the job of the film scholar is to attempt to locate culinary practices, so important as landmarks on the constructed mental geographies that individuals use to position themselves within particular cultures, and within their particular realities.

Because filmic texts operate within society rather than independently of it, it is necessary to contextualise and interrogate films in terms of their position, meaning and reception within the specific realities of a particular historical or social moment, especially if we hope to discern how they might have been understood by contemporary cinema-goers. While some recent work has started to rectify the previous marginalisation of the patron,[52] the relative paucity of primary evidence left by contemporary cinema-goers has meant that the writings of the film critics of the time have maintained an important position within film history. To move beyond the obvious limitations of the discourse established by the 1940s critics, contemporary documentation is vital. The National Archives (formerly the Public Record Office) is a mine of information, particularly in relation to government actions and attitudes, but also for papers dealing with the production and purpose of MoF publicity. Much of the material relating to government interaction with feature-film makers has been either lost or destroyed, however, so that supplementary sources take on greater significance. Contemporary newspapers, fan magazines and trade journals (for both cinema exhibitors and other, food-related industries) fill in some of these blanks. Other useful sources include the British Film Institute's Special Collections department, which holds many papers relevant to those sections of the project which deal with commercial feature films and the exhibition industry. The National Film and Television Archive contains many rarities that allow for a more complete understanding of British cinematic history. The Mass-Observation project encouraged Britons to record their thoughts about, and perceptions of, life in wartime; where appropriate I have used diary entries to suggest how MoF propaganda and commercial films were received by the public.

The book is composed of five chapters which, by addressing different themes and adopting different approaches, demonstrate the diversity of issues and material which inform analysis of the inter-relationship of food and cinema during the war. Although the majority of this work focuses on the years 1939 to 1945, the continuation of rationing in the decade after VJ Day meant that while food was a munition of war, the armistice did not lead to its immediate demobilisation. Consequently, some chapters also investigate the immediate post-war period, looking in particular at popular frustrations that attended the continuation of rationing in the age of austerity.

The first two chapters analyse the MoF's publicity work. Chapter 1 explores the MoF's position as publicist, demonstrating the effort expended by the Ministry in its attempts to establish food and consumption as prominent elements of wartime culture. Chapter 2 provides both a production history and textual analysis of the *Food Flash* films commissioned by the MoF and screened weekly in thousands of cinemas throughout Britain.

The final three chapters deal with some key thematic representations of food and consumption evident in wartime films, looking at some of the ways in which food was used by both government and commercial filmmakers. Although few, if any, commercial features adopted food as a primary narrative device, numerous films took advantage of food's special significance in wartime to communicate information and nuance meaning. Most significantly, food was used to explore issues of communality and individuality, and their relative values in wartime.

Chapter 3 investigates competing representations of consumption, positioning contemporaneously set films which used food as a site of community in opposition to examples of costume/period films from the later years of the war, which used it to celebrate the sensual pleasures available to the individual. Food's position as a communal signifier is also the focus of Chapter 4, which deals with the ways in which the illegal food transactions of the black market were represented in a series of wartime films. Chapter 5 charts the use of stereotypically British foodstuffs, most importantly tea, in films which sought to locate Britain in relation to its allies, most importantly the USA and the USSR, and its enemies.

The food-based community was a temporary construct able to resist most of the rigorous challenges arising from the war, but less well-equipped to solve the very different problems faced during the peace that followed. Food was used to communicate an idea of Britain to the people of the islands – for, as the narrator of *World of Plenty* asserted:

> Proper planning, rationing, [and] distribution of food according to need, not riches, can raise and sustain a nation on a level of healthy, willing, unforced, unyielding, but almost unnoticeable endurance. That is the mood of inevitable victory!

During the war food played a significant role in the material strengthening of British resolve. The pages that follow demonstrate that representations of food in wartime cinema had a similarly important cultural and social function.

Notes

1 Bodleian Library, Oxford: Woolton Papers (hereafter MS Woolton) 13: *Postscript*, 2 August 1942. Emphasis in original.

2 Hubert Beaumont, 18 July 1940. *Parliamentary Debates: House of Commons*, 5th Series, vol. 363, col. 527.

3 MoF Advertisement S. 40, July 1940; *Ministry of Food Bulletin*, No. 230, 18 February 1944, p. 1. See Food Facts No. 125, week of 23 November 1942, in which a soldier and a housewife shake hands, and each adopts a deferential posture in honour of the other's contribution.

4 Food Facts No. 59, week of 15 September 1941

5 The National Archives (hereafter TNA) MAF 102/53: Transcript of Lord Woolton's speech at the Queen's Hall, 5 April 1940.

6 Diary entry, February 1940, in Robert Malcolmson (ed.), *Love and War in London: A Woman's Diary, 1939–1942* (Stroud: History Press, 2008), p. 63.

7 Unnamed M-O diarist, 19 April 1941, in Angus Calder and Dorothy Sheridan

(eds), *Speak for Yourself: A Mass-Observation Anthology, 1937–49* (London: Jonathan Cape, 1984), p. 169.

8 Ina Zweiniger-Bargielowska, *Austerity in Britain: Rationing, Controls, and Consumption, 1939–1955* (Oxford: Oxford University Press, 2000); Robert Mackay, *Half the Battle: Civilian Morale in Britain During the Second World War* (Manchester: Manchester University Press, 2002), pp. 196–202.

9 Mary Douglas and Baron Isherwood, *The World of Goods: Towards an Anthropology of Consumption* (London: Allen Lane, 1979), pp. 5, 57.

10 Claude Fischler, 'Food, self and identity', *Social Science Information*, 27:2 (1988), pp. 275, 281.

11 Robert Boothby quoted in *Manchester Guardian*, 21 September 1940, p. 9.

12 For example, see reports of a different speech in *Daily Mirror*, 25 September 1940, p. 2.

13 *The Economist*, 1 March 1941, p. 265.

14 Memo from Churchill to Woolton, 25 February 1941. Martin Gilbert (ed.), *The Churchill War Papers: Vol. 3 – The Ever-Widening War, 1941* (London: Heinemann, 2000), pp. 265–6.

15 Christopher Tomlin, diary entry, 1 January 1940, in Simon Garfield (ed.), *We are at War: The Remarkable Diaries of Five Ordinary People in Extraordinary Times* (London: Ebury Press, 2005), p. 142.

16 Woolton in *Daily Express*, 9 July 1940, p. 1.

17 Rationing systems for non-food goods were also implemented: cosmetics and clothing schemes were administered by the Board of Trade; petrol was rationed by the Ministry of Fuel and Power.

18 Alan F. Wilt, *Food for War: Agriculture and Rearmament in Britain Before the Second World War* (Oxford: Oxford University Press, 2001), p. 194.

19 TNA INF 1/343: Broadcast on the Empire Programme, 'Food Supplies in Wartime', 15 November 1939.

20 Lord Woolton, 22 April 1941. *Parliamentary Debates: House of Lords*, 5th Series, vol. 119, col. 21.

21 Concerns about how German propagandists might react to British food control were evident in discussions about how to implement and publicise the initial rationing system. See TNA INF 1/343: Memo from Mr Bevan to Mr Hope-Jones, 16 December 1939.

22 Lord Woolton, 'Introduction', in The Tea Centre, *Tea on Service* (London: Graham Watson, 1947), pp. 75–6.

23 *Picture Post*, 12 July 1941, p. 27.

24 Diary entry, 18 April 1942, in Simon Garfield (ed.), *Private Battles: How the War Almost Defeated Us* (London: Ebury Press, 2006), p. 239.

25 Lord Woolton, *The Memoirs of the Rt. Hon. The Earl of Woolton* (London: Cassell, 1959), p. 212.

26 Norman Longmate, *How We Lived Then: A History of Everyday Life During the Second World War* (London: Hutchinson, 1971), p. 148. Total biscuit production was also dramatically reduced, with the MoF planning to reduce output by some 50 per cent in the year to May 1943. *Ministry of Food Bulletin*, No. 189, 7 May 1943, p. 1.

27 Robert Boothby, 18 July 1940. *Parliamentary Debates: Commons*, 5th Series, vol. 363, col. 451.

28 Lord Woolton, 10 June 1941. *Parliamentary Debates: Lords*, 5th Series, vol. 119, col. 359.

29 TNA RG 23/9a: Gertrude Wagner, 'Food During the War: A Summary of Studies on the subject of Food made by the Wartime Social Survey between February 1942 and October 1943', pp. 2, 3.

30 TNA MAF 75/67: 'General Account of the Work of Public Relations Division, 1939–50', p. 10.

31 A. J. P. Taylor, *English History, 1914–1945* (Harmondsworth: Pelican, 1970), p. 392.

32 H. E. Browning and A. A. Sorrell, 'Cinemas and cinemagoing in Great Britain', *Journal of the Royal Statistical Society*, 117:2 (1954), p. 134.

33 Jeffrey Richards, 'Cinemagoing in Worktown: regional film audiences in 1930s Britain', *Historical Journal of Film, Radio and Television*, 14:2 (1994), p. 147.

34 Central Statistical Office, *Annual Abstract of Statistics, No. 84: 1935–46* (London: HMSO, 1948), p. 72; Linda Wood (ed.), *British Films, 1927–1939* (London: BFI, 1986), p. 120.

35 James Chapman, *The British at War: Cinema, State and Propaganda* (London: I. B. Tauris, 1998), p. 86.

36 'Programme for Film Propaganda' (MoI, January 1940?) in Ian Christie (ed.), *Powell, Pressburger and Others* (London: BFI, 1978), p. 124.

37 James Chapman, '*The Life and Death of Colonel Blimp* (1943) reconsidered', *Historical Journal of Film, Radio and Television*, 15:1 (1995).

38 *The Times*, 2 June 1943, p. 5.

39 Andrew Higson, *Waving the Flag: Constructing a National Cinema in Britain* (Oxford: Clarendon Press, 1995), p. 176.

40 Dilys Powell, 'Films since 1939', in Arnold L. Haskell, Dilys Powell, Rollo Myers and Robin Ironside, *Since 1939: Ballet, Films, Music, Painting* (London: Phoenix House, 1948), p. 91.

41 Roger Manvell discusses the concept of 'poetic realism' in *The Film and the Public* (Harmondsworth: Penguin, 1955), pp. 90–5. See also John Ellis, 'The quality film adventure: British critics and the cinema, 1942–48', in Andrew Higson (ed.), *Dissolving Views: Key Writings on British Cinema* (London: Cassell, 1996).

42 For work on audience taste, see: Jeffrey Richards, 'Wartime British cinema audiences and the class system: the case of *Ships With Wings* (1941)', *Historical Journal of Film, Radio and Television*, 7:2 (1987); Julian Poole, 'British cinema attendance in wartime: audience preference at the Majestic, Macclesfield, 1939–46', *Historical Journal of Film, Radio and Television*, 7:1 (1987); Sue Harper, 'Fragmentation and crisis: 1940s admission figures at the Regent cinema, Portsmouth, UK', *Historical Journal of Film, Radio and Television*, 26:3 (2006).

43 Chapman, *The British at War*.

44 Ian McLaine, *Ministry of Morale: Home Front Morale and the Ministry of Information in World War II* (London: George Allen and Unwin, 1979).

45 R. J. Hammond, *Food: Vol. I – The Growth of Policy* (London: HMSO, 1951), p. 58.

46 R. J. Hammond, *Food*, 3 vols (London: HMSO, 1951–62).

47 Zweiniger-Bargielowska, *Austerity in Britain*.

48 *Programme of the National Film Theatre*, August 1998, p. 2.

49 Jane F. Ferry, *Food in Film: A Culinary Performance of Communication* (London: Routledge, 2003); Anne L. Bower (ed.), *Reel Food: Essays on Food and Film* (London: Routledge, 2004).

50 Gaye Poole, *Reel Meals, Set Meals: Food in Film and Theatre* (Sydney: Currency Press, 1999); Steve Zimmerman and Ken Weiss, *Food in the Movies* (Jefferson, North Carolina: MacFarland, 2005).

51 See, for example, Lisa Odham Stokes and Michael Hoover, 'Food fight, food fight: culture and economy in *Chicken and Duck Talk*', *Asian Cinema*, 14:2 (2003); or Terry Barr, 'Eating kosher, staying closer: families and meals in contemporary Jewish American cinema', *Journal of Popular Film and Television*, 24:3 (1996).

52 See Jackie Stacey, *Star Gazing: Hollywood Cinema and Female Spectatorship* (London: Routledge, 1994); Annette Kuhn, *An Everyday Magic: Cinema and Cultural Memory* (London: I. B. Tauris, 2002).

Not so quiet on the Kitchen Front: Ministry of Food publicity in the Second World War

On 8 May 1947, the Publicity Club of London gathered at Mansion House to present an award described as the 'Nobel Prize of Advertising' to the individual deemed to have made the year's most singular and important contribution to the advertising industry. The 1947 ceremony was the first since 1938, and was organised to proclaim the most effective and significant British publicist of the Second World War. Given the scale and cost of advertising commissioned by the government during the war, it is not surprising that the award was presented to a politician. However, rather than reward one of the wartime Ministers of Information, the Publicity Club instead decided to acknowledge Frederick Marquis, Lord Woolton, who had been Minister of Food between April 1940 and November 1943. A man whose department was essentially responsible for restricting consumption and telling people what they were not allowed might be considered something of an unlikely winner, but the Publicity Club's recognition of Woolton – and, by extension, his colleagues and successors – serves to demonstrate the pains the Ministry of Food (MoF) took to make rationing a key element of the prosecution of the war and a prominent aspect of British wartime culture.

The Publicity Club awarded its Cup primarily in recognition of the MoF's weekly Food Facts newspaper advertisements, which it described as a 'remarkable war-time advertising campaign', and which were still being issued at the time of the prize-giving. The prize also recognised that the Ministry had made use of numerous media when issuing 'advertising and publicity in a manner more widespread and comprehensive than anything previously attempted by a Government department in Great Britain'.[1] The ambitious scope and volume of the MoF's publicity saw information about food issued in newspapers (both in paid advertising and in editorial comment), on posters, on the radio (the regular *Kitchen Front* programme and single broadcasts), in cinemas (in slides, notices in foyers and in short *Food Flashes* and other films) and in various one-off stunts and publicity events.

An M-O report on Home Propaganda was in little doubt as to the effectiveness of the MoF campaign ('no Ministry has been more active and detailed in its publicity') or the fact that what propelled the MoF into the public consciousness was money, and lots of it (more than £500,000 spent on press advertising alone by June 1941).[2] By spending, in the words of the *Manchester Guardian*, 'lavishly and cleverly on publicity', the MoF became culturally omnipresent, issuing thousands of advertisements through various media and thereby promoting food and consumption as central elements of British wartime life.[3]

By providing the country with so much food information, the MoF aimed to cultivate respect and admiration for an organisation that might otherwise have proved unpopular. Woolton himself outlined the fundamental principles that had informed all aspects of the MoF's advertising campaigns when accepting the Publicity Club Cup: 'I have faith in the people of this country … I have always believed that advertising should be used to tell the facts and allow people to form their own opinion.'[4] While we might accept Woolton's claim that the majority of his department's publicity was factual, the way in which this information was presented had a significant impact on the opinion that consumers formed as a result of their interaction with it.

The MoF, and its integrated propaganda campaigns, was a ubiquitous and high-profile presence in wartime Britain. So prolific was the MoF's publicity department that, at times, Britons must have felt that it was impossible to escape its reach. This, though, was the point: food was crucial, an integral part of war effort and of people's experience of the war, and the government wanted the population to acknowledge this fact and respond accordingly. The aim was the creation of a 'food-conscious' nation.

The Ministry's impact on the population's diet, attitude to consumption and domestic gastronomic arrangements was reinforced by its continual forays into British popular culture. The implications of such publicity extended beyond the relationship between the individual consumer and the state, for such was the prominence of the MoF's publicity during the war that all representations of consumption in wartime culture became effectively politicised, mediated by the knowledge of the government's regulation of food. British popular culture, in terms of cartoons, newspapers and commercial films, frequently featured food imagery that was lent additional meaning and significance by the state's determination to make consumption and rationing defining characteristics of the British wartime experience, promoting the idea of the 'food-based community.'

As Ina Zweiniger-Bargielowska has noted, the Home Intelligence reports produced by the Ministry of Information (MoI) suggest that popular attitudes towards the rationing system were most heavily influenced by the availability of food.[5] Thus, the success (or otherwise) of MoF publicity was closely aligned to the Ministry's ability to fulfil its promise to feed the nation. However, the volume of publicity issued, and the skill with which it was produced, complemented the practical successes of the Ministry, and assisted in the creation of a largely positive attitude towards Woolton and his department. Food, as the MoF slogan insisted, was 'a munition of war'. Publicity was also a weapon, and one that the Ministry was determined to deploy to maximum effect.

9 down: Woolton, the man who made the food go round (8)

As the chosen recipient of the Publicity Club Cup, Lord Woolton was clearly very closely associated with both the Ministry of Food and the advertising campaigns it commissioned. Indeed, it is possible to understand Woolton's public persona as being one of the most important elements of MoF publicity, for without a knowable and sympathetic figure at the helm, the Ministry of Food would have had to work much harder to gain the nation's trust. Woolton's background as a retail executive had taught him to appreciate the importance not simply of publicity, but of appropriately conceived and targeted publicity. During his first speech as Minister of Food, Woolton demonstrated his skill as a publicist with a popular touch by coining several phrases which found public favour, talking of 'the Kitchen Front' and suggesting that the British tea-making adage 'one for the pot' be amended to 'none for the pot' for the duration.[6]

Until Neville Chamberlain appointed him Minister of Food, Woolton had been working in an important but nondescript position in the Ministry of Supply. Indeed, Woolton's subsequent high profile and popularity were related to his role as Minister of Food, rather than to any pre-existing reputation. Woolton's appointment was greeted with consternation in some quarters. Despite his undisputed organisational capabilities, he was a comparative unknown and his appointment had, as the *Daily Herald* suggested, 'a grave weakness': Woolton sat in the House of Lords. As such, he was not personally answerable to the public via their representatives in the House of Commons.[7] Although the rationing system at this time was still something of a novelty and supplies of food were not a cause for undue concern, the *Herald*'s criticism makes clear the importance that was coming to be placed on food and the understanding that the MoF would play a significant role in promoting democratic ideals through equality of sacrifice, and also that it was vital for morale that a close link be forged between the Ministry and the people of Britain.

Thus when Winston Churchill became Prime Minister just weeks after Woolton's appointment, the Minister of Food found himself on difficult ground: the new Premier was unconvinced that Woolton had the political experience needed to 'impress the public through the parliamentary process'.[8] Furthermore, Woolton was associated with the ineffectual Cabinet changes undertaken by Chamberlain during his last months in office. Woolton, however, was keen to point out that he was not a politician but a businessman, and was similarly intent on letting the British people know that the MoF was not some abstract, distant, parliamentary body, but a very real part of the life of ordinary Britons. Understanding that direct communication with the public was more important to the success of his ministry than was oratory in the House of Lords, Woolton took pains to ensure that the MoF addressed the public whenever practicable.

On 8 April 1940, just days after taking office, the new Minister of Food talked to the nation in a radio *Postscript* which followed the evening news. The hallmarks of Woolton's style were identifiable even in this first broadcast: the sincerity of his tone and the simplicity of his language.[9] Although this first broadcast was well received, Woolton would refine his style as he became more comfortable behind the microphone, working alongside Howard Marshall, the first director of the MoF's Public Relations Division (PRD) and a pioneer of live cricket commentary, to produce scripts that helped to create the public persona of the Minister of Food.[10]

On air, Woolton was also very clear about who he believed himself to be talking to: 'Food control really is a woman's affair, and that's why I talk to women in these broadcasts.'[11] Broadcasting on Christmas Day 1941, Woolton went out of his way to praise the efforts of 'the housewives of Britain':

> What a grand job you've done in these 28 months of war. Food has been difficult: shopping has been worse … we are fighting fit – and we wouldn't have been if you housewives hadn't risen to the occasion and fed your families and done it with knowledge and skill.[12]

Food Facts advertisements, which frequently made clear their address to a specifically female readership, were also keen to encourage women – and, it should be pointed out, those that they fed – to recognise the contribution that the nation's cooks were making to the war effort. In November 1941, one Food Facts advertisement declared that, 'The British Housewife is helping to make a second front – the Kitchen Front – against Hitler.' At a time when increasing numbers of Britons were calling on the government to demonstrate its commitment to the Anglo-Soviet alliance by launching a second front against the Nazis, it was suggested that the nation's women were capable of doing what, at that time, their uniformed countrymen were not – actively prosecuting the war. And while this advertisement was obviously not to be taken literally, it was sincere in its tribute to the women of Britain: 'Medals for you, Madam.'[13]

The scarcity of many foodstuffs that had previously constituted significant parts of the British diet meant that most women had little choice but to follow the MoF's advice and 'try new things' or to use meat or fish as a flavouring rather than as a major ingredient. The praise that the Ministry heaped on British housewives perhaps rang somewhat hollow. However, what this type of publicity demonstrates is the MoF's willingness to recognise the sacrifices, more often than not made of necessity, that British consumers were making in wartime, and to suggest to housewives that these sacrifices were aiding the war effort. Additionally, such publicity might also encourage British men to recognise that changes to their diet were the result of exceptional circumstances. (Not that this brought an end to complaints about food: separate publicity was issued to persuade men that dietary changes were not only vital but also actually desirable from a gustatory point of view.)[14] Direct appeals to British women seem to have been appreciated, even if the occasionally grandiose martial terms the MoF used to incorporate the housewives into the war effort were mocked and applauded in equal measure by one female Glasgow diarist who 'took to teasing [her mother] about the "Kitchen Front", telling her she was generalissimo and quite the most important member of the family'.[15]

Woolton's eagerness to communicate directly with British consumers was noted by German radio propagandists in their broadcasts to the United Kingdom. Claiming that his regular appearances on the radio were nothing more than an attempt to 'calm the people' as the food situation got worse, queues longer and shortages more acute, the Germans attempted to present Woolton's very public presence not so much as a sign of openness, but rather as a symbol of his failure.[16] Further, Workers' Challenge, a German radio station that claimed to be the voice of the British proletariat, attempted to drive a wedge between Woolton and those he was responsible for feeding when, in April 1941, it claimed that 'a deputation of tough workers [should go] to see

[Woolton] and beat him up ... And if old Woolton had to go to hospital for a fortnight, he'd be as much use to us there as anywhere else.'[17] Such attacks were essentially backhanded compliments, recognising both Woolton's prominent cultural position and the importance that the MoF placed on maintaining public faith in rationing.

British broadcasters were, on the whole, more appreciative of Woolton's abilities. J. B. Priestley, whose own *Postscript* radio broadcasts transformed him into a household name during the war, was generally critical of government ministers' attitudes towards the 'terrific power of the broadcast word',[18] but he singled out Woolton for praise:

> Having run big stores and having been compelled to study the public mind, [he] believes in getting into direct contact with the public and not hiding himself behind some gigantic wall of hush-hush bureaucracy. He talks to our housewives over the radio, reassuring them about our stocks of food but asking for their co-operation in seeing that nothing is wasted. They listen to him on the air. They write letters to him, explaining about this, grumbling about that, and he makes himself acquainted with the gist of these letters and acts accordingly.[19]

The confidence that Woolton expressed in the public's willingness to accept the necessity and reality of rationing was repaid by increasing British faith in the MoF in general and Woolton in particular. Rationing, it was believed, was in the charge of a knowable, likeable businessman-turned-politician, rather than a faceless Whitehall bureaucrat, and Woolton came to embody the humanity and approachability for which the MoF hoped to gain a reputation.

Woolton became a recognisable and trusted voice, and the easy familiarity with which he discussed food matters led one of his parliamentary secretaries to say of him that he had developed 'an avuncular [style of] government, and I think that it is as a kind of universal uncle that he is accepted'.[20] Woolton projected himself as ordinary and accessible, and these traits appear to have increased the success of his wireless broadcasts. Priestley, who, even more so than Woolton, was defined by his non-metropolitanism, understood that the Minister of Food's background – born and educated in Manchester and a successful businessman in Liverpool – was one of the foundations of his popular appeal: 'Like all people who are the salt of the earth, he comes from the North of England. He does not belong to the ruling or official class – thank God!'[21]

What Priestley understood instinctively took the BBC another two years to comprehend. In her history of wartime broadcasting, Siân Nicholas suggests that, by mid-1942, BBC producers had come to realise that those ministers who were able to cast themselves as ordinary were best placed to communicate effectively and popularly, and that many listeners conflated a regional accent with ordinariness and a lack of affectation and, therefore, sincerity.[22] Indeed, so successful was Woolton in bolstering both his personal and his ministry's profile and popularity that he was declared by one journalist to be the only member of the government other than the Prime Minister to 'carry any weight with the Common Man'.[23] Further, his name was often invoked in the MoF's own appeals to the public:

> Those who have the will to win
> Eat potatoes in their skin,
> Knowing that the sight of peelings
> Deeply hurts Lord Woolton's feelings.[24]

Other Food Facts were presented as if signed by Woolton – a decision that strengthened his association with the MoF publicity machine and moved *Advertiser's Weekly* to describe him as '"our" Lord Woolton'.[25]

Woolton became such a recognisable figure that he was '"perpetrated" in wax for public exhibition' at Madame Tussaud's.[26] He also gave his name to a number of recipes, the most famous of which was Woolton Pie, a combination of oats, vegetables and wholemeal pastry. The public remained suspicious, despite heavy promotion. The irony that such a popular minister could lend his name to such an unpopular dish was not lost on the cartoonists. When Woolton eventually left the MoF, the *Daily Mail* printed a cartoon in which a waitress suggests to a colleague that if they mentioned 'how [Woolton]'s been a guide, philosopher and friend to us all' the 'surplus Woolton Pie problem' would instantly be resolved.[27]

The Woolton Pie cartoon is representative of the attitude that the newspapers took towards Woolton, for although there was often criticism of specific details of rationing policy the press were kind to the MoF for most of Woolton's tenure. Because he sat as an independent peer, Woolton attracted less hostility from politically-aligned newspapers than a minister who toed a party political line might have done, but this was not to say that he did not work hard to cultivate good relations with Fleet Street. Woolton's desire to keep the press on-side was based not on a desire to bolster his own profile so much as on the belief that the Fourth Estate played a decisive role in influencing public opinion. Even if, as an M-O report suggested, newspapers were less able to influence the general public than popularly thought, many politicians, including Woolton, remained convinced that the press spoke for and, more importantly, to the population at large.[28]

Early on in the war, the *Daily Express* raised its voice in very vocal opposition to the introduction of any form of food control, arguing that the country had adequate supplies: 'We don't need food rationing at all. It is absolute nonsense. It gives the people a sense of insecurity.' Further, the paper argued, if supplies of commodities such as butter and bacon were to run short, the country could replenish stocks 'from our dairies and pigsties in the Empire': what Britain needed were 'warehouses, not … coupons'.[29] At least one MP was convinced that these criticisms had led the government to postpone regularised food control, and that papers hostile to rationing were continuing to bring pressure to bear upon the Cabinet.[30]

Soon after arriving at the MoF, Woolton convened a meeting of the proprietors of Britain's major newspapers and outlined both 'the potential gravity of the food situation' and his proposals for the extension of the rationing system. Similarly, the newspapers were informed in advance of major changes to the system, such as the introduction of points rationing, in the hope that they would then assist in selling such changes to the public.[31] Woolton's weekly press conferences were used as opportunities for senior MoF staff to discuss, 'off the record', the delicate minutiae of food policy with the dedicated food correspondents that many papers employed to keep their readers abreast of the rationing situation. This approach strengthened the bond between Woolton, the MoF and the papers, and thereby helped to maintain positive public attitudes to rationing or, rather, minimised damaging media carping about food control.

However, the rumpus that accompanied the introduction of egg rationing in mid-1941 suggests that neither the Ministry nor the Minister were beyond criticism, and that the general goodwill that characterised Woolton's relationship with the press was the result not only of popular acceptance of the need for food control, but also of the care that the MoF took to communicate with the public and the papers. For once, Woolton lost his touch when it came to outlining his policies. Admitting not only that egg rationing was likely to proceed by 'trial and error', but also, and potentially more damagingly, that the scheme would be 'imperfect', the usually consensual Minister of Food insensitively announced that he would push forward with his plans 'whatever the reception they met'.[32] The confrontational nature of the announcement, and the admission that the system was flawed, provided those who opposed the scheme with carte blanche to criticise it: the papers were soon printing letters from outraged readers who believed themselves especially hard done-by. A satirical poem published in the *Daily Mail* captures something of the confusion that accompanied the introduction of the scheme:

The little hen, with Anxious Face,
Proceeds to some secluded place,
And there, unburdening her mind,
She leaves a handsome Egg behind.

But now, although for Eggs I yearn,
The Woolton Wheels begin to turn,
My Egg is taken by the State,
I fill in Forms (in triplicate).

Having watched the men from the Ministry weigh, measure and classify the precious egg, the poet looks on disconsolately as it falls into the clutches of a party of civil servants.[33]

To a population used to eating, on average, three eggs a week, headlines which advised consumers that they would receive just 'two eggs per ration book in October' would have seemed more than faintly ridiculous had they not been so grim.[34] But in the summer of 1941, eggs were no laughing matter. In August, one cinema-goer had her enjoyment of *Ninotchka* (1939) – a Hollywood satire about the Soviet Union – spoiled by the intrusion of two recent real-world events into the fictional space of the film. The first was the German invasion of Russia, which led her to observe that it 'seemed in rather bad taste to be laughing at the Bolsheviks'. The second was the introduction of egg control. A key scene in which impoverished communists are forced to make a communal omelette because they are only allocated one egg per person now struck too close to home, and 'failed to entertain' as it might have done 'before our eggs were rationed'.[35] *Ninotchka* might have been the film in which, famously, 'Garbo laughs', but not all British consumers could bring themselves to join her.

In some instances the joke was turned to good effect on the Ministry itself. Released in September 1941, the comedy *I Thank You* found Arthur Askey masquerading as a cook in a wealthy household. When called upon to make a pudding, he opens up a cookbook and begins to read: 'Take three eggs...' Having read this, Askey quietly tears the page out, crumples it in his hand, and throws it to the floor. His eloquent silence, which provides time for the audience to laugh, was appreciated by *Picture Show*, which observed: 'There is no need for further words ... the house roars.'[36] The joke benefited from its topicality, and is part of a longer sketch, in which the floor of the kitchen becomes littered with paper as recipes were discussed and deemed unfeasible under contemporary conditions.

It was not only films that made fun of the MoF's difficulties. While newspaper cartoons generally tended to treat shortages and rationing as a source of stoical

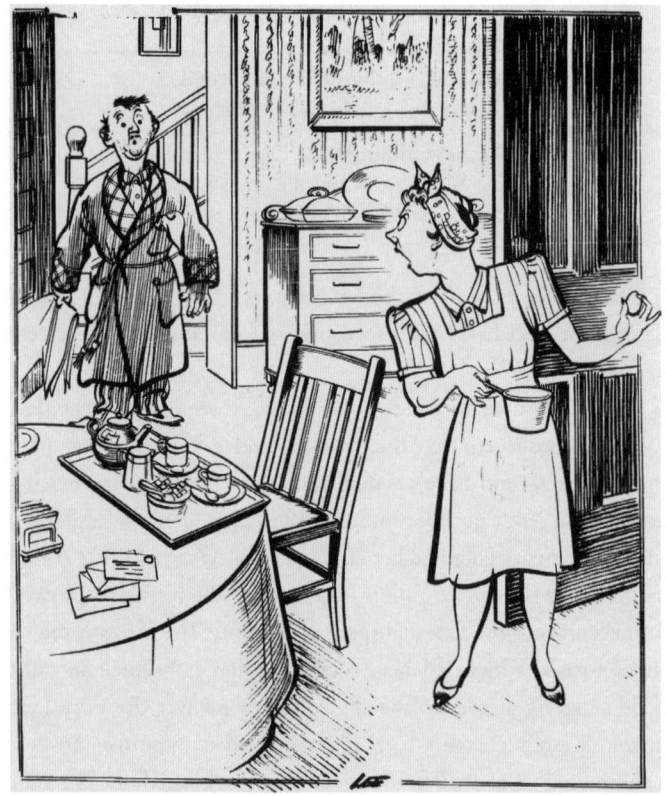

I   Occasion: 'Go back and shave and dress at once, John. The idea! Coming
down to breakfast like that when we're having our fortnightly egg.'
Joseph Lee in the *Evening News*, 30 October 1941.

pride and self-deprecating humour, attempting to demonstrate that the British
were doing their best to carry on as normal in straitened circumstances, those
that lampooned egg rationing were notably more pointed. The seeming illogi-
cality of the scheme was manna for the cartoonists, who made fun of the
system in such a way as to point an accusatory finger at the government. In
one cartoon from October 1941 (see figure 1), a wife reprimands her ill-kempt
husband with the words: 'Go back and shave and dress at once, John. The idea!
Coming down to breakfast like that when we're having our fortnightly egg.' The
cartoon encapsulates perfectly the impact that food shortages had on the lives
of ordinary people, and the absurdities that became evident when these same
people tried to maintain a semblance of normality in extraordinary situations.

Worse still for the MoF's reputation was the initial inefficiency of the system.
The Ministry's admission that the redistribution of eggs was causing a greater

number to go bad prompted fresh criticism, from both press and public. A letter in the *Daily Herald* suggested that: 'Mismanagement of food distribution is helping Hitler more than his bombs or threats', while one journalist noted that, 'Chaos and misunderstanding are everywhere … faith in the system has crashed.'[37] A claim made by an MoF official that, 'We are finding something wrong [with the system] every day' can have done little to assuage public doubts.[38] Since the introduction of rationing, the MoF had endeavoured to gain the public's trust, predicating its relationship with British consumers on its ability to honour their rations, and on its refusal to make promises that it could not keep. When a newspaper could report that 'you will get one egg per ration book next week … if you are lucky', the MoF risked undermining its previous hard work; luck had no place in rationing, and diarist Vere Hodgson was surely not alone in expressing exasperation: 'No eggs again this week … 3rd in succession, rotten!'[39]

Part of the problem with egg control arose because, for once, the Ministry's publicity campaigns were ineffectual: 'we are being badly put across to the public', Woolton confided to his diary.[40] Relatively little publicity attended the launch of the scheme – especially in comparison to the launch of dried eggs a year later[41] – and it was January 1942 before a Food Facts column discussed the reasoning behind, and the purpose of, egg rationing: 'Is it fairer for very few people to have as many eggs as they please, or for everybody to have his two or three a month?'[42] That said, the Ministry took to the airwaves more quickly, and a series of radio talks was organised in which British consumers were able question MoF officials, including Woolton, about the food situation. The broadcasts seem to have poured oil on these temporarily troubled waters, helped, no doubt, by the eventual stabilisation and normalisation of egg production and distribution. Individual consumers were granted a regular allocation, usually of two and in some instances three eggs a month, and although this was obviously fewer than many had hoped for, it did grant more people regular access to a product that many city dwellers had previously found difficult to obtain. As the teething troubles that plagued the introduction of egg rationing were overcome, and as the relentless progress of the war lessened Fleet Street's interest in eggs, the press's attitude to the MoF became more positive once again. 'Popularity's a fickle jade', Woolton noted, wryly.[43]

The regular meetings between Woolton and the press are mentioned in *Unpublished Story* (1942), a feature film which uses the power and tenacity of the newspapers to expose a group of pacifists as Nazi agents. Encouraged by her editor to 'get down to the Ministry of Food and beard Woolton in his den', reporter Carol Bennett (Valerie Hobson) reads with limited enthusiasm the press release of the story she is being sent to cover: '"Ministry of Food are considering the question of price control for herrings, the present price of which for cran, creel or casket…" Well, that ought to thrill the nation.' The paper's editor is quick to criticise this dismissive attitude, and reminds the surly reporter that 'There's a good story in it, Carol. An army isn't the only thing which marches on its stomach.'

Woolton actually appeared in *World of Plenty* (1943). The film stresses both Woolton's popularity – he is affectionately introduced as 'Old Woolton' – and his familiarity – an early version of the script would have encouraged Woolton to describe himself as 'the unseen guest at ten million breakfast tables'.[44] Further, the film's writers were eager for Woolton to contribute a 'filmic drama-punch' and hoped that the Minister's words could provide 'a phrase, a thought, an expressive force at the end which will leave the film watcher just rocking'.[45] Although Woolton's final contribution, a filmed interview at a desk, is somewhat flat compared to these dramatic ideals, the filmmakers' belief that the Minister of Food was an appropriate figure to attempt such a sequence testifies to both his fame and his reputation as a skilled communicator.

When he stood down as 'Minister of Girth Control' to become Minister of Reconstruction,[46] Woolton was praised by *The Times*:

> Of the two Ministers who have both done their best, men curse the President of the Board of Trade as they gaze on their baggy old trousers because he will not let them buy new ones. Yet as their eyes fall on the ever more fluttering and cavernous gap at the top of them they rain blessings on the … Minister of Food.[47]

Such was the praise heaped on Woolton that Mollie Panter-Downes, in her regular letter to the *New Yorker*, wrote that 'Seldom, if ever, has a Minister bowed his way offstage … in the applauding atmosphere of a successful first night; such departures usually resemble a post-mortem.'[48]

Woolton's synonymy with the MoF – a synonymy that extended into the post-war period, when he was singled out for recognition by the Publicity Club of London – meant that crossword compilers could drop his name into their clues to introduce a gastronomic aspect to a cryptic puzzle. Woolton was the subject of six crossword clues in *The Times* and two in the *Manchester Guardian*.[49] All of *The Times* clues about Woolton related to his position as Minister of Food; as Minister of Reconstruction he had no further appeal to the crossword compilers. It was as the man, like the turnspit, who made the food go round that Woolton was most noteworthy.[50]

The Public Relations Division

As an extensive, complex and well-capitalised organisation dedicated to the purchase, regulation and distribution of food, the MoF required a similarly extensive, complex and well-capitalised publicity department dedicated to explaining to the British people the intricacies and continual evolution of rationing policy. MoF publicists would later admit that 'one of the principal aims' of food publicity was 'the cultivation of public confidence in the Ministry', acknowledging an awareness of the need to enter into a perpetual dialogue with the British public if the rationing system was to function smoothly.[51] Woolton encouraged consumers to write to the Ministry with their grievances rather than grumble among themselves, and answered in person a proportion of the letters sent to him. Such decisions led one correspondent to address his letter to 'Mr Get-at-able Minister'.[52] 'We don't just cope, we care', was the Ministry's wartime motto, intended to humanise the MoF and strengthen its bond with those it served. Obviously, the best way to gain credibility was to feed the people, but by instilling popular ownership of food control, consumers were encouraged to become active participants in the MoF's publicity strategy rather than passive recipients of it.

The Ministry's Public Relations Division was responsible for food publicity, and devised one of the most far-reaching and ambitious domestic propaganda campaigns of the war. Maintaining the MoF's high profile with an integrated publicity campaign of which *Kitchen Front* radio broadcasts, Food Facts newspaper advertisements and *Food Flash* cinema trailers were the most regular features, the PRD also employed other media:

- press conferences, leading to editorial publicity
- leaflets
- poster advertising
- exhibitions and demonstrations
- speakers for meetings
- information bulletins for women's organisations, schools, etc.
- photographs.[53]

Unlike most government ministries, which issued publicity through the MoI, the MoF was, from early 1940 onwards, responsible for devising, running and funding its own campaigns. The Ministry continued to issue propaganda through the MoI – *Eating Out with Tommy Trinder* (1941), for example, was part of the MoI's 'Five Minute Film' programme – but on the whole it was happy to take responsibility for delivering its own messages to the public.

The PRD was fiercely protective of its position as the mouthpiece of the MoF and, when called upon to justify its post-war existence, powers and (most importantly) budget by the Public Accounts Committee, produced the following defence, which also neatly summarises its wartime role:

> With a continuous advertising programme of the size required by the Ministry of Food it is ... essential to have specialist officers in the Ministry's Public Relations Division to handle the work ... The subject matter of the Ministry's advertising is complex, because food control is itself complex. Instead of telling one straight-forward story – such as fuel economy or road safety – the Ministry has to cover such diverse subjects as ration book procedure, points changes, special rations for particular sections of the population, issue of feeding stuffs for domestic poultry keepers, the recovery of jam jars and milk bottles, and food advice for the housewife. This last item has to be kept in line with the frequent changes in food supply. This complexity of the subject matter means that each advertisement, which generally includes two or three different items, is the product of very close co-operation between the Public Relations Division, several other Divisions of the Ministry, and the Advertising Agents. Consultation is frequent during each week and last minute changes are often necessary.[54]

In the late-1940s, as food controls were repealed and rationing scaled back, the MoF conceded many of its publicity functions to the Central Office of Information (the post-war equivalent of the MoI).[55] Until that time, however, the MoF remained a major publicist. With the exception of the MoI, which handled accounts for several other ministries, the only Department to coordinate its own advertising and exceed the MoF in terms of budget for Home Front publicity was the National Savings Committee, the body responsible for persuading the public to invest their money in government savings schemes. In 1943–44, the peak year for MoF advertising expenditure, the PRD's 70-strong staff spent £599,153 on publicity – a figure which equates to a little under a quarter of the MoI's total Home Information budget for the same period.[56]

It is possible to divide MoF propaganda into three broad categories: information that the MoF *required* the public to know for food control to function properly; information that the MoF *wanted* the public to know; and information geared towards satisfying public demand for recognition, reassurance and recipes. The first category included straight, factual information on subjects such as changes to the points values of particular foods, the issue of new ration books and the logistical practicalities of rationing. The second contained messages aimed at changing behaviour, and promoted the importance of a balanced, nutritional diet and the benefits of certain foodstuffs, particularly vegetables, in relation to the health of both adult and, particularly, juvenile

Britons.[57] The third acknowledged British consumers, declaring their efforts to be a central component of the war effort rather than an adjunct to it. Simultaneously, MoF propaganda of this nature reassured British cooks that the changes to diet brought about by the war need not necessarily undermine morale, and that changes to pre-war domestic norms were not a sign of poor housekeeping but rather of the impact that the war was having on the nation as a whole. Issuing recipes that helped British cooks make the most of available foods was crucial in this regard, as was publicity that provided tips on dietary and domestic economies.

Thus, although much of the publicity sponsored by the MoF was of an informative or instructional nature, it also served a psychological purpose, making it very clear that the sacrifices demanded of Britain's army of cooks linked the Kitchen Front to the front line. As a review of Woolton's first months in charge of the Ministry of Food explained:

> many women, who wondered if they were doing anything to help, have been heart-ened by the partnership [the MoF] has invited them into by the revelation of what shiploads of difference a little saving or ingenuity in millions of kitchens makes.[58]

The use of different mass media to advance this message not only elevated the visibility and the stature of the nation's cooks, but also provided for a shared experience by raising the profile of food in the public consciousness and helping to create and strengthen a spirit of consensus among British consumers.

Communality and equality were prevalent concerns in much of the MoF's early publicity. In late 1939, the MoF, which was at this time still issuing its publicity through the MoI, launched a campaign to promote acceptance of food control on the grounds that 'the main object of British rationing will not be to combat shortage so much as to ensure equality of distribution and, by minimising the effects of the unevenness of wealth, to ensure evenness of sacri-fice'.[59] These themes informed a newspaper advertisement which announced the advent of rationing in January 1940: 'Rationing divides supplies equally. There will be ample supplies for our 44½ million people, but we must divide them fairly, everyone being treated alike. No one must be left out.'[60]

Although price controls and rationing implicitly benefited the poorest sections of British society to the greatest extent, MoF publicity tended to focus on the sense of community that the system might engender. By privileging the community and the national while taking pains not to ignore the continued appeal of the individual and the local, MoF advertising used food to position the individual within society, as a member, as one Food Facts advertisement put it, of 'a family of 45,000,000'.[61]

The positive attitude that the majority of this extended family had towards rationing meant that the MoF did not need to expend too much effort or money defending or selling the system. The joint MoF-MoI campaign accepted early on in the war that 'nothing strikes the public as more ridiculous than earnest attempts to make them accept something which they would in fact have accepted without any urging at all'.[62] As such, initial campaigns that had adopted justificatory and somewhat didactic tones were superseded by more informative and entertaining publicity.

This was perhaps just as well, for the MoF's early publicity campaigns came in for some criticism. One Conservative MP insisted that the MoF would only reach 'the masses' once it abandoned its dry, 'highbrow methods' and became attuned with more popular tastes.[63] Further, a later survey commissioned by the MoF to explore the reception and popularity of its Food Facts newspaper advertisements found that those which contained 'Exhortation to the house-wife' were least popular – 'a long way last on the list'. While this does not mean that no such publicity was subsequently produced – and there was, after all, enough to merit inclusion of this advertising style as an option in the survey – the MoF's willingness to accept the likely failure of such an approach helped it avoid excessive use of a 'very dull and not well read' style.[64]

By declining to take a hectoring tone, and by understanding the psychological difference between telling and asking, the PRD demonstrated an inclusiveness that transformed what might otherwise have been viewed as fussily bureaucratic statements into something altogether more 'friendly and informal'.[65] It might be argued that this policy was dictated by the sheer amount of food-related information there was to communicate. Needing to maintain goodwill towards the Ministry's publicity if the public were to be receptive to its messages, Woolton and the PRD understood that if 'the public was either going to laugh or cry about food rationing … it was better for them that they should laugh – even if it was only a somewhat wry smile – than that they should contemplate too much on the misery of the position'.[66]

This does not mean that the PRD's output was flippant or inappropriately light-hearted, but it is possible to discern a positive, humorous and encouraging style in much of its work. Stating that, 'All publicity was designed to promote morale as well as material health', the PRD did its best to produce propaganda that would engage and entertain the public.[67] There is an interesting contrast to be drawn between the MoF and the MoI, for while the latter was relatively slow to understand that humour was, in the right circumstances, a very effective means of communicating with the public, the MoF was much quicker to recognise the possibilities offered by a comic approach.[68]

The PRD frequently demonstrated a popular touch, recruiting well-known entertainers to front campaigns, thereby making more accessible what might otherwise have become strictly functional, informational publicity campaigns. The possibility of using variety and music hall stars had been considered by MoF publicists very early in the war, when in December 1939 it was suggested that Arthur Askey, star of the hugely popular radio comedy *Band Waggon*, might write and perform a song called 'The Sugar Rat' to castigate those who wasted imported food resources.[69] While this scheme does not appear to have come to fruition, it is significant in that it demonstrates the desire to embed MoF publicity in the cultural mainstream, as an integral element of popular culture (albeit with a very obvious propagandistic purpose).

In this spirit of reaching out to the public, one of Woolton's first acts as Minister was to recruit Elsie and Doris Waters to make a series of radio broadcasts in mid-April 1940. Better known to the British public as Gert and Daisy, the Waters sisters were established music hall comedians whose characters' appeal was founded on their almost extreme ordinariness. Although surprised to be asked to assist the MoF, they were soon persuaded by Woolton that their style might be suitable for food publicity.[70] The result was *Feed the Brute,* a series of eleven five-minute broadcasts put out after the 6 p.m. news on the BBC Home Service, beginning on 9 April 1940. In the *Daily Express*, Jonah Barrington described the first programme as a 'curious (though effective) broadcast: part Saturday night music hall, part Whitehall statistics'. He suggested that if the Waters sisters could step out of the 'shadow of Whitehall', they would be able to establish a more meaningful rapport with the women of Britain.[71] The radio critic of the *Manchester Guardian* also enjoyed the broadcast, but felt that it should have been twice as long, so as to provide more time for both an increased number of jokes and more detailed food information.[72]

An M-O survey found that Gert and Daisy's broadcasts were greeted with 'a quite exceptional degree of interest and appreciation'. Of those women questioned, eight out of every nine approved of the talks, and the accessible and sympathetic tone, communicated via the hosts' comic approach, was singled out for special praise. Further, more than half of those working-class housewives contacted by M-O had listened to the talks 'with some sort of regularity'. While the broadcasts' status as entertainment, and the presence of the Waters sisters, might go some way towards explaining listener enthusiasm, the large number of women who wrote to request further information suggests that the overtly instructional elements of the show were neither unnoticed nor resented.[73] The success of these broadcasts, which combined informality, propaganda and a pretty direct appeal to and association with women, did not go unnoticed by the MoF; *Feed the Brute* was used as the template for *The Kitchen Front*, which took to the air two months later.

The sisters made such an impression that they were often approached to appear alongside Woolton and other MoF officials when meetings about rationing and food control were held in towns where the Waters were performing. Gert and Daisy also appeared at many cookery demonstrations and food control centres, where it was found, in the words of one local educator, that their 'subtle combination of sound food campaign propaganda with humour … gets a message home when straight tutoring fails'.[74]

Aware that the power of celebrity might be boosted yet further by combining it with royal glamour and gravitas, the MoF considered approaching the Queen to host an episode of *The Kitchen Front*. Although nothing came of this conceit – mainly, it seems, because no-one could decide on the appropriate protocol for making such an invitation – the fact that such a bravura idea was considered at all suggests that the PRD was rarely willing to rest on its laurels.[75] Both E. M. Delafield, the author of *Diary of a Provincial Lady*, and Clemence Dane, who would later win an Academy Award for her screenplay for *Perfect Strangers* (1945), were 'anxious to help' and appeared on MoF radio broadcasts, as did the comedian Vic Oliver and the American radio broadcaster, and narrator of *London Can Take It!* (1940), Quentin Reynolds. At a 'sherry party' held in March 1941 for those who had spoken on *The Kitchen Front*, a thrilled and somewhat star-struck Woolton noted that the presence of well-known West End actors and famous authors was testament to the importance of the MoF and its publicity. He also observed dutifully that many of the dieticians who had helped the Ministry were in attendance, too.[76]

Gert and Daisy returned to the MoF's wireless campaign in December 1940, hosting *The Kitchen Front* during Christmas week. Asking the Waters sisters to host the programme was a bold move, not because they lacked the skills necessary for successful wireless broadcasting, but because choosing to employ a comic approach at such a time was potentially controversial. Christmas 1940 was a very bleak period for many Britons: following the defeat of France earlier in the year, the United Kingdom fought alone and the *Luftwaffe*'s defeat in the Battle of Britain had replaced the threat of invasion with the reality of the Blitz. Further, families were often affected by loss, evacuation, bomb damage or conscription and might be understood to have felt the sorrow associated with such events all the more acutely during the festive season. However, amid the jokes and songs which constituted the majority of each of Gert and Daisy's broadcasts were moments of candour and pathos, dealing with separation and sacrifice and reinforcing the shared experiences of communality and good humour.[77]

Other well-known performers were recruited to front food-related publicity. In May 1941, the MoI released *Eating Out with Tommy Trinder*, in which the eponymous star demonstrated the appeal of the newly established British Restaurants (subsidised, state-run canteens) by taking his fiancée and her family to one. Trinder's constant comic patter – he celebrates the quality of the meals available by declaring the British Restaurant to be 'a place where they never let bygones be rissoles' – demonstrates his star status and adds glamour to a potentially mundane setting. The lack of pretentiousness in his comic persona, on the other hand, helped to counter allegations of disingenuousness that might otherwise have been thrown at the film's central premise.

The *Food Flash* short films also featured famous names. In spring 1945, humorous poet Cyril Fletcher, best known for his 'Odd Odes', provided the narration for three films, while in late 1946 comedian Charlie Chester was brought in to perform the last five *Flashes* in the series. Chester, who had toured Europe with the 'Stars in Battledress', had by this time established a reputation as a talented and popular comic performing on the *Stand Easy* and *Merry-Go-Round* wireless broadcasts. In the *Flashes*, he (mis-)applied his skills to topics as diverse as cod liver oil and the preparation of cabbage.

The public, it seems, was on the whole receptive to such a light-hearted, star-driven approach. Writing to *Picturegoer* magazine about the MoI short film *The Nose Has It* (1942), John Roy of Nottingham insisted that Britons should 'rejoice that … the official mind has realised the possibilities of humour when putting over a "dry" subject'.[78] By singling out a public information film featuring Arthur Askey for special praise, Roy points to the potential that such an approach had to engage the public. While this should not lead to the conclusion that films that did not feature well-known actors or entertainers were doomed to failure, it does suggest that the mobilisation of a star persona could serve official propagandists very well.[79]

When the MoF launched a campaign to promote the wheatmeal National Loaf (which required the importation of less wheat), well-known newsreader Alvar Lidell was cast as one of the (caricatured) faces of the new product. A Food Facts column published in April 1941 features a parody of the lines with which Lidell introduced the news. The broadcaster is shown sitting behind a microphone and holding a slice of bread, intoning: 'Here is national wheatmeal bread – and this is Alvar Lidell eating it' (see figure 2).

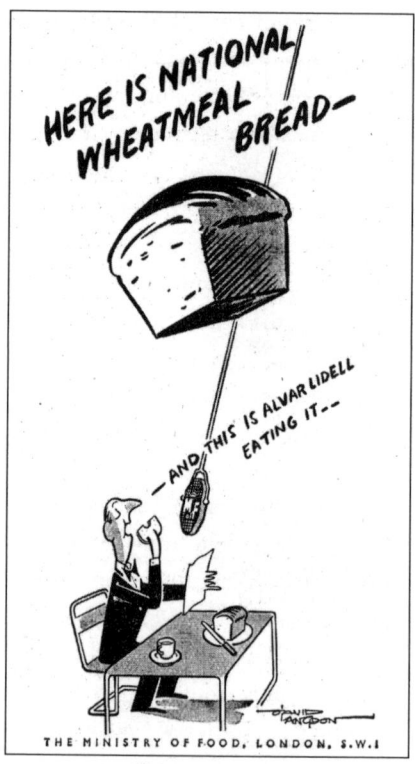

2   Food Facts No. 38, week of 21 April 1941.

Lidell on his own, though, was not enough to wean the British public off its preference for white bread. Bread was one of the most important staples of the wartime diet, and the Ministry of Food was not prepared to risk morale by forcing people to eat the National Loaf.[80] Instead, it relied on propaganda in an attempt to persuade consumers to voluntarily make the switch. As a result, Gert and Daisy could be heard boosting the wheatmeal loaf, claiming that they preferred it 'because white [bread] always makes the table cloth look dirty!' The MoF also created a most intriguing-sounding device, the 'Effluviator' – also known, somewhat less appealingly, as the 'smell machine' – to pump the odour of products baked with National Flour onto the street from a shop on Piccadilly.[81] Britons remained unconvinced. One consumer wrote to the MoF and complained that the National Loaf was 'nasty, dirty, dark, coarse, indigestible bread'.[82] Even the suggestion that the National Loaf had aphrodisiacal qualities failed to bring about an upswing in its popularity.[83] There were some things, it seemed, that even the PRD found it difficult to get the British public to swallow.

The Kitchen Front

Research undertaken on behalf of the MoF found that, in 1942, more than three-quarters of British households had a radio.[84] The MoF was keen to use the wireless to gain access to the homes of ordinary Britons – particularly to the women who queued for food and prepared their family's meals – and so initiate a more intimate form of contact with those it served. As food control and rationing were subjects affecting family life, the domestic wireless was considered an ideal medium to communicate information about the MoF's work. Indeed, the MoF had a seemingly boundless enthusiasm for wireless broadcasting: by early June 1945 a total of 1,196 programmes on the BBC had been dedicated to, or featured, food or rationing, a number that dwarfs the totals for programmes which dealt with the work of other departments.[85] There were also numerous incidental references to the Ministry's work in news bulletins. Cinematic examples of such broadcasts can be heard in both *Millions Like Us* (1943) and *Back Room Boy* (1942), where an announcement Woolton has made regarding eggs is inserted into the newsreader's script at the last minute.

Although the MoF had issued information via the radio from very early in the war, it was not until the debut of *The Kitchen Front* on 13 June 1940 that the Ministry and the BBC developed a format that was able to fully harness the communicative power of the wireless. Described by one historian as the 'most important radio campaign' of the war, this series of five-minute broadcasts was transmitted at 8.15 a.m., six mornings a week.[86] In case listeners were in any doubt about the reasons for the programme, or its target audience, the first *Kitchen Front* broadcast was introduced with the following words: 'Food is such an important section of the Home Front that today we are starting a regular series of short talks about it to reach the housewife before she sets out on her morning's shopping and plans the meals for the day.'[87]

The significance of food in wartime Britain was demonstrated by *The Kitchen Front*'s prominent position just after the 8 o'clock news bulletin. The MoF was fiercely protective of the programme's time-slot, and with good reason. The breakfast-time scheduling had the effect of making the show a regular feature of many families' daily routine, allowing husbands and children to learn about the difficulties that wives and mothers faced in wartime, and placing issues of food and consumption in a familial, and therefore communal, context. The BBC's Listener Research Department estimated that by October 1940 each *Kitchen Front* broadcast was heard by 5.4 million Britons.[88] The programme was still prominent enough in January 1945 for a *Daily Mail* cartoon to suggest mischievously that the recipes broadcast by Freddie Grisewood (a 'genial soul' whose potato cakes went down very well in Barrow-in-Furness, according to M-O diarist Nella Last) were responsible for a temporary potato shortage, just as they had earlier helped the MoF dispose of a glut of carrots.[89]

Although from the second half of 1943 it would have to share two of its six 8.15 a.m. time-slots with other government departments, a move which resulted in the programme being renamed *Household Front*, the MoF retained a great deal of power in its relationship with the BBC.[90] Technically, an independent BBC production, *The Kitchen Front* was scripted in conjunction with the MoF to avoid the transmission of material that ran contrary to official policy. With its feet thus under the table, the Ministry soon became dominant in determining the content of *The Kitchen Front*; censoring scripts, insisting that certain broadcasts be amended or cancelled, and inviting guests and presenters onto the programme without always consulting the programme's producers.[91] Indeed, so powerful did the MoF become in its dealings with the broadcaster that a BBC memorandum bemoaned the fact that the Ministry had gained the 'position of would-be dictators'.[92]

While the MoF was generally content for its publicity to adopt a genial tone, it appears initially to have disagreed with the BBC about the format and style of *The Kitchen Front*. These arguments seem to have arisen from the two bodies' different conceptions of what the broadcast was intended to do: initially, and in contrast with much of its later thinking on propaganda, the Ministry wanted an informative programme which communicated essential rationing information, whereas the Corporation believed that such an educative format might soon come to alienate listeners. A compromise between these two positions was reached and different presenters, each with their own style, were introduced to specialise in certain areas. Charles Hill, who would continue to broadcast once a week for the next decade, started work on the programme in 1941, although it was not until he was introduced as 'the Radio Doctor' rather than simply as 'a doctor' that he gained both an identity (despite his pseudonymity) and a good deal of popularity.[93] However, despite both *The Kitchen Front*'s popularity and the tentative agreement between the MoF and the BBC regarding who had the final say over content, tension caused by squabbles concerning who had control would continue through much of the war.[94]

The friction arising from the genesis of each programme does not appear to have been evident on-air, where a spirit of general good humour and heartiness came to dominate proceedings. The success of the Waters sisters' cheerful chars inspired the MoF to turn to the Bugginses, an East End family created and performed by the comedian Mabel Constanduros. By replacing Gert and Daisy with the family Buggins, including the cantankerous Grandma who had a deft line in malapropisms, *The Kitchen Front*'s producers demonstrated their belief that comic characters might attract and communicate with large audiences. The journalist and novelist S. P. B. Mais – previously something of a straight act – became 'a whirlwind comic, snapping out wisecracks'.[95] Ambrose Heath, a noted cookery writer, whose quiet practicality provided a thoughtful counterpoint to the boisterously convivial Mais and Grisewood, was moved to apologise for his style of delivery in just his second broadcast: 'One or two of my friends have told me that I sounded very miserable yesterday morning. I wasn't really: it's just the sort of voice I have.'[96]

Some listeners found the upbeat, Pollyanna-ish tone adopted by the programme, and by the Ministry, both tiresome and grating. This was especially true at those times of year, such as weeks before Christmas, when housewives were forced to contend with long queues and short tempers. In 1943, J. J. Llewellin, who had replaced Woolton as Minister of Food, announced plans to supplement basic rations with special festive bonuses, a move reported by the *Daily Mirror* under the headline 'An egg (real) and pork for Christmas.' 'Pork', insisted the new minister, 'goes very well with turkey.' The impact of this generosity was tempered by the fact that Llewellin was obliged to add a caveat: 'if you can get the turkey.' Although the press noted that this last line was intended to be humorous and self-deprecating, not everyone was in the mood for jokes.[97] Edie Rutherford, of Sheffield, made her frustrations clear in her diary:

> I dislike the mention on BBC and in the paper that pork goes well *with* turkey. Surely it will be fairer if those who don't get a turkey get a bit of pork. I find it hard to believe that there will be so much of either that anyone will get either for sure.[98]

Humour and good cheer, especially when expressed subtly, had their limits.

On other occasions, criticism was aimed at individual presenters, or the food information they provided. Mrs Ingillson was described by a Mrs Spencer of Stevenage as having the second worst voice on radio after Lord Haw-Haw, while Mrs Radmar of London was appalled by Robert Westerby, who was: 'not polite enough and obviously unfit for his duties'.[99] S. P. B. Mais received a hostile letter from a family in Farnborough that described one of his recipes as 'quite the most horrid dish we have ever attempted to consume; after only one mouthful each, there was a general dash for strong peppermint tablets'.[100] For the most part, the recipes, each of which was carefully tested in the Ministry of Food's own kitchens, were warmly welcomed by cooks looking to adapt their menus in the face of shortages of pre-war staples and the introduction of novel wartime ingredients.[101]

Although both the BBC and the MoF recognised that *The Kitchen Front* was aimed at a predominantly female audience – 'I don't suppose many men listen in at this time of morning' said the host on the morning of 3 July 1940 – the early weeks of the show were dominated by male voices. Indeed, it was the end of July before the first woman took charge of a broadcast.[102] And not only were these men talking to women: these were middle-class broadcasters talking to working-class listeners.[103] Bruce Blunt frequently talked about his housekeeper, Dorcas, and Freddie Grisewood was often heard conversing with his cook. That these men were not often responsible for either procuring or preparing the majority of their food (and the subtitle of Grisewood's *Kitchen Front* talks, 'A Man in the Kitchen', suggests the novelty of his position) seems to have been unimportant. This was, after all, the BBC; and male broadcasters were considered, initially at least, to have a greater degree of authority than their female counterparts.[104]

After a few months, a better balance between male and female presenters was achieved. Janet Chance, Helen Burke, Mrs Bosanquet and the actor Sunday Wilshin all hosted programmes during *The Kitchen Front*'s first year. As with their male counterparts, many of these women were middle class and southern. However, the presence of the occasional presenter with a regional accent, such as Mrs Ingillson from Yorkshire, was likely to have been welcomed in the north of England even if it did risk alienating some parts of the Home Counties. For the most part, though, listeners were inclined to be generous to the programme and its various hosts, perhaps because each broadcast attempted to present practical information in a way that blended entertainment and propaganda to the detriment of neither, while speaking to shoppers, cooks and consumers of their own wartime experiences.

The Kitchen Front made a sustained attempt to be inclusive. Ordinary Britons were encouraged to contribute to the show, and enough recipes and cooking tips were submitted from all corners of the country for the programme to become something of a national forum, which, day by day, built up a picture of British food during the war. Such was the kudos of contributing to *The Kitchen Front* that the MoF came to suspect that some of the food stories described by correspondents – such as the Bristol man who wrote to the programme about his 'teeny-tiny cauliflower' – were 'obviously concocted' in the hope of getting them read out on air.[105]

In 1942, the MoF published a collection of recipes submitted by listeners. The cover of *The Kitchen Front* featured a cartoon showing a woman holding a frying pan over her wireless set. The message was clear: the radio enabled her to cook. While each of the recipes in the book had been submitted by listeners, and tested by the MoF, the Ministry admitted that certain problems arose when it came to publishing retrospective collections of recipes. Foodstuffs that had been 'in good supply at the particular time' of broadcast might now prove rather more difficult for housewives to procure.[106]

By including material contributed by listeners, *The Kitchen Front* was positioned as a responsive medium, and its dialogical format further promoted the programme's psychological significance. By emphasising the crucial role of the warriors on the Kitchen Front, each five-minute broadcast contributed to a sense of national communality and encouraged individuals, in the words of one historian, to 'identify their day-to-day hardships with the wider national endeavour'.[107] Harassed housewives, bachelors and hungry schoolchildren were all made to understand that the problems they were experiencing were not unique to them; rationing and food shortages affected everyone, and all Britons had to adapt to a wartime situation in which one's diet evolved continually and the affordable luxuries of peacetime were often little more than a memory. One M-O diarist noted, with a mixture of frustration and pleasure, that she was finding it much harder to obtain the bones from which she had always made soups and stocks:

> No one used to bother with jelly bones or sheep heads or bacon bones from the grocer and I used to feel like little orphan Annie sometimes when I asked for them! Now I think the *Kitchen Front* talks are making people 'soup-conscious'.[108]

Housewives from poorer backgrounds who had for many years cooked with limited resources saw many of their 'dodges' and 'economies' find favour with previously more affluent households as *The Kitchen Front* broadcast 'bits and bobs' recipes that reflected a restricted national diet.[109]

The end of the war saw a reduction in government influence over the BBC. *The Kitchen Front* proved to be an early casualty: the programme ceased broadcasting in October 1945, although certain elements of it – in different formats and under a variety of names – would continue into the 1950s. The MoF, now powerless to dictate content, found itself marginalised in the programme's production, accelerating a process begun by an increasingly confident BBC during the last year of the war. Accustomed to having the upper hand in *The Kitchen Front* production process, the Ministry became little more than a repository of official information, a passive resource rather than an active collaborator. But despite the Corporation's eagerness to rid itself of ministerial shackles, the success of *The Kitchen Front* suggests that the BBC and the MoF were able to overcome their rivalry and produce effective and arresting radio publicity.

Food Facts

While the immediacy and communality offered by radio broadcasting were among the medium's greatest strengths, they could also be something of a disadvantage. As William Mabane, Parliamentary Secretary to the Ministry of Food, observed, 'The wireless is useful, but you may not hear it when the important announcement is made. If you do hear it, you may not get the details right, or you may not have time to make a note.' Mabane contrasted the radio with newspaper advertising:

> there … you have the details set out, in print, for you to study at your leisure. So far as the Ministry of Food is concerned, I say, read the newspaper and you are likely to hear something to your advantage [and] you will be making a direct and important contribution to the war effort.

Recognising the benefits of print advertising, and reminding Britons that 'In these days, it is the daily duty of every citizen to read the newspaper', the Ministry undertook a prolonged and expensive publicity campaign in broadsheets, tabloids, periodicals and magazines, developing the Food Facts series and purchasing space for single-issue promotions and one-off advertisements.[110] The first Food Facts column (see figure 3) was published in the week of 29 July 1940, with the series initially intended to run for three months. However, the MoF was so pleased with the advertisements that after just six editions the decision was taken to prolong the series indefinitely.[111] More than 500 editions would eventually be commissioned before Food Facts was finally discontinued in 1950. The PRD hoped that the advertisements would become the MoF's 'national noticeboard', carrying essential rationing information and recipes, promoting the consumption of non-rationed vegetable produce and explaining the functions and decisions of the MoF.[112] Despite a continued drive for paper economy, which would see the size of Food Facts reduced in line with the newspapers that carried them, and which led to the widespread promotion of recycling, readers were encouraged to keep the advertisements because it was felt that Food Facts could in many instances replace the leaflets that the MoF would otherwise have to print.[113] Such an attitude seems to have been justified, for in August 1948 a survey carried out for the MoF found that more than a third of those questioned had followed the MoF's advice and kept hold of Food Facts advertisements for later reference.[114]

The advertisements also pointed readers in the direction of alternate, and complementary, sources of food information. For example, Food Facts No. 5 advised readers to listen to *The Kitchen Front*:

Do you feel, as many women do, that war-time housekeeping would be easier if only you could count on getting a little special advice from a kitchen expert? Here's your chance – without trouble, without cost, without even having to leave your own home. Just switch on your radio every morning at 8.15. You'll hear the answers to your own kind of food problems.[115]

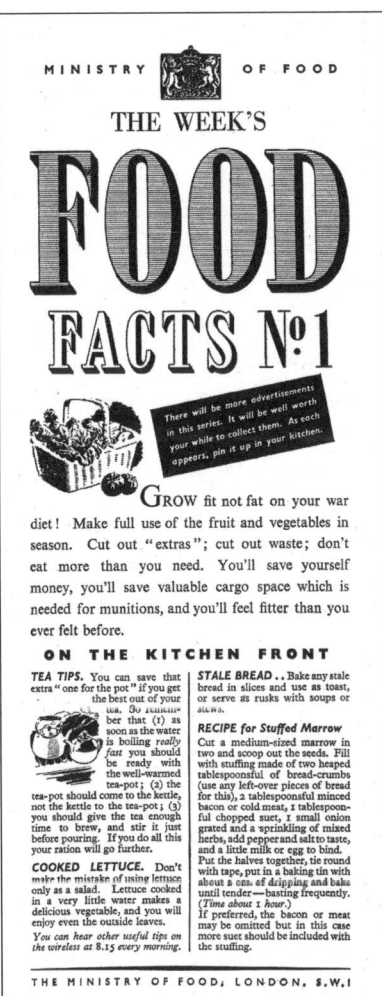

Food Facts No. 1, week of 29 July 1940.

Later advertisements mentioned the host of the corresponding week's *Kitchen Front* broadcasts by name – a move which suggests that the MoF was becoming increasingly aware of the appeal of the different personalities who fronted the programmes, and which has echoes of the decision taken at the beginning of the war that all news broadcasters introduce themselves at the start of each bulletin.

A survey conducted in the winter of 1942–43 established that almost half of the women questioned read MoF newspaper advertisements regularly, and a further quarter read them on an occasional basis. The opinions of men were not sought. Of the Ministry's advertisements, the most popular were Food Facts, although slightly less than 25 per cent of women could actually remember the title of the series – a result that might well have disappointed the PRD. The same survey discovered that MoF adverts were more likely to be read by younger women and those from higher income groups.[116]

It was not difficult for Britons to find a copy of Food Facts, for some 1,150 different newspapers and journals with an estimated combined weekly circulation of some 43,000,000 carried the advertisements. As the PRD itself conceded, this did not necessarily equate to a similar number of actual readers.[117] Wartime newspapers, with advertising space at a premium, were crowded with advertisements for all kind of products and services; there was no guarantee that Food Facts, arrestingly designed though they often were, would stand out sufficiently to turn occasional readers into regulars. Indeed, readers of different newspapers were sometimes treated to slightly different layouts, with the tabloids carrying slightly wider, shorter advertisements than those found in the broadsheets.

It is worth noting that paid advertising in newspapers and magazines was supplemented by liaison between the PRD's Press Branch and journalists. The MoF briefed newspaper employees with innumerable press releases and at frequent news conferences (it was to such a briefing that Carol Bennett was sent in *Unpublished Story*). The Press Branch passed on information, often linked to the theme of the current edition of Food Facts, in the hope that some of it might be included in the following day's papers thereby reinforcing the Ministry's messages. The MoF was aware that the newspapers would soon come to resent being fed material to be repeated verbatim. Press briefings were therefore most often used to provide the journalists with straightforward factual information that they could incorporate into their stories as they saw fit. The tactic seems to have worked, for Woolton, who held a press conference every Tuesday, boasted that although he 'never gave them sherry or any other inducement to come' more than eighty journalists would regularly attend because of 'the frankness and liveliness of the discussion that took place'.[118]

'Frank' and 'lively' are also suitable descriptions of the content and the style of the Food Facts advertisements.[119] Produced for the Ministry by three advertising agencies (Mather & Crowther, C. Vernon and Sons and Saward, Baker and Co.), there was no aesthetic uniformity: a bewildering array of fonts and layouts was employed in an attempt to attract readers and keep the advertisements from becoming stale. The MoF conceded that there was so much food information that it was not always easy to maintain reader interest, and so developed 'a special "magazine" format … to present a number of topics in a single advertisement'.[120] While this makes generalisations about style difficult, it is possible to suggest that official administrative information tended to be presented in a more conservative way, whereas commodity information and food advice were often expressed more informally. Short, humorous poems were a regular feature, often used to add a touch of levity to a serious advertisement, sugaring the pill of what might otherwise have been unpalatable messages.

The inclusion of cartoons made the advertisements more visually appealing; David Langdon was just one of the artists who contributed work to the campaign, while Walt Disney presented the MoF with a family of anthropomorphic root vegetables: Pop Carrot, Clara Carrot and the monocle-wearing Carroty George.[121] Despite the touch of Hollywood glamour offered by Disney's creations, the two longest serving animated conscripts on the Kitchen Front were Potato Pete and Doctor Carrot, with the latter being credited with some 'unexpected little talents', one of which was helping Britons to 'see better in the blackout'.[122]

The playfulness evident in many of the advertisements was not to everyone's taste. Describing the £78 that the MoF paid to place its Food Facts 'Puzzle Corner' in *The Times* in December 1944 as 'an absolute waste of the taxpayers' money', Maurice Petherick MP attacked the column as 'wholly puerile'. The offending advertisement quizzed readers about their knowledge of the food situation, testing how closely they had followed the year's Food Facts. J. J. Llewellin rejected Petherick's criticism, suggesting that although the piece might not appeal to all, it had been 'very generally appreciated' in 'a lot of houses up and down the country'.[123]

As with *The Kitchen Front*, most Food Facts assumed a predominantly female audience, speaking specifically to British women about their daily lives and concerns, and offering information about how best to feed a family in wartime.

It was assumed that those who queued for, purchased and prepared food would be women, whereas those who sold food and orchestrated rationing policy were men. Woolton's name was invoked on several occasions as an analogue for state authority, while the various grocers, milkmen and butchers who populated the Food Facts columns were all male, to say nothing of the cast of merchant mariners, Royal Navy sailors, dockers and lorry drivers, who, under the aegis of the government, were shown importing food from overseas and distributing it within Britain.

Some of the instructions contained in MoF propaganda might therefore have been considered patronising by housewives, especially those on lower incomes, who had successfully fed their families for many years without state intervention. These same women might not always have taken kindly to the Ministry of Food, containing a number of men who had rarely set foot in a kitchen before the war began, dictating dietary policy. Nella Last was surely not alone in the frustrations she expressed regarding this imbalance, especially in terms of the constitution of the government:

> I think it's a pity there are no women in the War Cabinet … I'd like to have some of them [politicians] to come and stay for a weekend. I'd show them a few things, and tell them what women thought – real everyday commonplace women like myself, who had to budget on a fixed income, and saw ordinary things wasted and no shortage of unnecessary things.[124]

Women like Nella Last prided themselves on their ability to cook and might not always have appreciated being told how to make the most of their rations. Two Food Facts were issued in autumn 1944, which toyed playfully with the idea of unwanted advice. In these advertisements, a younger woman was shown using MoF recipes to teach her sceptical grandmother how to prepare cabbage and how to make a rice pudding (although not how to suck powdered eggs).[125]

Perhaps concerned that adopting too dictatorial a stance might irritate British consumers, the MoF launched regular appeals for, and frequently printed, information submitted by those who read Food Facts. In one instance, recipes were solicited for inclusion in what was described as a 'Potato County Championship':

> Can the women of Somerset make better dishes than Kentish women? Can Devon cooks go one up on the Cornish Pasty? Lancashire Hot-Pot is praised the world over, but what can the women of Surrey or Hampshire do with potatoes? … Now is your chance to win honour for your county.[126]

The MoF's recognition of the regional nature of the United Kingdom extended to its production of specific propaganda for inclusion 'in newspapers published

North of the Border'. While, for the most part, this meant little more than substituting the word Scotland for England in phrases 'where the word "England" [did] not form part of a recognised phrase' – such as 'England expects', the inclusion of which in Food Facts No. 46 prompted a Scottish MP to complain about the Anglocentric language employed in MoF propaganda – it also, on occasion resulted in the creation of campaigns aimed specifically at Scottish consumers.[127]

Food Facts advertisements offered instructions on food preparation to women who had never been taught how to cook; information on nutrition, vitamins and health to housewives who had not previously thought about these aspects of their family's diet; and advice on how best to make use of novel or unusual ingredients like flat fish, turnip juice and wholemeal bread. Numerous advertisements contained recipes suggesting ways of cooking the unrationed vegetables that were cheap, British grown and in plentiful supply. A diet composed in the main of potatoes, carrots and cabbage was soon likely to lose its appeal if interesting ways of preparing them were not found, and Food Facts contained recipes for dishes such as devilled potatoes, carrot cookies and coleslaw. One advertisement from November 1944 suggested ways in which a man who was tired of cabbage might be made to eat more of it: 'How to fool your husband … three easy ways to make him eat his words – and his cabbage, too.'

> No husband can be expected to like over-boiled, mushy, tasteless cabbage. So be a gay deceiver just for once [and try one of these new recipes]. The first time, your husband won't recognise it as cabbage. Second time he'll ask for more.

So fooled, a 'silly goose' of a man would be transformed from a table-banging ogre into a charming dining companion who politely and enthusiastically asked, 'What's this delicious new vegetable?'[128]

British men, via their wives' cooking, were the eventual beneficiaries of much of the propaganda issued by the MoF, but it took the Ministry until April 1942 to produce a column that recognised that so significant were the changes afoot in wartime Britain that it should also target male readers:

> 'Man-about-Kitchen.' Now that thousands of wives and mothers are helping in the factories, or evacuated to the country, many men are having to do their own cooking. No wonder they ask their women-folk for easy recipes![129]

While it recognises the novelty of the 'man-about-kitchen' phenomenon, and pokes fun at the helplessness of the British male in matters of household economy, the advertisement positions this trend as being strictly temporary:

women are 'helping', rather than working, in the factories until such time as they can return to their domestic duties. There is no suggestion that cooking is a natural activity for the man of the house – although men who lived on their own had for many years honed their skills in this regard, as recognised by later Food Facts[130] – but, rather, is an inconvenience to be borne stoically in wartime. (Just how many men became competent in the kitchen and how many followed the lead of the widower Jim Crowson (Moore Marriot) in *Millions Like Us*, who, left to fend for himself following the conscription of his daughters, survived on a diet of fish and chips eaten off unwashed plates, is open to debate.)[131]

Food Facts provided the MoF with the regular noticeboard it desired, but the Ministry also paid to advertise in the Press during special single-issue campaigns. The 'Eat More Potatoes' drive saw the MoF place additional advertisements in papers at a total cost of more than £130,000.[132] Consumers were encouraged to 'Eat Home-Grown Potatoes Instead' of bread as part of a national 'Potato Plan':

1. Serve potatoes for breakfast three days a week.
2. Make your main dish a potato dish one day a week …
3. Refuse second helpings of other food until you've had more potatoes.
4. Serve potatoes in other ways than 'plain boiled'.[133]

A fifth part of the plan – 'Use potatoes in place of flour' – was soon added, and advertised in 'Potatoes Dishes', the *Food Flash* sent to cinemas in the week of 22 February 1943. In the film, a Food Facts column featuring a burning ship is shown to the camera. However, perhaps wary of disturbing members of the public during their precious leisure hours, the film's commentator concludes with an upbeat, rather than a sombre, message. The film cuts from the brutal Food Facts column to a table covered in food: '[Using potatoes] Makes sense, and makes lovely grub!'

Green vegetables were also heavily promoted. In September 1944, the MoF ran an advert in 'popular and women's weeklies' that demonstrated its prepared-ness to exploit traditional notions of femininity in an attempt to shift a few tons of brassicas. Cheekily taking advantage of the unpopular cosmetics rationing scheme run by the Board of Trade, the advertisement describes a '"Skin Food" [that] is not on a quota!' Cabbage, it was claimed, 'does remarkable work in clearing the complexion, making cheeks pink, lips red and infusing you with fascinating vitality'. Advocating that 'as with every beauty routine, regularity brings the best results', the text encouraged cosmetics-starved women to 'have cabbage in some form every day'.[134]

The ambitious nature of both the Food Facts and the single-issue campaigns required significant expenditure. Although the PRD selected papers to carry Food Facts and its other advertisements based on strict criteria to ensure maximum coverage for minimum cost, the bill for the MoF's print advertising campaigns was still large.[135] Peaking at an annual total of £531,712 in financial year 1942–43, the money spent on press advertising accounted for more than 90 per cent of the Ministry's entire publicity budget.[136] This figure remained largely similar until 1946–47 when a noticeable drop, to £344,172, reflected both a general tightening of ministerial belts and increased scrutiny of the amounts spent on government publicity campaigns in post-war Britain.[137] This decrease in expenditure brought about changes in the way Food Facts were disseminated: from August 1946, national daily and London evening papers only carried the advertisements in alternate weeks, a change which was extended to national Sunday papers in January 1947.[138] By the autumn of 1948, approximately £3,000 was still spent each week placing Food Facts, but this figure equates to less than a third of the cost of placing the advertisements during the years of peak food propaganda.[139]

Following the election of the Labour government in July 1945, Food Facts came under increased, and increasingly political, scrutiny. In December 1948, Edith Summerskill, Parliamentary Secretary to the Ministry of Food in Attlee's administration, was asked by the Conservative MP Sir Waldron Smithers if she was aware that 'many people think that these Food Facts are just a joke, that they are only Socialist propaganda'. Smithers' colleague George Drayson offered an alternate name for a series: 'Should not the title be altered to "Food Fables"?' Smithers himself chipped in with the idea of rebranding the series 'Food Failures'. Summerskill, unamused by such slights, informed the honourable gentlemen that they were 'completely out of touch' with British housewives.[140]

Despite such criticisms, Food Facts limped on until the summer of 1950. It is questionable, though, how effective the series was by this date. As more foods were taken off the ration, and as the amount of money made available for advertising declined, the decision was taken to discontinue the Food Facts series.[141] The war that had necessitated the campaign was over, and MoF publicity now did little more than point to the inability of post-war governments to lift the burden of food control. Many of the final advertisements reflected the relative scarcity of novel food information in the summer of 1950, with a large amount of blank space surrounding the text. This was in obvious contrast to the crowded multi-topic magazine format of the war years.

Without the war to justify rationing policy or publicity expenditure, Food Facts was quietly retired at the end of August, safe in the knowledge that, as the Publicity Club of London recognised, the campaign had played an important part in helping the MoF feed the nation.

The Ministry of Food at the cinema

The cinema was the most popular form of entertainment in the United Kingdom during the war, and the MoF was keen to use it to communicate with the British public. Furthermore, there was evidence to suggest that the cinema was likely to be a particularly effective propaganda medium for the Ministry of Food to employ. A wartime survey found that women were slightly more likely than men to visit the cinema on a weekly basis (34 per cent as opposed to 28 per cent). In addition, poorer sections of British society – less likely to read newspaper advertisements, least likely to own a working radio – were found to be the most regular cinemagoers.[142] The cinema could therefore complement, and extend the scope of, the MoF's publicity, simultaneously reinforcing and expounding the messages contained in both Food Facts and *The Kitchen Front*.

Having previously made use of slides and films produced by the MoI, in 1942, the MoF took greater control of its own cinematic publicity and commissioned a series of short, weekly film trailers called *Food Flashes*. These films are analysed more thoroughly in Chapter 2, but it may be useful here to outline the extent and style of this series and the contribution it made to MoF propaganda during the war. More than 200 *Flashes*, most with running times of 15–30 seconds, were released between March 1942 and November 1946. Understanding that the multi-subject magazine format, which had character-ised many of the Food Facts advertisements, would not work if used in the *Flashes*, the films instead offered a brief, and where possible humorous, expla-nation of a single point of rationing policy. As a visual medium, the *Flashes* were well suited to short instructional subjects and offered advice on how to bone a fish, measure a level teaspoon or collect a new ration book.

Each *Flash* was distributed to thousands of cinemas nationwide, appended to newsreels, and viewed by a weekly audience estimated to be in excess of 20 million people. In auditoriums deemed too small to merit the exhibition of a *Food Flash*, the MoF instead showed a specially prepared slide. These film slides were sent to 1,500 cinemas each week and contained a message of about twenty words such as: 'There are plentiful supplies this week of apples, plums and green vegetables – make the most of them.'[143] These slides also often referred cinemagoers to MoF displays in cinema foyers. Given that the Cinematograph Exhibitors' Association (CEA) had agreed to show the films and slides gratis, these campaigns were, unsurprisingly, considered by the MoF to represent excellent value for money. For instance, in 1941–42, the £2,884 spent by the MoF on cinema slides would have been an estimated £50,000 higher had screening fees not been waived.[144] The exhibitors' generosity made cinema advertising particularly cost-effective, especially when compared to press publicity, which was paid for at commercial rates less a small government discount.

Just as the MoF's relentless quest for wireless publicity strained its ties with the BBC, so its insistence on screening weekly *Flashes* introduced an element of tension into its relationship with the CEA.[145] Although the PRD would later claim that the production of *Food Flashes* was halted because exhibitors were suggesting that audiences were no longer responding to the films,[146] the CEA's commercial motive for advising the MoF to discontinue the series should not be discounted.[147]

The MoF's involvement in cinematic propaganda extended well beyond this single, extensive series. Issued in July 1940, *Food for Thought*, directed by Adrian Brunel, was the first film commissioned by the Ministry of Food. This short, which was shown in commercial venues, starred Mabel Constanduros (of Buggins family fame) as the host of a tea party to which guests bring their own sugar. *Kinematograph Weekly* thought the film 'entertaining' and anticipated the release of further food-related shorts.[148] It did not have long to wait: six short films called *Cookery Hints* were produced and released later in the year by Verity Films. Most often shown at non-theatrical venues, such as cookery demonstrations or women's organisations, the films had running times of five minutes or more and were able to discuss their chosen subject at some length. Pronouncing the films to be 'uncommonly well made', a reporter for the *Manchester Guardian* believed that they would be useful 'even to women who have long experience of cooking'.[149]

By 1942, government mobile film units were exhibiting food films to as many as five millions viewers each year at non-theatrical venues that could offer 'a blacked-out hall and an audience of not fewer than 100 people'.[150] MoF films could also be borrowed by individuals or organisations possessing their own projection facilities. However, while the number of Britons reached through non-theatrical screenings was relatively impressive, they pale in comparison to the tens of millions of patrons who visited Britain's cinemas each week. It is not surprising that the MoF decided that frequent and regular access to the nation's auditoriums would ensure better exposure for its publicity.

The production and distribution of weekly short films allowed the MoF to respond swiftly to the rapidly changing social conditions of wartime Britain and so avoid screening out-of-date material, which it had done to some embarrassment in the past. In April 1942, just as the first *Flashes* were being exhibited, eyebrows were raised by the screening of an older film which had been produced prior to recent alterations to the meat rationing scheme, and which advised women to: 'Take two pounds of neck mutton and some onions.' At this, many of the women in the audience were heard to laugh. The scarcity of previously easily obtainable foodstuffs invested shots of prosaic ingredients such as onions and mutton with a real and immediate power that had the potential to damage the MoF's reputation.[151] A newspaper correspondent who was present at the screening and witnessed the audience's reaction, adopted a whimsical tone and observed that the film was 'like a dream of the golden days'. *Today's Cinema*, a trade paper read by exhibitors whose integrity might be undermined by the inclusion of such out-of-date material, took a far more critical view. It declared the film to be 'a complete failure. It should not have been in the programme.'[152]

Even after commissioning its own films, the MoF continued to provide subject material for, and work in partnership with, the MoI. Consequently, *Eating Out with Tommy Trinder* (issued in the week of 10 May 1941) and *Queen's Messengers* (week of 12 July 1941), which explained how special convoys fed Britons displaced by the Blitz, were issued as part of the MoI's Five Minute Film programme. While the latter film is largely factual, the self-consciously humorous tone of the former anticipates the light-hearted approach that many *Food Flashes* would adopt.

Similarly comic is *The Way to His Heart*, a two-minute film made by Strand for the MoF and released through the MoI in December 1942 as part of the 'Eat More Potatoes' campaign. Noticeably longer than the *Food Flashes*, by this time a well-established element of British cinema programmes, *The Way to His Heart* constructs a simple narrative and deftly tells the story of how a man driven to drink by his wife's cooking is lured home from the pub after she prepares a potato dish according to a recipe found in a Food Facts advertisement. Thematically, then, the film is similar to many *Kitchen Front* broadcasts and newspaper advertisements. What is especially interesting about this film is its playful inventiveness: *The Way to His Heart* is shot as a pastiche of silent, First World War-era propaganda – and also of early twentieth-century temperance films – complete with static-yet-shaky camera, stylised inter-titles, Edwardian costumes and make-up, and a piano soundtrack.[153] While the film's parodic nod to an earlier cinematic style is hardly subtle, its knowing self-reflexivity promotes both the idea of food publicity as mischievous and non-exhortative and, through this conceit, potato consumption. Further, by choosing to finish with a cheeky, vulgar request for the audience to 'Eat more spuds!', *The Way to His Heart* gives a very distinct impression that the MoF is laughing at itself (see figure 4). This aligns the Ministry with the viewer, be they cook or consumer, who would no doubt groan at the prospect of having to face the 199 other potato recipes the wife promises to make.

It was almost always women, both old and young, who were shown cooking. In *Two Cooks and a Cabbage* (1941), two girls are called away from playing cricket with their brothers and taught by their grandmother how to properly prepare vegetables. (The girls are also shown setting the table while the boys, having put bat, ball and stumps aside for the day, fly paper aeroplanes in the garden.) One of the girls, Sally, is a walking MoF advertisement, following Ministry instructions to the letter, while the other, Jane, makes the wrong decision at every opportunity and serves up a very unappetising plate of cabbage, much to the distress of her brothers. Jane, though, is told not to worry about this temporary setback and informed by her grandmother that

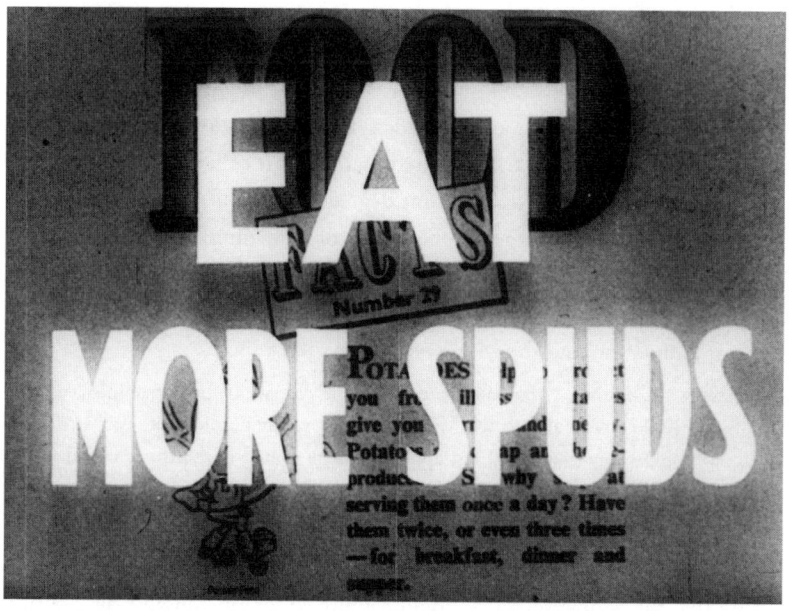

Inter-title from *The Way to His Heart* (1942).   **4**

she will 'do quite alright tomorrow'. The boys, on the other hand, receive no culinary training.

The MoF also worked alongside local exhibitors to devise special advertising campaigns that used commercial feature films to promote the work of the Ministry. In May 1943, the Regal in Levenshulme displayed posters that read, apropos the ongoing MoF campaign and the critically acclaimed 1942 naval drama, 'Eat More Potatoes and Help Save the Ships *In Which We Serve*.' A local MoF official addressed patrons at afternoon screenings of the film and a Canadian merchant seaman discussed his experiences at evening shows, while easels displaying Food Facts advertisements were placed in the foyer of the cinema and recipe cards were distributed to cinema-goers.[154]

This determination to address the people while they were at leisure demonstrates the single-mindedness of the MoF's approach, for by using the cinema to communicate with Britons, the Ministry encouraged consumers to understand that the battle on the Kitchen Front required constant vigilance. However, having taken the decision to make use of the nation's auditoriums, the Ministry's decision to employ a humorous style spoke of its desire not to alienate the public. By exhibiting numerous, short, amusing films it was able to integrate itself into British leisure culture (reiterating the prominence it enjoyed in British culture more generally) and thereby attempt to construct and define itself, and its audience, as good humoured, generous and food conscious.

'Helpful information, well presented'

The PRD did not find it easy to assess the contribution that its publicity made to wartime Britain, and admitted that, while it believed its campaigns to have earned the Ministry a significant degree of goodwill, this was difficult to quantify because of the large number of factors contributing to the formation of public opinion. Reviewing its work in the early 1950s, the PRD adopted a positive attitude when summarising the nature of the relationship between the general population and the Ministry:

> There is no doubt ... that during the war the climate of public opinion was, on the whole, favourable to the Ministry ... They [the public] were prepared to accept almost any hardships that appeared to be shared fairly; this enabled the Minister to be frank with the public and assured him a sympathetic acceptance of unpleasant news.[155]

On leaving the MoF, Woolton gave a speech in which he told staff that he was proud that the Ministry had 'got public approval for an equitable distribution of food in [this] country' before adding:

in these times of stress, when tempers are likely to get short in the stress of personal emotion, we kept the country steady, *feeling* that it was well fed and that the Government had a sense of justice and equity behind it.[156]

The public appears to have remained largely positive towards both rationing and the MoF throughout the war, and the Ministry's publicity can be understood to have played a part in shaping such attitudes. The work of the PRD was important: its newspaper, radio and cinematic advertising campaigns suggested openness and a willingness to communicate with the people it served. It also suggested that as far as food control was concerned the MoF, in Woolton's words, 'foresaw and knew how to handle the situation'.[157]

Reports were commissioned in an attempt to discover the impact and success of different campaigns. Many such reports discovered that heavy promotion of certain foods coincided with an increase in their consumption. In early 1940, having imported a significantly larger amount of sultanas than was usual, the MoF turned to the MoI for assistance in devising a campaign which would increase sales and prevent the sultanas from going bad. For an outlay of approximately £25,000, year-on-year sales rose by 42,000 tons, an increase of some 200 per cent.[158] The MoF also funded special advertising campaigns warning of the health problems caused by rats and promoting the nutritional benefits of fresh-salted cod, carrots, National Household Milk and dried egg. This last campaign was considered to be especially successful; the £42,500 spent on advertising resulting in a 50 per cent increase in weekly consumption.[159] According to the official history of the MoF, the publicity that attended the scheme to provide subsidised oatmeal to poorer consumers in winter 1940–41 proved to be 'all too successful' as the product rapidly became practically 'unobtainable'.[160]

However, it must be remembered that these special campaigns were often devised to help the MoF promote the sale of foodstuffs of which it found itself with a sudden glut, or to encourage consumers to rely less on ingredients which were becoming increasingly difficult to procure. As such, as the Wartime Social Survey noted, it is difficult to assess the extent to which changes in consumption patterns might be attributed to advertising as opposed to the easy availability of a promoted foodstuff when compared to shortages of alternatives.[161] That said, the £131,679 the MoF spent advertising potatoes in 1942–43 was claimed to have brought about a 500,000-ton increase in sales compared to the pre-war average. The Ministry noted that much of the growth was accounted for 'by precisely those usages advocated in [MoF] publicity, e.g. potatoes for breakfast, potatoes in home baking', suggesting a strong correlation, in this case at least, between the work of the PRD and British consumption patterns.[162] The near-continual promotion of potatoes – described by one historian as 'not [an] altogether promising ware for publicity' – led one women's magazine writer to claim in 1944 that 'There are certain words which, to the end of my life, I shall never be able to hear without being instantly reminded of this war. "Potatoes" is one, "Waste" is another.'[163] In this instance, the MoF's advertising strategy seems to have hit home.

The advertising on its own, however, was not enough, and could not in itself help the MoF fulfil its prime – in reality its sole – objective of keeping the people of Britain fed. It comes as no surprise to learn, then, that the Ministry's propaganda was least successful during periods when it was unable to honour the ration, or during prolonged spells of bad news on the Kitchen or other fronts. The early part of 1941 was one such period: even though it took the step of reducing the meat ration, for several weeks in January, the Ministry was unable to provide all consumers with their weekly allocation. In an era before most houses had the means of storing meat for more than few days, and in a period of general food scarcity, the problem was acute. In an attempt to manage the shortage, the meat ration was set on a week-by-week basis, a decision that threatened the MoF's reputation for efficient long-term planning.[164] This was clearly an unsettling event for many, coming at the same time as the Blitz, and also because of the symbolic importance of meat in the British diet: 'The British soldier is far more likely to be right than the scientists', Winston Churchill had claimed in the summer of 1940, '[and] all he cares about is beef'.[165] At such a time, what consumers did *not* want to hear was the Minister of Food advocating increased vegetable consumption:

> I find it hard to tolerate this incessant nagging, these endless exhortations and scoldings, those pompous official lectures from Lord Woolton – whose utterances, far from encouraging us to endure our monotonous and restricted diets with good grace, infuriate us and are anything but conducive to the maintenance of good morale. If carrots and potatoes are the only things we can get to eat, all right we'll eat them; but it really is *too much* to be lectured all the time about the excellence of carrots and potatoes, and scolded for not having eaten more of them before, and nagged at for having eaten too much of other things.[166]

Although the Ministry worked hard to repair the damage done by this temporary failure, Woolton's personal standing was far from assured. In June 1941, with the 'Great Egg Scramble' just beginning, almost a third of those questioned for a Gallup poll expressed dissatisfaction with the way that Woolton was going about his job. A year later, with the food issues resolved (and with Britain, now allied with the USSR and America, no longer fighting alone), this figure had fallen to just 12 per cent; those happy with his performance – seemingly always in the majority – had increased from 57 to 79 per cent.[167]

Some of the individuals who lent their talents to the PRD's work were able to make use of the resulting publicity to further their interests in other fields. Elsie and Doris Waters, for example, became closely enough associated with food after their *Feed the Brute* broadcasts and food talks to secure a contract with Foster Clark to make cinema advertisements for soup.[168] More gener-ally, the increased prominence the sisters enjoyed as a result of their radio broadcasts can be seen as a catalyst in their transition to feature film acting. Tellingly, both of their first two films (*Gert and Daisy's Weekend*, 1941, and *Gert and Daisy Clean Up*, 1942) have substantial food content. Charles Hill, the Radio Doctor, was in 1950 accused of using the fame he gained through his (supposedly) apolitical *Kitchen Front* broadcasts for personal gain when he successfully ran for Parliament.[169]

The positive reaction to particular performers and campaigns, though, should not obscure the fact that not all were so successful. The 'Eat Potatoes instead of Bread' campaign serves as an interesting example. Although adver-tisements encouraging potato consumption appear to have achieved their goal, those discouraging the eating of bread were less effective, with figures suggesting that the level of bread consumption remained largely static.[170] In the public mind, 'instead of' became 'as well as'.

Commentators in the advertising industry noted that by resisting the temptation to *tell* the public to consume less bread, and by not setting specific targets, the Ministry itself may have been to blame for the campaign's failure:

> They are trying by *indirect* means to persuade the public to eat less bread. Why not *base their copy* on that simple theme? Such a series could be made forceful and dramatic … If less stress is placed on potatoes and more emphasis is given to the slogan 'Eat Less Bread,' we may yet obtain more favourable results.[171]

Given the MoF's dislike for exhortation, and the possibility that by overusing dramatic images and wording the Ministry might desensitise the public to such an approach, their faith in a more subtle campaign is understandable. The Ministry might also have been concerned that imploring people to eat less bread could be regarded as an admission that bread was in short supply and that rationing might soon follow. Bread rationing carried such awkward political and psychological implications that Woolton feared its introduction 'would certainly be interpreted as the first sign of surrender'.[172]

However, while the MoF found evidence to support its belief that the public was generally appreciative of the PRD's positive approach to publicity, it was also aware that the advertisements which appear to have had the greatest impact, and which stuck longest in the public consciousness, were precisely those which employed dramatic imagery and text to focus on the plight of the merchant ships importing food into Britain.[173] *Advertiser's Weekly* welcomed the Ministry's forays into dramatic advertising, and insisted that the MoF should be more willing to 'give it to the public hot and strong' and not shy away from 'the horrific stuff ... in favour of the kid-glove stuff'.[174] Thus, while the journal praised much MoF publicity as 'helpful information well presented', it did not mince words when criticising advertisements which adopted a tone of 'patronising heartiness': 'the impression that one is being talked down to by the Government, spoils too much Government advertising'.[175]

Such criticism misses the point, however. While *Advertiser's Weekly* is probably correct to assume that condescending publicity was unlikely to have the desired impact on consumers, the sheer scale of the campaigns run by the MoF to maintain the prominence of the Kitchen Front necessitated a combination of different advertising styles. In addition, the Ministry wanted regular access to British consumers. Too dramatic an approach, as well as becoming less effective over time, might also make Britons less willing to welcome MoF propaganda into their homes, thereby undermining the personal relationship the Ministry sought to establish with the British public. The MoF even held back advertisements that it considered to be too distressing: one featuring a photograph of merchant seamen clinging to an upturned lifeboat was never issued for fear that it went 'a little too far'.[176] Although the adoption of a patronising attitude is likely to have alienated certain consumers, the idea that the government cared enough about the gastronomic tribulations of the individual to take the time to assist them was probably a comfort to many and a contributory factor in the maintenance of British morale.

The regular use of humour not only created a positive impression of the MoF but also demonstrated the Ministry's willingness to play with and confound public expectations, thereby exhibiting a real confidence in both the success of its own advertising and the public's acceptance of it. Trusting the audience to get the joke, especially if that joke was made at the expense of established preconceptions about the nature of government publicity in general, and MoF publicity in particular, suggests that the PRD was reasonably certain of the Ministry's position in the public affections.

The publicity campaigns orchestrated by the Ministry also had the effect of reminding British consumers of their position within a clearly defined food community. Just as rationing, a key component of the British wartime reality, influenced a great number of food transactions, MoF publicity about rationing pervaded the nation's most important communication media. The widespread nature of these campaigns, and the success they enjoyed, promoted and reinforced the notion of a collective attitude regarding consumption.

The different strands of MoF publicity fulfilled separate, although inter-linked, functions. While each type of advertisement was inherently and primarily communicative, allowing for the transmission of information about rationing and consumption, the three mass media employed provided the MoF with different ways to address (and construct) the food-based commu-nity. First, Food Facts columns, intended primarily for solitary reception, allowed individuals to personalise their position vis-à-vis the state, to find a space within the corporate nature of the rationing system. The option to retain the advertisements also encouraged an individual investment in and ownership of rationing. Second, radio broadcasts, although simultaneously addressing millions of people nationwide, tended to be listened to in intimate and domestic environments, thereby formulating the family group as an important building block of the rationing system and the community it helped to define. Third, *Food Flashes* and other MoF films were screened in cinemas which, by the late 1930s, had an average of 900 seats.[177] Even allowing for half-full auditoriums, this allowed the Ministry to address large groups of consumers en masse, facilitating the recognition of the communal nature of the rationing system. As shown in Chapter 2, the *Food Flashes* spoke to both the individual and collective nature of the cinematic experience.

All three campaigns were aimed primarily at women, but were conducted in the full view of the public gaze, so were also accessible to men and children. This served to raise food consciousness among those who might not have paid much attention to where their food came from, and also made the entire country more aware of the difficulties facing the nation's cooks in wartime. What had previously been very much a domestic concern was now integral to constructions of the public and the national.[178] The Ministry was keen to bang the drum for the vital contribution that women – so much more likely to be serving their country in civvies than in uniform, and responsible for the overwhelming majority of food shopping and cooking – were making to the war effort.[179] This celebration of the efforts made by British women should be understood as being aimed not just at British women, but also at British society as a whole. British cooks were shown as being active front-line combat-ants, as an integral part of the nation's mobilisation for total war. While it is easy to contest the factual accuracy of Norman Longmate's bold observation, made after the war, that 'the Kitchen Front was the only one where Great Britain never lost a battle' by pointing, for example, to the activities of the wartime black market and the occasional breakdown of the rationing system, what his claim makes clear is the perception that rationing in Britain was regarded as a success.[180] Given his use of the phrase 'Kitchen Front', coined by the MoF in the early days of food control, we might also understand the importance of the Ministry of Food's propaganda campaigns in facilitating and publicising this success.

The campaigns worked to concentrate attention on food not just as the single most important factor in the rationing system but also as an integral element of British wartime culture. Although food control was the wartime norm it was also a historically distinctive parenthesis in British consumer society; to adhere to the principles of rationing was to participate in a specifically British reality and signal one's belief in the state, its agency and its aims. To adhere to the principles of rationing was to position oneself within a food-based community. On the other hand, to transgress these norms located an individual as an outsider. Consumption therefore became politicised and the act of eating and drinking became associated with the extraordinary social conditions that necessitated food regulation, price control, queues and shortages. The prominence and cultural currency that food enjoyed because of the MoF's relentless publicising transcended the strict limits of the state–consumer relationship that had initially incubated it, and played a central role in constructing ideas of Britain and Britishness in wartime.

Notes

1 *Announcer*, 19 April 1947, p. 1.

2 Mass-Observation, *Home Propaganda (Bulletin of the Advertising Service Guild*, No. 2) (London: Curwen Press, 1941), p. 14.

3 *Observer*, 7 May 1944, p. 3.

4 History of Advertising Trust Archive: 'Official History of the Publicity Club of London, vol. 3' (unpublished, n. d.), pp. 263–4.

5 Ina Zweiniger-Bargielowska, *Austerity in Britain: Rationing, Controls, and Consumption, 1939–1955* (Oxford: Oxford University Press, 2000), pp. 60–98.

6 The National Archives (TNA) MAF 102/53: Transcript of Lord Woolton's speech at the Queen's Hall, 5 April 1940. The tea industry was swift to react to Woolton's speech, and Brooke Bond advertised the fact that such was the quality of their Dividend Tea that consumers had never been required to use 'one for the pot'. *Advertiser's Weekly*, 18 April 1940, p. 91.

7 *Daily Herald*, 4 April 1940, p. 6.

8 Lord Woolton, *The Memoirs of the Rt. Hon. The Earl of Woolton* (London: Cassell, 1959), p. 176. Woolton's lack of political experience created tension with the civil servants at the Ministry of Food. Hugh Dalton, then President of the Board of Trade, quotes Woolton as saying, during his early days in office, to his Permanent Secretary that 'you are trying to delay because you think I may not last very long as a minister, then you may get somebody who will let you go on doing what you like'. Diary entry, 4 August 1942, in Ben Pimlott (ed.), *The Second World War Diary of Hugh Dalton, 1940–45* (London: Jonathan Cape, 1986), p. 471.

9 In his diary entry for 11 October 1940, Woolton claimed that he 'always tried to use words of two syllables' when broadcasting to the nation. Bodleian Library, Oxford: MS Woolton 2.

10 Woolton placed such importance on his radio broadcasts that he took as long as eight hours to prepare for a twelve and a half-minute talk. Woolton, *Memoirs*, pp. 250–1. See also *Picture Post*, 1 June 1940, p. 42; Anthony Weymouth, diary entry, 10 July 1940 in *Plague Year, March 1940–February 1941* (London: George G. Harrap, 1942), pp. 125–6.

11 MS Woolton 11: Broadcast by Minister of Food, 3 December 1940.

12 MS Woolton 12: *Kitchen Front*, 25 December 1941.

13 Food Facts No. 69, week of 17 November 1941. Housewives were instructed to award themselves a medal for 'acting on recipes and hints from Kitchen Front wireless talks, Food Advice Centres and Ministry of Food magazine announcements'.

14 See Food Facts No. 88, week of 23 March 1942, where a man is shown excitedly telling his wife 'I used to think one didn't oughter / Make a soup from vegetable water / But this, my dear – this IS a snorter!'

15 Pam Ashford, diary entry, 10 May 1940, in Simon Garfield (ed.), *We are at War: The Remarkable Diaries of Five Ordinary People in Extraordinary Times* (London: Ebury Press, 2005), p. 218.

16 MS Woolton 11: fol. 39.

17 Quoted in J. A. Cole, *Lord Haw-Haw – and William Joyce: The Full Story* (London: Faber & Faber, 1964), p. 190.

18 J. B. Priestley, *Postscripts* (London: William Heinemann, 1940), p. vi.

19 Transcript of a broadcast made to North America, 21 June 1940. J. B. Priestley, *Britain Speaks* (New York: Harper and Brothers, 1940), p. 40.

20 William Mabane, 13 May 1943. *Parliamentary Debates: House of Commons*, 5th Series, vol. 389, col. 824.

21 Transcript of a broadcast made to North America, 21 June 1940. Priestley, *Britain Speaks*, p. 39.

22 Siân Nicholas, *The Echo of War: Home Front Propaganda and the Wartime BBC, 1939–45* (Manchester: Manchester University Press, 1996), p. 100, n. 145.

23 *Advertiser's Weekly*, 25 November 1943, p. 172. In a diary entry made on 25 October 1940, Woolton noted that Churchill had described him as 'one of his three successful ministers'. MS Woolton 2.

24 Food Facts No. 14, week of 28 October 1940.

25 See Food Facts No. 22, week of December 30 1940; *Advertiser's Weekly*, 18 June 1942, p. 221.

26 Diary entry, 6 January 1944. MS Woolton 3.

27 *Daily Mail*, 13 November 1943, p. 4. As chairman of the Conservative Party, Woolton remained a popular figure both within the party and in the country more generally. Indeed, in 1952 a jealous Churchill, then party leader, tried (and failed) to dismiss Woolton. John Ramsden, *An Appetite for Power: A History of the Conservative Party Since 1930* (London: Harper Collins, 1998), pp. 335–6.

28 Mass-Observation, *Home Propaganda*, p. 20.

29 *Daily Express*: 2 November 1939, p. 6; 4 November 1939, p. 4.

30 A. V. Alexander, 8 November 1939. *Parliamentary Debates: Commons*, 5th Series, vol. 353, col. 277.

31 Diary entry, 17 October 1941. MS Woolton 2.

32 28 May 1941. *Parliamentary Debates: House of Lords*, 5th Series, vol. 119, cols. 331–3; *The Times*, 29 May 1941, p. 4. Woolton suggests in his memoirs that 'foreign' agitators used the shortage and inequitable distribution of eggs to stoke dissatisfaction with rationing more generally. Woolton, *Memoirs*, p. 241.

33 'Bee', 'No good for the system', in *Daily Mail*, 11 July 1941, p. 3.

34 Norman Longmate, *How We Lived Then: A History of Everyday Life During the Second World War* (London: Hutchinson, 1971), p. 146; *Evening Standard*, 30 September 1941, p. 5.

35 Maggie Joy Blunt, diary entry, 12 August 1941, in Simon Garfield (ed.), *Private Battles: How the War Almost Defeated Us* (London: Ebury Press, 2006), p. 148.

36 *Picture Show*, 17 January 1942, p. 11.

37 *Evening Standard*, 26 August 1941, p. 5; Letter from L. R. Hills, Hayes, in *Daily Herald*, 9 July 1941, p. 2; *Daily Herald*, 27 June 1941, p. 3. See also Vere Hodgson: 'My one egg during a fortnight was bad – and they refused to give me another!' Diary entry, 28 November 1941, in *Few Eggs and No Oranges: A Diary Showing How Unimportant People in London and Birmingham Lived Through the War Years, 1940–1945* (London: Dennis Dobson, 1976), p. 195.

38 *Daily Mail*, 11 July 1941, p. 4.

39 *Daily Herald*, 28 June 1941, p. 1; Vere Hodgson, diary entry, 1 October 1941, in *Few Eggs and No Oranges*, p. 187.

40 Diary entry, 16 July 1941. MS Woolton 2.

41 See, for example, Food Facts No. 103, week of 30 June 1942, which promised consumers 'EXTRA EGGS!' and provided them with three recipes in which to use them.

42 Food Facts No. 77, week of 5 January 1942.

43 Diary entry, 23 September 1941. MS Woolton 2.

44 TNA INF 1/214: 'The Strategy of Food', 27 January 1942, p. 13.

45 TNA INF 1/214: Letter from Eric Knight to Arthur Calder Marshall, 28 January 1942. For Woolton's role in promoting the film see Richard Farmer, 'Exploiting a universal nostalgia for steak and onions: the Ministry of Information and the promotion of *World of Plenty* (1943)', *Historical Journal of Film, Radio and Television*, 30:2 (2010).

46 Diary entry, 8 April 1943. MS Woolton 3. Woolton did not achieve the same success or popularity as Minister of Reconstruction as he had as Minister of Food.

47 *The Times*, 17 November 1943, p. 5.

48 'Letter from London', 19 November 1943, in William Shawn (ed.), *London War Notes, 1939–1945* (London: Longman, 1972), pp. 298–9.

49 *The Times*, 12 March 1941, p. 6; 22 November 1941, p. 6; 7 December 1942, p. 6; 15 June 1943, p. 6; 19 October 1943, p. 6; 23 October 1943, p. 6; *Manchester Guardian*: 22 August 1940, p. 2; 29 September 1941, p. 2.

50 *The Times*, 7 December 1942, p. 6.

51 TNA MAF 75/67: 'General Account of the Work of Public Relations Division, 1939–50', p. 9.

52 *Daily Mail*, 29 March 1941, p. 3; TNA MAF 102/59: Minister's Public Relations: Correspondence; *Picture Post*: 1 June 1940, p. 42.

53 TNA MAF 75/67: 'General Account, 1939–50', p. 2.

54 TNA MAF 138/163: 'Notes for the use of the Accounting Officer on the Ministry's Vote Appropriation Account for 1946–47', pp. 15–6.

55 *Report of the Committee on the Cost of Home Information Services* (London: HMSO, 1949), p. 7.

56 3 February 1944. *Parliamentary Debates: Commons*, 5th Series, vol. 396, col. 1405; TNA MAF 138/162: 'Notes for the use of the Accounting Officer on the Ministry's Vote Appropriation Account for 1943–44', p. 25; *Report from the Committee of Public Accounts* (London: HMSO, 1945), p. 180. In April 1945, an article in *Kinematograph Weekly* reported that approximately 550 government films had been shown on British screens during the war, of which 160 had been issued by the Ministry of Food, 90 by the National Savings Committee and the vast majority of the rest by the MoI. *Kinematograph Weekly*, 5 April 1945, p. 5.

57 Publicity that promoted nutrition often encouraged British consumers to recognise the importance of three main types of food: 'energy', 'protective' and 'body-building'. A more detailed analysis is contained in Mass-Observation, *Home Propaganda*, pp. 14–15.

58 *Picture Post*, 1 June 1940, p. 42.

59 TNA INF 1/343: 'Home Publicity: Scheme of Campaign relative to Rationing', 29 October 1939.

60 MoF advertisement 'Reasons for Rationing', week of 8 January 1940.

61 Food Facts No. 72, week of 1 December 1941.

62 TNA INF 1/343: Memo from Mr F. Darvell to Mr A. Hope-Jones, 23 November 1939.

63 Sir Leonard Lyle, 18 July 1940. *Parliamentary Debates: Commons*, 5th Series, vol. 363, col. 474. Lyle was talking in particular about radio programming.

64 TNA MAF 75/67: PRD, "Food Facts' Survey', 12 February 1949, p. 2. Four categories of Food Facts were ranked according to popularity: 1) official rationing news; 2) cooking methods; 3) recipes; 4) exhortation to the housewife.

65 TNA MAF 75/67: 'General Account, 1939–50', p. 10.

66 Woolton, *Memoirs*, p. 251.

67 TNA MAF 75/67: 'General Account, 1939–50', p. 1.

68 On the Ministry of Information's attitudes to humour, see Anthony Aldgate and Jeffrey Richards, *Britain Can Take It: The British Cinema in the Second World War* (Edinburgh: Edinburgh University Press, 2nd edn, 1994), p. 76.

69 TNA INF 1/343: Memo, 'Food Publicity Campaign: Phase 3', 21 December 1939.

70 Woolton, *Memoirs*, pp. 251–2.

71 *Daily Express*, 10 April 1940, p. 11.

72 *Manchester Guardian*, 10 April 1940, p. 8.

73 Mass-Observation, *Home Propaganda*, pp. 29–30.

74 *The Times*, 24 August 1940, p. 9.

75 Jennifer Davies, *The Wartime Kitchen and Garden* (London: BBC Books, 1993), pp. 47–8.

76 Diary entry, 15 March 1941. MS Woolton 2.

77 TNA MAF 102/2: *Kitchen Front*, 23 to 28 December 1940.

78 *Picturegoer*, 20 January 1945, p. 14.

79 Askey's comic partner, the debonair Richard 'Stinker' Murdoch, was engaged as the 'compère' of a special Food Facts newspaper advertisement in December 1944. Food Facts No. 234, week of 24 December 1944.

80 *The Economist*, 28 December 1940, p. 794.

81 *The Times*, 11 April 1942, p. 2; *Advertiser's Weekly*, 9 April 1942, p. 22.

82 Letter quoted in Woolton, *Memoirs*, p. 247.

83 Longmate, *How We Lived Then*, p. 154. By December 1941, the £29,000 the MoF had spent on advertising the National Loaf had resulted in it accounting for just 7 per cent of total bread sales. Gwilym Lloyd George, 11 December 1941. *Parliamentary Debates: Commons*, 5th Series, vol. 376, cols. 1713–14.

84 TNA RG 23/18: Wartime Social Survey, 'Food: 1) Food Schemes, 2) Publicity, 3) Shopping and Shortages' (May 1942–March 1943), p. 45.

85 Asa Briggs, *The History of Broadcasting in the United Kingdom: Vol. III – The War of Words* (Oxford: Oxford University Press, revised edn, 1995), p. 36.

86 Nicholas, *Echo of War*, p. 72.

87 TNA MAF 102/2: *Kitchen Front*, 13 June 1940.

88 R. J. E. Silvey, 'Listening in 1940', in *BBC Handbook, 1941* (London: Hazell, Watson and Viney, 1941), p. 79.

89 *Daily Mail*, 11 January 1945, p. 4; diary entry, 24 October 1941 in Richard Broad and Suzie Fleming (eds), *Nella Last's War: The Second World War Diaries of Housewife, 49* (London: Profile, 2006), p. 167; Frederick Grisewood, *The World Goes By* (London: Secker & Warburg, 1952), pp. 211–12.

90 *The Ministry of Food Bulletin*, No. 210, 1 October 1943, p. 1. The *Bulletin* presented this change as being 'consented to' by Woolton following a 'request' from the BBC.

91 Davies, *Wartime Kitchen*, p. 47.

92 BBC memorandum, 5 August 1943. Quoted in Briggs, *War of Words*, p. 37, n. 145.

93 Charles Hill, *Both Sides of the Hill* (London: Heinemann, 1964), pp. 106–7.

94 Nicholas, *Echo of War*, p. 78.

95 S. P. B. Mais, *Calling Again: My Kitchen Front Talks with Some Results on the Listener* (London: John Crowther, 1941), p. 6.

96 TNA MAF 102/2: *Kitchen Front*, 26 June 1940.

97 *Daily Mirror*, 27 November 1943, p. 8.

98 Diary entry, 27 November 1943, in Sandra Koa Wing (ed.), *Our Longest Days: A People's History of the Second World War* (London: Profile, 2008), p. 183.

99   TNA MAF 102/59: Minister's Public Relations: Correspondence.

100 Mais, *Calling Again*, p. 148.

101 Home Intelligence Reports compiled for the Ministry of Information refer to the appreciative comments made by many women about the MoF's willingness to distribute recipes. See, for example, report from 7 August 1940 in Paul Addison and Jeremy A. Crang (eds), *Listening to Britain: Home Intelligence Reports on Britain's Finest Hour, May to September 1940* (London: Bodley Head, 2010), pp. 307, 309.

102 TNA MAF 102/2: *Kitchen Front*, 3 July 1940. Mrs Ingillson was the first female host.

103 A survey analysing MoF propaganda found that working-class women were the most likely to listen to *The Kitchen Front*. See TNA RG 23/18: Wartime Social Survey, 'Food', p. 49.

104 Nicholas, *Echo of War*, p. 75.

105 TNA MAF 102/59: The letter from 'E. M. L. T.' of Bristol is discussed in an undated summary of correspondence.

106 William Mabane, 18 June 1942. *Parliamentary Debates: Commons*, 5th Series, vol. 380, cols. 1700–1.

107 Nicholas, *Echo of War*, p. 70.

108 Nella Last, diary entry, 10 February 1941, in Wing (ed.), *Our Longest Days*, pp. 69–70.

109 Nella Last, diary entry, 3 October 1941, in Broad and Fleming (eds), *Nella Last's War*, p. 165.

110 *The Times*, 17 October 1942, p. 2. Mabane also told reporters that without the papers, the MoF 'could not do its job.' *Daily Mirror*, 17 October 1942, p. 2.

111 *MoF Bulletin*: No. 45, 2 August 1940, p. 1; No. 49, 30 August 1940, p. 1.

112 TNA MAF 75/67: 'Work of the Publicity Branch, 1939–50', p. 3.

113 *MoF Bulletin*, No. 141, 5 June 1942, p. 1. The MoF estimated that it had printed 12 million fewer leaflets as a result of British consumers retaining Food Facts columns.

114 TNA MAF 75/67: PRD, '"Food Facts" Survey', August 1948, p. 2.

115 Food Facts No. 5, week of 26 August 1940.

116 TNA RG 23/18: Wartime Social Survey, 'Food', pp. 58, 61. Other reports suggested an even greater degree of popularity: 'A survey carried out by a commercial firm showed that 86 per cent of the public notice the advertisements, while 50 per cent read them through from beginning to end.' *MoF Bulletin*, No. 241, 5 May 1944, pp. 1–2.

117 TNA MAF 75/67: 'Work of the Publicity Branch, 1939–50', p. 7.

118 Woolton, *Memoirs*, pp. 248, 253.

119 TNA MAF 75/67: 'Work of the Publicity Branch, 1939–50', p. 3.

120 TNA MAF 138/163: 'Notes for the use of the Accounting Officer, 1946–47', p. 20.

121 Diary entry, 10 November 1941. MS Woolton 2.

122 See MoF advertisement C5, week of 2 February 1942.

123 17 January 1945. *Parliamentary Debates: Commons*, 5th Series, vol. 407, col. 165. The offending advertisement was Food Facts No. 234, week of 25 December 1944.

124 Diary entry, 1 July 1940, in Broad and Fleming (eds), *Nella Last's War*, p. 57. It would be 1945, when Edith Summerskill became Parliamentary Secretary to the Ministry of Food, before a female politician became associated in the public mind with the MoF. That said, every post-war Minister of Food was male.

125 Food Facts Nos 223 and 224, weeks of 9 and 16 October 1944.

126 Food Facts No. 119, week of 12 October 1942.

127 3 July 1941. *Parliamentary Debates: Commons*, 5th Series, vol. 372, col. 1520. A 1944 campaign, run in conjunction with the Ministry of Health for Scotland, encouraged vegetable consumption among Scots.

128 Food Facts No. 228, week of 12 November 1944. As Nella Last said of her husband, 'he doesn't like economy dishes – if he realises they *are* economy [dishes]!' Diary entry, 26 November 1941, in Broad and Fleming (eds), *Nella Last's War*, p. 171.

129 Food Facts No. 93, week of 27 April 1942.

130 Food Facts No. 213, week of 31 July 1944.

131 Many commentators assumed that government-subsidised canteens would be especially popular with men whose wives had been evacuated. See *Cambridge Daily News*, 27 December 1940, p. 4.

132 TNA MAF 138/161: 'Notes for the use of the Accounting Officer on the Ministry's Vote Appropriation Account for 1942–43', p. 23.

133 MoF advertisement P. 14, week of 4 January 1943.

134 TNA MAF 102/65: MoF advertisement S. 101, September, October and November 1944.

135 TNA MAF 75/67: 'Work of the Publicity Branch, 1939–50', pp. 3–4. Only papers with a circulation of more than 5,000 and with a maximum advertising rate of 6*d* per single column inch per thousand circulation carried MoF advertisements. William Mabane, 29 July 1943. *Parliamentary Debates: Commons*, 5th Series, vol. 391, col. 1813.

136 TNA MAF 138/161: 'Notes for the use of the Accounting Officer, 1942–43', p. 22.

137 John Strachey declared that MoF advertising expenditure for 1946 was 'considerably reduced compared to that spent under my predecessors'. 24 March 1947. *Parliamentary Debates: Commons*, 5th Series, vol. 435, col. 840.

138 TNA MAF 138/163: 'Notes for the use of the Accounting Officer, 1946–47', pp. 18, 21; *The Times*, 10 May 1947, p. 7.

139 Edith Sumerskill, 1 December 1948. *Parliamentary Debates: Commons*, 5th Series, vol. 458, col. 177. Certain Food Facts were considered worthy of more widespread dissemination (at a proportionally greater cost). In the run-up to Christmas 1949, for example, approximately £5,400 was spent on placing Food Facts No. 495. 14 December 1949. P*arliamentary Debates: Commons*, 5th Series, vol. 470, col. 262.

140 6 December 1948. *Parliamentary Debates: Commons*, 5th Series, vol. 459, cols. 12–13.

141 TNA MAF 75/67: 'General Account, 1939–50', p. 4.

142 TNA BT 64/4747: Wartime Social Survey, 'Ministry of Information inquiry into cinema audiences', pp. 2, 4; TNA RG 23/18: Wartime Social Survey, 'Food', p. 45.

143 *Kinematograph Weekly*, 20 November 1941, p. 11; TNA MAF 75/67: 'General Account, 1939–50', p. 5; *Daily Film Renter*, 28 August 1941, pp. 1, 5.

144 TNA MAF 138/160: 'Notes for the use of the Accounting Officer on the Ministry's Vote Appropriation Account for 1941–42', p. 6.

145 The CEA reported that some patrons had complained that many government shorts were 'of no interest from an entertainment point of view, and entertainment is what [patrons] pay their money at the box office for'. *Kinematograph Weekly*, 26 April 1945, p. 40.

146 TNA MAF 75/67: 'General Account, 1939–50', p. 5.

147 See, for example, *Kinematograph Weekly*, 5 April 1945, p. 26.

148 *Kinematograph Weekly*, 18 July 1940, p. 7.

149 *Manchester Guardian*, 13 December 1940, p. 4.

150 *The Times*, 18 April 1942, p. 2.

151 Although by 1942 supply had increased, the memory of the acute shortage of onions in 1940–41 would still have been fresh in the memories of many British housewives. See Longmate, *How We Lived Then*, pp. 144–5. In autumn 1941, an enterprising showman from Middlesbrough attracted patrons to the Elite cinema by displaying in a glass case some onions that he had brought to Teeside from Leeds, some 50 miles distant, 'on loan'. Onions were still enough of a rarity for the display to become 'the talk of the town'. *Kinematograph Weekly*, 2 October 1941, p. 43.

152 *Manchester Guardian*, 18 April 1942, p. 4; *Today's Cinema*, 21 April 1942, p. 2.

153 TNA INF 6/1831: 'Rough Treatment for Trailer on: Potatoes', p. 1. This treatment envisioned the film as 'a potted version of an old silent domestic drama – complete with jerky movements and dark, scratchy printing.'

154 *Kinematograph Weekly*, 20 May 1943, p. 47.

155 TNA MAF 75/67: 'General Account, 1939–50', p. 9.

156 Lord Woolton, quoted in *The Times*, 16 November 1943, p. 2. Emphasis added.

157 Woolton, *Memoirs*, p. 187.

158 *Report from the Committee of Public Accounts, Session 1941–42* (London: HMSO, 1942), p. 194.

159 TNA MAF 138/162: 'Notes for the use of the Accounting Officer, 1943–44', p. 26.

160 R. J. Hammond, *Food: Vol. I – The Growth of Policy* (London: HMSO, 1951), p. 183. See Food Facts No. 24, week of 13 January 1941.

161 TNA RG 23/46; Gertrude Wagner, '"Eat More Potatoes": An enquiry into the effect of a publicity campaign', July 1943, p. 1.

162 TNA MAF 138/161: 'Notes for the use of the Accounting Officer, 1942–43', p. 24.

163 R. J. Hammond, *Food: Vol. II – Studies in Administration and Control* (London: HMSO, 1956), p. 146; Monica Dickens in *Woman's Journal*, March 1944. Quoted in Jane Waller and Michael Vaughan-Rees, *Women in Wartime: The Role of Women's Magazines, 1939–1945* (London: Optima, 1987), p. 5.

164 *Daily Express*, 9 January 1941, pp. 1, 6.

165 Memo from Churchill to Woolton, 14 July 1940. In Martin Gilbert (ed.), *The Churchill War Papers: Vol. 2 – Never Surrender, May 1940–December 1940* (London: Heinemann, 1994), p. 514.

166 Unnamed M-O diarist, 18 February 1941, in Amy Helen Bell, *London Was Ours:*

Diaries and Memoirs of the Blitz (London: I. B. Tauris, 2008), p. 74. Emphasis in original.

167 *Daily Mail*, 28 August 1941, p. 2; *The Gallup International Public Opinion Poll: Great Britain 1937–1975: Vol. 1 – 1937–1964* (New York: Random House, 1976), pp. 46, 60. The second Gallup poll was taken in May 1942.

168 *Advertiser's Weekly*, 10 October 1940, p. 26.

169 *The Times*, 13 February 1950, p. 5.

170 *Advertiser's Weekly*, 11 March 1943, p. 209.

171 *Advertiser's Weekly*, 18 March 1943, p. 242. Emphasis in original.

172 TNA PREM 4/2/2: Lord Woolton, 'Policy of the Ministry of Food', 30 July 1940, p. 5.

173 *Advertiser's Weekly*, 21 October 1943, p. 45.

174 *Advertiser's Weekly*, 21 January 1943, p. 66.

175 *Advertiser's Weekly*, 26 March 1942, p. 250.

176 Hammond, *Food: Vol. II*, p. 146.

177 Linda Wood (ed.), *British Films, 1927–1939* (London: BFI, 1986), p. 120. Wood's figures are taken from *Today's Cinema*, 27 June 1936.

178 For more on this, see Gillian Swanson, '"So much money and so little to spend it on": morale, consumption and sexuality', in Christine Gledhill and Gillian Swanson (eds), *Nationalising Femininity: Culture, Sexuality and British Cinema in the Second World War* (Manchester: Manchester University Press, 1996), pp. 70–1.

179 For examples of contemporary views, see Elaine Burton, *And Your Verdict?* (London: Frederick Muller, 1942), p. 15; J. B. Priestley, *British Women Go to War* (London: Collins, 1943), p. 13.

180 Longmate, *How We Lived Then*, p. 140. That contemporary critics were equally as positive about the work of the MoF can be seen in the title of Thomas G. Jones's *The Unbroken Front: Ministry of Food, 1916–1944 – Personalities and Problems* (London: Everybody's Books, 1944).

2

Food Flash! Ministry of Food short film publicity

During the winter of 1942–43, London bore the brunt of the Ministry of Food's (MoF) relentless 'Eat More Potatoes' publicity campaign. In addition to material directed at the entire nation – Food Facts newspaper adverts, *Kitchen Front* radio broadcasts and a short *Food Flash* publicity trailer entitled 'Potato Resolution' (which encouraged the population to make a New Year's pledge to 'Save on bread, eat potatoes instead') – a special *Food Flash* was exhibited in the capital's cinemas to advertise 'Potato Pete's Fair'.[1]

Taking place on Oxford Street, on the site of the bombed-out John Lewis department store, and attracting more than 100,000 visitors during its fortnight run in December 1942, the fair was seen as an MoF attempt to '"go gay" in its campaign to increase potato consumption'. Its success was assisted by the relative scarcity of competition: 'Gone are the days when every shop in the street vied with the others to produce the gayest, most exciting show, and Potato Pete, holding the field to himself, is proving a great draw'. The fair was opened by Lord Woolton, the Minister of Food, with the assistance of Potato Pete, a 'utility model' Father Christmas, six clowns, two midget ponies and a baby elephant named Comet.[2] (Comet, Mollie Panter-Downes informed readers of the *New Yorker*, proved to be too heavy to perform his duties in full, 'perhaps from too much patriotic spud-eating'.)[3] Such publicity stunts contributed to a 50 per cent rise in potato consumption during the first four years of the war, with the free baked potatoes handed out on Oxford Street by Father Christmas in lieu of presents no doubt contributing to this increase.[4]

The majority of the Ministry's publicity took more conventional forms, however. At the fair, a temporary cinema was constructed to exhibit a continuous loop of MoF cartoons and weekly *Food Flashes*, presumably for the benefit of those who had missed such films when they were given a theatrical release. By screening at the fair the forty *Flashes* it had already released in Britain's cinemas, the MoF emphasised the importance it placed on the films' ability to communicate food information, but also simultaneously to contribute to the fun of the fair.

The MoF was a firm believer in the ability of the moving image to complement the food-related information it issued through other media. At the forefront of the Ministry's cinematic publicity were the two hundred or so *Food Flash* films made for the Ministry by National Screen Service Ltd (NSS) and issued in the years between the screening of the first film, 'Bakers' Deliveries', in the week of 2 March 1942, and the last, 'Charlie Chester 5', in the week of 4 November 1946.

Given that many of the *Flashes* are no longer extant and that the NSS archive detailing this period of the company's history has been either lost or destroyed, there are, naturally, gaps in our knowledge of the company's involvement in the production process. However, material held in the National Archives, although often frustratingly incomplete (nothing, for example, appears to have been kept concerning the process of choosing the subject or writing the script for individual films), allows for a more confident assessment of the MoF's role in this long-running partnership.

Almost half of the films survive and can be viewed in various British archives. They tend to follow a regular format: following a standardised opening sequence in which the MoF's logo is transformed into the words 'Food Flash' by way of an animated explosion accompanied by the sound of a cymbal crash, a single point of rationing policy is presented and discussed. The majority of the films lasted less than thirty seconds, making them among the shortest films ever screened in British cinemas. The films' brevity was not regarded as a weakness by contemporary critics, with *The Times* describing as 'admirable' the *Flashes*' ability to 'make their point in a few seconds'.[5] The longevity of the typical *Food Flash* format, which could easily be adjusted in response to changing publicity imperatives, is testament to the confidence that both the Ministry and NSS had in it; the humorous approach that the films frequently adopted is suggestive of the MoF's desire to arrest the interest and maintain the goodwill of cinema patrons.

The ability of the *Food Flashes* to address simultaneously each member of a group of cinema-going consumers, thereby transforming individuals into a corporate body, strengthened the notion of a collective gastronomic identity established by the communal imagery presented in the Ministry's other publicity campaigns. Annette Kuhn has written that *Desert Victory* (1943) had a style 'characterised largely by an appeal to the unit, most apparent in an address which renders the spectator as a member of a collectivity'.[6] Such an approach is also evident in the *Food Flashes*, which can be understood as attempting to construct a cinema audience as a group and encouraging this audience to understand itself as such.

Production

As with other major strands of food-related publicity, the MoF, rather than the Ministry of Information (MoI), was responsible for the commissioning, content and financing of the *Food Flashes*. The MoF envisioned the nationwide exhibition of a new *Food Flash* each week, and in commissioning 218 films it came close to achieving this goal: during the series' run, only 29 weeks saw either a reissued *Flash* or no film at all.

The *Food Flashes* were made by National Screen Service Ltd,[7] a company that specialised in film trailers, the production and distribution of which it virtually monopolised during the 1940s.[8] NSS had been founded in America in 1919, and its British subsidiary opened in 1928 and subsequently made trailers for all of the major studios, leading to the development of a brief, arresting style able to summarise broad narrative themes in a few quick sequences. Working for commercial advertisers and government departments (for example the MoI), NSS also made short publicity films. The company's capacity to shoot and edit new footage on limited budgets and to very tight deadlines meant that it was an obvious choice of partner when the MoF decided that it wanted to directly address British cinema audiences.

The trailers produced by NSS were frequently designed to coincide with the wider promotional campaign, most importantly in terms of advertising posters, which accompanied a film's release. As such, NSS was called upon to produce trailers that highlighted a particular aspect of a film – a star, a theme, a technical novelty – while simultaneously summarising a 90-minute narrative in 90 seconds in such a way as to 'secure orders' from cinema managers and patronage from cinema-goers.[9] The MoF, which also put out promotional material across a wide range of media, therefore found in NSS a company that was able to satisfy its criteria for filmed publicity, namely the ability to 'convey essential topical information quickly and dramatically to the public', but also able to integrate the *Food Flashes* with more general promotional activity.[10]

Each *Flash* was made by NSS's Documentary Department, which remained in central London even after those responsible for making feature film trailers had been evacuated to Perivale, Middlesex. The speed with which the films were made allowed for the messages contained within them to respond to a rapidly changing rationing situation, and, in some instances, individual *Flashes* seem to have been released too early (that is, before the issues they discussed came into effect). For example, in November 1943, *Daily Film Renter* reported that traders in Lambeth had complained to the MoF regarding a *Flash* which informed consumers that tinned jam was now available, when no new stocks of jam had been released.[11] However, such problems seem to have been relatively rare, and for the most part the films issued were able to address topical gastronomic matters in a timely manner.

Individual *Flashes* were the result of consultation between NSS personnel and the MoF's Films Officer, who ensured that a particular film's content corresponded with the Ministry's wider publicity plans. The films were simply, quickly and cheaply shot by directors such as Norman Cobb and Cecil Hepworth, the latter a film pioneer who had joined NSS after his own studio had gone out of business. Although Hepworth appears to have directed the majority of films in the series, he was not particularly impressed with the work that he undertook for the MoF, comparing what he considered to be the 'ineffective' *Flashes* with the 'snappy little propaganda films' his own company had made during the First World War.[12] Acting, for example, as a grocer in 'Fats Reduced' (week of 16 July 1945, see figure 5), Hepworth appeared in several

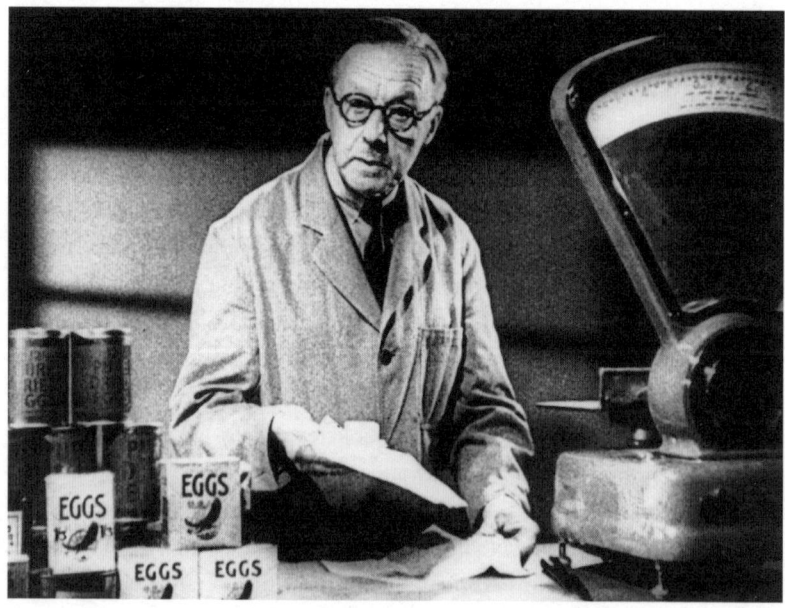

5   Cecil Hepworth in 'Fats Reduced', week of 16 July 1945.

Flashes and co-opted members of his family – or at least their identity papers – into starring alongside him. Documents belonging to Hepworth's second wife Olive feature in 'Ration Book No. 1' and 'Ration Book No. 2' (weeks of 13 and 20 May 1946) and his daughter Valerie's ration book and papers feature in 'Identity Card' (week of 19 April 1943). Their presence suggests a familial, ad hoc and, above all, cheap mode of production. Hepworth's was not the only face to gain national exposure as a result of appearing in the *Food Flash* films: the series featured a stock company of British men, women, boys and girls, each of whom was placed before the camera at regular intervals to populate the food-based community that the MoF and NSS aimed to create.

As NSS made the majority of its profits from selling its trailers directly to cinemas, it had developed an independent distribution network of which the MoF availed itself. Completed films were sent to cinemas around the country, where they were often shown immediately after the newsreel.[13] Initially, the *Flashes* targeted larger venues – those seating more than 1,000 people – and six weeks into the series Woolton announced that each film was being exhibited in nearly 2,000 cinemas, more than 40 per cent of the total number of screens.[14] The number of cinemas showing the *Flashes* rose throughout the war, eventually reaching 3,000, or about 65 per cent of the total.[15]

The expansive nature of the campaign led to an increase in the MoF's budget dedicated to cinematic publicity. During 1941–42, the Ministry had spent just under £3,000 on the production of cinema advertising slides, but the production of a weekly film necessitated an increase in advertising expenditure: in the year following the first *Food Flash*, £10,352 was spent on production and distribution. As with the cost of showing the slides, this figure would have been significantly increased had the Cinematograph Exhibitors' Association (CEA) not instructed its members to waive their normal screening fees, an act which meant that in their first year the *Flashes* enjoyed £85,000 worth of screen time 'without payment'.[16]

The decision to exhibit the *Flashes* was not universally welcomed by all cinema managers. Although each film was brief, it was usually accompanied by at least one MoI film, and often a series of slides eliciting donations to local and national charities, too. *Kinematograph Weekly* reported exhibitors' fears that entertainment-hungry patrons would come to resent the amount of screen time dedicated to the war: one correspondent observed that during a recent visit to a cinema, half of the evening's programme had consisted of 'national effort films'.[17] Such was the prevalence of government shorts that a *Kinematograph Weekly* columnist worried that cinema audiences might come 'to think that the cinema exists to act the role of an "interfering marm" in all areas of life – domestic as well as social and governmental'.[18]

While the concerns of exhibitors were most often couched in terms of their 'duty to the paying patron', some cinema managers took a more openly commercial stance. One even suggested that the government and local charitable organisations should be made to pay for screen time, thus remunerating the trade for any potential loss of goodwill that might result from having to show excessive amounts of screen propaganda while also discouraging the further proliferation of slides and films.[19]

Another issue which concerned exhibitors was the fact that some state-sponsored films were not registered as British at the Board of Trade, meaning that they did not count towards the quota of domestically-produced films that each cinema was legally obliged to show. In this matter the government sided with domestic short-film producers, who feared that the appeal their films held for exhibitors would be undermined if they were forced to compete for quota space with MoI and MoF films, which the CEA had already agreed to screen.[20] Exhibitors were thus committed to show not only those cheap British films of variable quality produced to satisfy the requirements of the quota, but also numerous 'national effort' films.[21]

Estimates as to how many patrons saw each *Flash* vary, from 18,000,000 to, a frankly unlikely, 30,000,000.[22] The Ministry's own calculation of 21,500,000 weekly viewers favours the more conservative end of this scale, but is still suggestive not only of the number of Britons who regularly attended the cinema during the war, but also of the potential of this form of publicity, especially given the relatively small amounts spent on producing and distributing the films.[23] *Kinematograph Weekly* was clearly impressed, and when it discussed the films in December 1944, it began its article with a joke: 'Printer! Run me off a few extra noughts…'[24]

Expenditure on *Food Flashes* doubled in 1945 when the number of cinemas screening the films rose and the length of each film was increased by a few seconds.[25] Although the MoF would later concede that the desired expansion was 'limited by the amount of film footage available',[26] it successfully lobbied the Board of Trade to increase the stock it was allocated by some 20 per cent.[27] Indeed, the MoF's faith in its *Food Flashes* led to the films' proportion of the Ministry's publicity budget more than tripling, from 1. 77 per cent in 1942–43, to 5. 44 per cent in 1945–46.[28]

However, as competition for limited supplies of film stock increased, the ubiquity of the MoF's films provoked criticism, and there were some reports of exhibitors simply dropping government films from their programmes.[29] In April 1945, with the end of the war in sight, C. J. Burow, a member of the Devon and Cornwall branch of the CEA, described the *Food Flashes* he had recently been sent as 'a complete waste of film' that 'nobody could understand'. Worse, Burow declared that so acute was the shortage of stock that some film renters were unable to provide exhibitors with a full programme, meaning that 'some distributors had to refuse good money while Government departments could waste it on flashes'.[30] This shortage was, exhibitors believed, the result of increased government involvement in film production, for although the total amount of stock processed each year had risen between 1939 and 1945, the amount made available for commercial interests had declined.[31] The MoF, though, clearly considered its expenditure of both money and film stock to be justified. In December 1944, Minister of Food J. J. Llewellin thanked CEA members for helping the MoF 'speak to many of the people whom we most want to reach'.[32]

Britain's cinemas were obvious locations for the display of MoF publicity; they attracted tens of millions of patrons each week. In late 1941, Woolton had requested that CEA members display additional rationing information in their foyers, and the brevity of the *Food Flashes*, which prevented them from discussing the minutiae of complex subjects, made them ideal for directing public attention towards such displays.[33] Hoping to encourage patrons to view this information as a supplement to, rather than a replacement for, the entertainment for which they had paid, those *Flashes* which discussed the foyer's function as a site of MoF advertising typically used actuality shots of patrons leaving a cinema.[34] In 'Ration Book "B"' (week of 18 May 1942), the standard *Flash* opening sequence was inverted; instead of the MoF roundel moving towards the viewer, it moved away, towards the cinema exterior over which it is superimposed. This has the effect of drawing the viewer into the building, which here functions as a repository of rationing information. Whereas most *Flashes* passed information from the screen to the patron, in this instance the patron needed to be proactive. At the film's conclusion, the MoF logo reappears, moving this time towards the audience, restoring normality and repositioning viewers within the auditorium.

However, the audience which the MoF was so keen to reach with its cinematic propaganda was not always appreciative of its efforts. In January 1943, the London *Evening News* printed a cartoon (see figure 6) in which a woman stands outside a cinema and, seeing a board advertising the presence in the programme of an MoF film entitled 'Eat More Potatoes', asks the

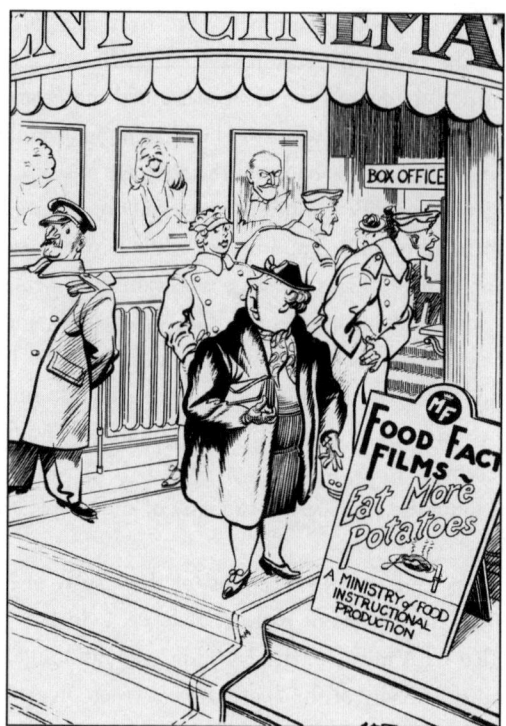

6

Food for thought: 'Anything else on the menu today, Mister?'
Joseph Lee in the *Evening News*, 12 January 1943.

commissionaire if there is 'anything else on the menu'. Although the cartoon calls this MoF release a 'Food Fact Film', this inaccurate description, which confuses the names of print and cinematic promotional campaigns, is suggestive of the Ministry's omnipresence in British wartime culture. It also predicts the title of a *Food Flash* released just two months later, although this act of clairvoyance is perhaps not surprising given the effort the Ministry put into placing this particular message before the British public. Hinting at the zeal with which the MoF attempted to communicate with the British people, the cartoon also recognises the occasional tensions that arose from the Ministry's insistent intrusions into cinemas, newspapers and other popular media.

The antagonism that developed in some quarters towards the *Flashes*, and towards state-sponsored films more generally, arose not only from the fact that valuable moments of screen-time were being taken up by propaganda films, but also because such films brought the real world into the fantasy space of the cinema. As the war ground on, and as rationing and food control became more burdensome, the constant reminders that as soon as patrons stepped foot outside the theatre they would be reclaimed by a world of queues, coupons, potatoes and points grated to an ever greater degree.

However, as if aware that its weekly forays into British cinemas might attract such criticism, the MoF occasionally mocked its own position as propagandist, joyfully subverting the intrusiveness of its films. In 'Dried Milk and Eggs' (week of 26 October 1942), the narrator, over shots of the foods in question, announces that:

> Two old friends turned up again last week, and they'll keep coming every eight weeks. Here's one for you: dried milk. And here's another for you, with a double ration for the under fives: dried eggs.

There follows a cut to a shot of a darkened auditorium in which a man stands and gesticulates towards the screen. The narrator, adopting a working-class accent to speak for this cinema-goer, delivers the film's punch-line: 'And here's one for you: Dry up!' *Fin.*

When the *Food Flashes* were eventually discontinued in November 1946, the decline of public responsiveness was cited as the cause.[35] It should come as little surprise that the MoF lost some of its popularity after the cessation of hostilities, for while it could use the Fascist menace during the war to justify its existence and its enthusiasm for cinematic propaganda, the end of the war left the Ministry with no external threat to dramatise. Whereas in early 1943 three *Flashes* used shocking images of German naval vessels sinking British wheat ships to discourage bread consumption, the introduction of bread rationing in 1946 was accompanied by four films which did little more than list regulations and tell the public that their diet was about to become even more restricted. British cinema-goers were, for the duration, prepared to tolerate the *Flashes'* intrusion into an evening's entertainment; but weary and hungry after the end of the war, they were less willing to stomach such films.

Format

As might be expected of a series of more than 200 films concerned with so broad and varied a subject as rationing and food control, the *Food Flashes* addressed a diverse range of issues, from the best way to cook cabbage so as to minimise vitamin loss to the need to preserve food stocks, via the sudden availability of certain foodstuffs and the correct way to complete personal information in a ration book. The MoF understood that film had significant demonstrative capabilities, and the *Flashes* became an important source of practical advice on how to prepare powdered milk or measure a level spoonful.

Although such instructional films had a tendency to dullness, many attempted (not always successfully) to lighten their tone and raise a smile.

For all the diversity of content, though, the opening few seconds of each film remained largely unchanged throughout the series (see figures 7–10). Designed to arrest the attention of the viewer, this simple sequence sets the tone for the film which follows. The destruction of the crown-topped logo – which carries the imprimatur of government – appears to occur when it reaches the screen, as if the official publicity message potentially contained in each film is unable to negotiate the fabric, and is therefore unable to ignore the entertainment norms, of the cinema.[36] As such, it is effectively reshaped by the rules of a popular entertainment medium.

The opening sequence, and the other on-screen typography, was most likely the work of George White's Art Department at NSS. Having produced title and credit sequences and trailers for feature films, the style which White and his staff had developed was often integrated into the *Flashes*. In one *Food Flash*, which advertises the availability of National Milk Cocoa for workers under 21, a succession of slogans appear on the screen in a manner which is reminiscent, albeit in a less hyperbolic way, of the overblown trailer for the fictional film 'Flames of Passion' in *Brief Encounter* (1945). Yet whereas the lettering announcing the approach of the 'Stupendous! Colossal!! Gigantic!!!' cinematic experience appears over exotic African footage, the *Flash's* claim that 'National Milk Cocoa warms you through and through' is superimposed over silhouettes of factories, the industrial connotation of such an image communicating the significance of nutrition to a worker's productivity, just as an exotic locale is required for a romantic adventure. Further, such *Flashes*, by adopting a knowing and mock-epic style, could be inserted less jarringly into a cinema's programme.

The *Flashes'* desire to entertain, or, rather, to disrupt as little as possible the cinema's ability to entertain, saw the adoption of a playful tone where possible, with many films featuring excruciating puns and tenuous wordplay. 'Marmalade', from Easter 1945, had the narrator claim that an increase in the preserves ration was 'An Easter egg for you, just like Mamma laid'. Elsewhere, 'Dried Fruit – Dates' (week of 25 November 1945) had fun with the different meaning of the word 'date', which suggested that consumption of the fruit would increase the likelihood of a romantic tryst, while 'Swedes' (week of 10 May 1943) also had fun with homonyms: (vitamin) C, sea, see. The series also made use of more visual forms of comedy, most noticeably the slapstick associated with drunkenness, a subject which permitted the MoF to condemn

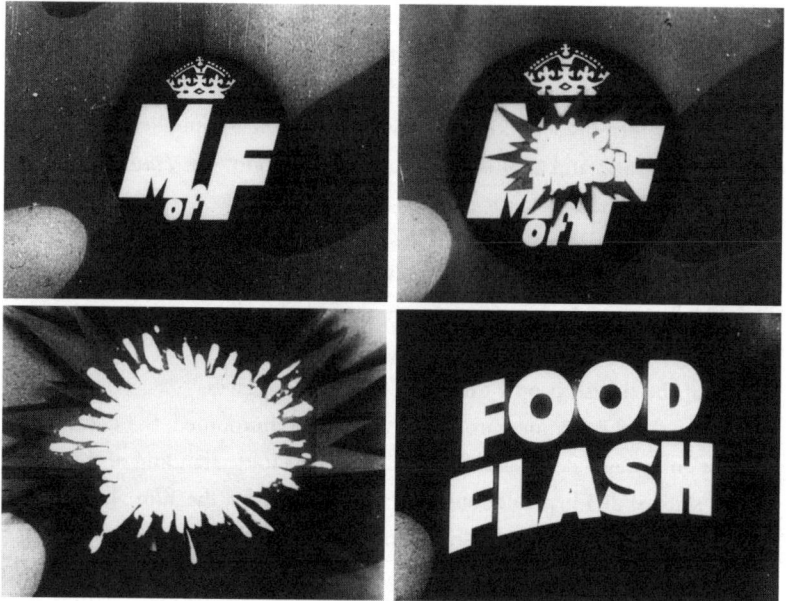

The *Food Flash* opening sequence.   **7–10**

(in a mild way) the selfishness of over-indulgence in an era more commonly characterised by the communality and restraint of its consumption practices. In 'Carrots' (week of 14 September 1942), the eponymous vegetables are said to help 'night blindness', although not the sort, the narrator adds, as a man weaves along a street and clings to a lamp-post, associated with a trip home from the pub. The narrator of 'Canned Jam' (week of 12 April 1943) told viewers, over a shot of two inebriated men, that as far as their preserves were concerned 'bottled or canned, they're very much the same'.

Many of the films were quite inventive – within the limitations imposed by their restricted budgets and short running times – when it came to photography, with some utilising simple special effects to enliven their subjects. In 'Clean Milk Bottles' (week of 24 August 1942) the film is run in reverse to reassemble a broken bottle, while a similar technique is used to un-cut, and therefore prevent the squandering of, a loaf in 'Waste Bread' (week of 23 November 1942). 'Double Egg Ration' (week of 6 November 1944) used a different type of trick photography, doubling the image on the screen – first of a bus, then a packet of dried eggs, then a basket of eggs – to reinforce the message contained in its title. In one of the more bizarre sequences in the *Food Flash* series, Potato Pete is dismembered and chopped into pieces to represent the different elements of the five-part 'Potato Plan' (week of 21 June 1943).

While verbal dexterity, physical comedy and trick photography rarely overwhelmed or distracted from the information the films were intended to impart, they added a touch of levity to what might otherwise have been a series of dry sermons, marking the MoF as a cinematic publicist hopeful of presenting a warm and approachable face to the nation. The *Flashes*' unnamed and exclusively male narrators, whose upper-middle class accents spoke with, and for, the authority of the MoF, usually mustered at least a modicum of enthusiasm for their subject, and although the films' simplistic messages occasionally patronised audiences, on the whole, they were inclusive and attempted to demonstrate what the state was doing to feed the British people, and what the British people might do to feed themselves.[37]

The tone of the commentator, most often good humoured, but occasionally stern or encouraging, was crucial to an audience's understanding of the nature of the state–individual relationship as envisioned by the film. Indeed, the small budget allotted to each film did not often stretch to synchronous sound; non-diegetic voice-overs were the norm. Viewers were, therefore, dependent on the commentator to an unusual degree. This reliance on the commentator was made all the more acute because the brevity of each *Flash* did not provide much opportunity for alternative interpretation: the way that each film was construed was largely dependent on the attitude adopted by the omniscient narrator.

The narrators' frequent emphasis on particular dates (often complemented by close-ups of calendars or a Food Facts column) lent the films a historic specificity, making the viewer's relation to, and understanding of, each *Flash* temporally and culturally immediate, positioning the audience as a community defined by shared experiences. Further, by most often directly addressing their viewers as 'you', a pronoun with both singular and plural connotations, the narrators positioned the individual as the recipient of the film's message, but also encouraged the individual to understand themselves as a member of a larger group (in the obvious sense of the cinema audience, and in the more abstract sense of the national community).

These 'yous', of course, were very often women. Women were understood to constitute a larger proportion of the cinema audience than men, and the chance to talk to them directly was too great for the MoF to pass up. Yet the appeal the Ministry made to female cinema-goers was perhaps less explicit than might be expected. Within the films, many of the basic practicalities of food preparation are often explained to female protagonists, and there is an obvious assumption in many *Flashes* that women will be shopping and preparing food.

Women, then, were still presented as being the cooks of the nation, but they are less explicitly coded as active participants in the war than they are in, for example, the Food Facts advertisements. The intention of the films was not so much to publicly laud the contribution that housewives were making to the war effort as to pass on practical information in as lively a manner as possible.

There were, of course, some *Flashes* that praised the women of Britain. 'Pool Delivery', from the week of 1 March 1943, suggested that 'shoppers [were] doing their bit, and more than their bit', and that the country was benefiting as a result. The shoppers shown are all women – the grocers are all men – and the film cuts to a shot of a woman with a shopping basket returning home on foot along a suburban street as the commentator delivers his final line: 'This petrol [saved by the pooled delivery of groceries and careful shopping] goes to the war effort, but the credit goes to you.'

If the *Flashes* were somewhat restrained when it came to praising Britain's housewives, they were less circumspect about pointing out where women could get food information. Many *Flashes* make reference to either *Kitchen Front* broadcasts, or to Food Facts advertisements. 'New Ration Book No. 2', from the week of 24 May 1943, has a commentary featuring a deliciously tenuous pun, but makes clear the way in which the different strands of MoF propaganda were to be understood as complementary and interlocking rather than as stand-alone campaigns:

> Some buy papers, some achieve papers, and some have papers thrust upon them. But which ever you do, take a good look at Food Facts in this week's papers. It tells you the first and last word about the ration books; instructions, information, everything.

While these words are being spoken, Food Facts No. 151, issued in the same week as the film, appears on the screen.

Screened outside London in the week of 21 December 1942, 'Food Information' ties cinema advertising to other important aspects of the MoF's advertising campaigns, using the *Flash* format to accentuate its message. The film starts with two speeded-up shots of shoppers walking along a generic High Street, over which a male voice announces: 'Bit quick this, you know, isn't it? Like a *Food Flash*. But you can always get fuller food details from Food Facts in the papers…' – there is a cut and a zoom into a close-up of a finger pointing to an MoF advertisement (No. 126, week of 30 November 1942) – '… and from the radio every morning at 8. 15'. There is another close-up, this time of an alarm clock, showing the appropriate time, which dissolves to a shot of a wireless set. 'So look out.' In just fifteen seconds – slightly shorter than most

Flashes – all three of the MoF's major wartime campaigns are mentioned. The swiftness with which the narrator imparts information is matched by the quick cutting of the five different shots (not including the opening sequence) that constitute the film. Allowing the temporal limitations of the *Flash* format to dictate content, 'Food Information' self-consciously accentuates, and therefore celebrates, the *Flashes'* brevity.

'Food Information' also suggests that the MoF was aware that the cinema was a site of escape suited to a very specific mode of address. Many *Flashes* understood the counter-productivity of exposing cinema audiences to lengthy lectures after they had paid to be entertained. Thus the MoF preferred to make short, pithy statements – these, after all, were as capable of encouraging personal and national food consciousness as a lengthier lecture – and refer viewers to propaganda media where they were more able to interact with food publicity at their own convenience. Obviously, this is not to suggest that the MoF's films were not intrusive, only that the frequent references to other propaganda media suggest a degree of sensitivity to possible audience reactions.

Yet whereas the fear of antagonising the audience persuaded the MoF to address women, likely to be regularly interacting with other types of food propaganda, in a relatively low-key way, the potential number of men that could be reached via film led the Ministry to more regularly talk to this section of the audience than it did in its other propaganda. While men could easily switch off a radio or choose not to read a Food Facts column (or, in the case of 'Food Facts Recipes', week of 21 January 1946, simply pass an advertisement to the wife and wait for a delicious meal to appear as if by magic) it was more difficult to ignore a *Food Flash*. The *Flashes* therefore made more appeals to male consumers – both directly and in terms of featuring male protagonists for British men to identify with – than did either *The Kitchen Front* or Food Facts.

On occasion the homonymic word play in some of the male-oriented films is little more than a sniggering double entendre catering to male desire. For example, in April 1944 British cinema-goers were presented with a film that told them that potatoes, like a young lady who is shown removing her coat as she smiles for the camera, are 'equally good with jacket on, or off' ('Small Potatoes', week of 17 April 1944). Eighteen months later, a film about the availability and points value of dried dates shows a young lady in profile, as the narrator asks the audience 'what's the best point about [this kind of date]'? ('Dried Fruit – Dates', week of 25 November 1945.) Other films were more restrained and saw men, many of whom were having to fend for themselves for the first time following the evacuation of their families or the conscription of their wives, being taught how to do all manner of useful things, such as boning a herring.

However, while the *Flashes* are intriguing in their attempt to get British men to think about food, they still conformed to normative attitudes concerning gender roles: women were, on the whole, shown preparing food, and men selling and consuming it. Indeed, on the few occasions when men are shown as active agents in the kitchen, such as Charlie Chester's feeble attempt to cook a cabbage, the situation is played as comedy, as a temporary inversion necessitated by extraordinary circumstances. Yet these films, despite the gendered division of labour that they presented, might also be understood as having persuaded British men to recognise the efforts of British women. *Food Flash* films that featured a male protagonist might have encouraged male viewers to contemplate who was responsible for their own food, and to get them to think, even momentarily, about the amount of time spent by their mothers, wives and daughters on shopping and cooking, compared to the time they themselves spent on these essential tasks.

While many of the films centred on interesting topics or benefited from scripts that encouraged narrators to adopt a personal or energetic tone, not all *Food Flashes* could embrace such an approach. Some were unable to escape the restrictions imposed by their instructional purpose and/or their rapid and cheap production: such films were little more than a series of static shots, inter-cut with inserts and stock footage, with a non-synchronous soundtrack. However, though many *Flashes* were made about unglamorous subjects, such uninspired films are surprisingly rare. Some *Flashes*, unable to find interesting ways of communicating with their audiences, settled for listing dates and facts while shots of calendars, ration books and potatoes reproduced visually, and often with dogged literalness, the accompanying narration. 'New Ration Period' (week of 20 July 1942), for example, consists of a single shot of a woman entering her personal information into a new ration book and placing her old one in the drawer of her desk. While a slow downwards tilt attempts – and fails – to add a degree of visual interest, the flat narration makes no attempt to engage the viewer, imparting instructions in an insipid monotone.

Seemingly aware that dull publicity ran the risk of alienating the very people to whom the *Flashes* were intended to appeal, the Ministry and NSS introduced elements into the films which toyed with expectations and gained the viewer's attention. Understanding that the opening sequence had great potential, several *Flashes* rejected the standardised format and replaced it with something more novel. Of course, such an approach, akin to an in-joke, was constituted on the understanding that viewers were familiar enough with the films to be able to recognise, and appreciate, such a change. That the audience was trusted in this matter is testament to the confidence of the Ministry, both in its own abilities as a publicist, and in the public's attitude towards it. In the week of 3 August 1942, six months into the series, a *Flash* called 'Sour Milk' was released which replaced the sound of the cymbal with a thunder clap, using this meteorological sound effect as the basis for a wry explanation as to why dairy products spoil, using science to disprove an old wives' tale which held that bad weather caused milk to turn.

A more dramatic alteration of the standard opening accompanied a sequence of three *Flashes* exhibited in early 1943. Linked to the 'Eat More Potatoes' campaign, the films graphically illustrated the dangers faced by the merchant ships which imported wheat to Britain, and hence the cost, in human lives and military materiel, of a loaf of bread.[38] Each of the three 'Bread Costs Lives' films (weeks of 18 and 25 January and 1 February 1943) began with the sound of German naval guns, and the juxtaposition between the seriousness of this message and the more light-hearted tone that the *Flashes* usually adopted was further accentuated by an additional alteration to the opening sequence. By replacing the animated explosion with a shot of a real one and, at the moment that the words 'Food Flash' usually appeared, cutting to a shot of the guns being fired, the film ties the work of the MoF, and the dietary habits of the British people, directly and graphically to the war effort.

The decision to discard the standard opening sequence prepares the viewer for the directness of the Ministry's appeal. Distressing shots of torpedoed ships and merchant seamen adrift in the Atlantic – shots captured, the viewer is told, from a German raider – drive home the three films' messages with rare force, further confounding audience expectations. The commentary was also different; a dispassionate narrator granting the images the space to speak for themselves stood in obvious opposition to the puns and word play found in so many previous (and, indeed, later) *Food Flashes*.

The novel visual and formal style of these three *Flashes* was mirrored in two Food Facts columns (numbers 133 and 134) released to coincide with the films; shocking imagery and a spare style of commentary were utilised in these advertisements, too, in a radical deviation from the established good-natured and consensual format. Clever use is made in the advertisements of the restrictive dimensions of the newspaper column; the narrowness of the photographs, the first used in Food Facts advertisements, accentuates the vertical axis and so focuses the reader's attention on either the prow of a ship standing unnaturally upright as it waits to sink beneath the waves, or the plumes of smoke issuing from the fires aboard a stricken merchant vessel. Attention is also focused on the images by the limited textual content of these particular advertisements.

Advertiser's Weekly described the campaign in glowing terms, claiming that such publicity proved the MoF had 'its coat off and its sleeves rolled up', and that its impact was such that 89 per cent of those questioned about it understood the 'Eat More Potatoes' campaign as having a 'ship saving motive'.[39] Although an MoF report observed that many consumers felt that they were already eating 'as many potatoes as they can stomach' and noted that a significant minority expressed 'disbelief in the nutritional value and harmlessness of the potato', such was the success of the campaign that its slogan was thrown in the face of the Ministry during a tuber shortage during the winter of 1944–45.[40] Indeed, when the Wartime Social Survey conducted research into the 'Eat More Potatoes' drive, it found that some Britons were unwilling to admit that they had not increased their potato consumption for fear of appearing unpatriotic, a fact that speaks to the visibility, and the limits, of the campaign.[41]

The linkage of potatoes to the war effort, and the elevated position that they occupied in the British national diet, meant that it was not only government films that made mention of them. In *Millions Like Us* (1943), a family gathers after dinner to listen to the news on the radio. They soon descend into bickering; the only story that can be heard concerns the importance of potatoes to the national diet, an ironic interjection given the disappointing nature of the meal they have just eaten. Further, in *The Life and Death of Colonel Blimp* (1943), the humble potato is the inspiration for one of the two alimentary nicknames attached to central protagonists. Lieutenant Wilson (James McKechnie) is known as 'Spud', and uses modern and, the film suggests, somewhat ungentlemanly military techniques during an army exercise against the Home Guard. His nickname succinctly communicates his role as a wartime necessity: somewhat unpalatable, but essential if victory is to be won. On the other hand, Clive Candy (Roger Livesey), the charming if anachronistic colonel of the title, is known as 'Sugar', a name which creates a degree of sympathy, but which also suggests, given that sweets rationing had been introduced in 1942, that his chivalrous approach was a luxury that the country could not really afford in time of war, but to which it no doubt hoped to return to on cessation of hostilities.

Child health was another subject deemed worthy of the use of shock tactics, although pathos was more common in this regard than the more martial imagery that accompanied the 'Bread Costs Lives' films. While other MoF publicity occasionally used overt scare tactics to point to the link between poor child nutrition and ill health – witness, for example, Food Facts No. 178, which began 'Your child may be another picture-book baby today, but…'[42] – the cinema was often more subtle in its approach. Many of the *Food Flashes* concerning child health tended to focus on the general benefits of vitamins and dealt with the administrative questions arising from how parents could gain access to special foods for their children.

More arresting images feature in 'Rickets' (week of 2 October 1944), which opens with a shot of a column of young boys whose limbs have been misshapen by the disease, caused by an insufficient intake of vitamin D. The image is reminiscent of injured soldiers filing past newsreel cameras, and an inter-title reading '1918' and the narrator's comment that 'many European children were like this at the end of the last war' accentuates this similarity, positioning the afflicted youngsters as unwilling veterans of conflict. By displacing such unsettling images into a foreign past, the *Flash* declares that such scenes are preventable, and therefore unthinkable, in contemporary, progressive Britain: 'If the children get plenty of vitamin D, and the government has made it theirs for the collecting, it'll never happen here.' Within the context of the film 'here' is obviously Britain, but the image accompanying the narrator's confident declaration is specifically rural. Healthy children sit in a field and enjoy a picnic, giving the impression that the sunshine and verdant lushness of the countryside have healing properties and that the children, products of this pastoral, natural landscape, are integral parts of a healthy British future. The vibrant, well-fed bodies are stable and comfortable in front of the camera, offering a dramatic contrast to the freak-show of rickety youths paraded earlier in the film for the purpose of exposition and exhibition. The two shots invite comparison, but also, when combined with the significant 'if' which informs the narration, provide for the possibility that without government intervention British children might succumb to disease and malformation.

While most of the *Flashes* which addressed matters of health and nutrition maintained the serious attitude visible in 'Rickets', the three which featured Charles Hill, the Radio Doctor made famous by his *Kitchen Front* broadcasts, adopted an approach more in keeping with Hill's jowly, avuncular persona. Screened in the weeks of 17 December 1945, and 7 and 28 January 1946, the films follow the standard opening sequence with the title 'Presents the Radio Doctor', preparing the viewer not only for the medical consultation to follow, but also for Hill's lugubrious style. Hill was described by *Time* magazine as having a 'rich, soothing voice that … sounds like a ham actor's impersonation of a family doctor'.[43] Hill's style was not to everyone's taste, and he was an often controversial broadcaster. He would later claim in his memoirs that he was

> rebuked by some and praised by others for my blunt indelicacy about bowels and prunes – 'black coated workers' and 'the smallest room in the house' – and other embarrassing intimacies.[44]

Hill believed that what popularity he enjoyed came from understanding that the average Briton was more interested in disease than prevention or cure: 'If I want to discuss the circulation, I start by mentioning varicose veins. I know then that I'll have the sympathetic ear of most.'[45] The 'Radio Doctor' *Flashes* pertaining to nutrition during pregnancy and infancy, adopted a similar approach, suggesting that, in order to be healthy, a newborn baby 'needs its extras, its cod liver oil and orange juice. Unless, of course, you want a rickety child, a bandy, knock-kneed, large-headed pale and rickety article.' The films further proposed that 'the baby looks just like other babies, but don't tell mother that'.

Easing his transition into the cinema, each film begins with a shot of a radio (see figure 11), lending the weight of Hill's established credibility to the *Flashes*, and suggesting that the films should be regarded as an extension of his work

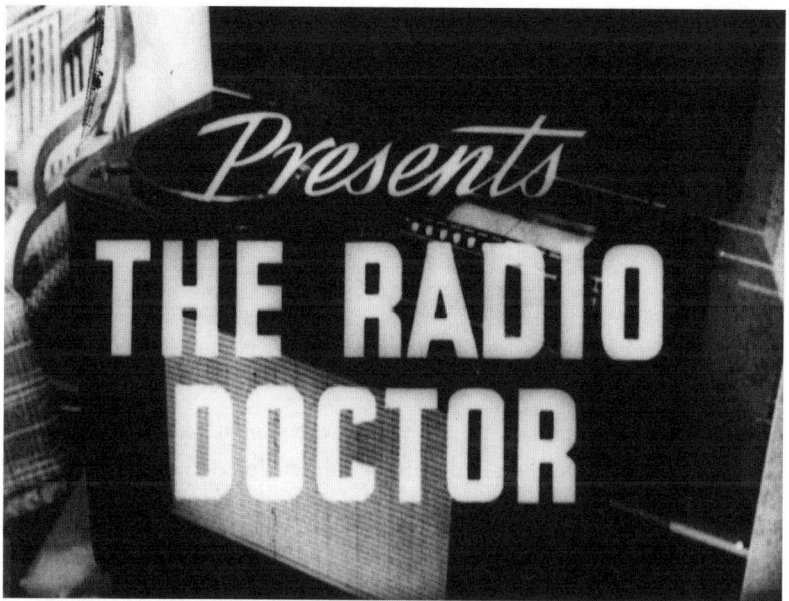

Introducing the Radio Doctor to the cinema audience. 'Radio Doctor No. I', week of 17 December 1945.

on the wireless. These three *Flashes* are visually undistinguished. As with his broadcasts, the Radio Doctor remains unseen and pseudonymous, a decision that serves to focus attention on the narration and the aural qualities that Hill had taken such care to establish. The 'Radio Doctor' films Hill made are representative of the increased interest in health that the *Food Flash* series took after the war; although more than a dozen *Flashes* had dealt with this topic during the conflict, the relative frequency of such films increased after VJ Day.

Bread was another subject that featured with greater regularity after the accession of the Labour government in July 1945. The end of the war had not brought an immediate end to wartime dietary conditions, and post-war *Food Flashes* explained the continued need for rationing. In the week of 17 September 1945 the MoF asked Britons not to 'Waste Bread', informing them that even though the war is over 'the whole world is short of food for a while'. These words are accompanied by a shot of a map of the Earth, reinforcing the global nature of the events that necessitated the maintenance of rationing while also suggesting that Britons were not alone in experiencing ongoing deprivation. The seriousness of the message is, if anything, strengthened by the gallows humour of the film's final line, delivered in an almost apologetically deadpan style: 'Bread is worth more than dough these days.' Following a disappointing harvest, in February 1946 the possibility of a global food crisis was real enough for Ben Smith, then Minister of Food, to make the following appeal to the British public via Food Facts:

> In the first six months of this year the world will have to do with at least five million tons of wheat less than it needs.
> In many countries this means hunger and, unless they get relief, starvation and death.
> On your behalf the Government have agreed to help these countries by cutting down our imports of wheat. To make up some of the loss, we are going back, for the time being, to the war time loaf...
> Don't buy any more bread than you can eat. In canteens and restaurants don't ask for bread unless you intend to eat it. Bread means lives. Don't waste a crumb.[46]

Bread became an important issue in post-war food policy, and thirteen of the 37 *Flashes* exhibited in 1946 deal with the subject. Ten of these thirteen films, representing more than half of the total number of *Flashes* screened between mid-February and early July, attempted to persuade Britons of the need to reduce bread consumption and waste, dealing with matters of storage, preservation and economy. These ten *Flashes*, and the more extensive MoF campaign of which they were a part, were unable to change dietary habits to the extent needed to prevent the introduction of bread rationing, which came into effect on 21 July 1946.[47] Winston Churchill, then leader of the opposition, was not slow to place the blame for additional food control at Clement Attlee's door: 'At home people are having to undergo a greater hardship than they ever had in the war, although there is a full peace and the seas are free from U-Boats.'[48]

Three films were produced explaining how bread rationing was to operate – 'B[read] U[nit]s – Food Facts' (week of 8 July 1946), 'Issue of BUs' (week of 22 July 1946) and 'L. BU Coupons' (week of 5 August 1946) – but these brief, rather dry films are the last *Flashes* to discuss the issue, prompting the thought that the Labour government was unwilling to discuss bread rationing at length for fear of reminding cinema audiences of the administration's travails and thus alienating the electorate. Unsurprisingly, Conservative politicians were keen to focus on the Labour government's shortcomings. In 1947, Brendan Bracken, Minister of Information from 1941 to 1945 and a Conservative MP, noted that 'angry housewives are the most formidable enemy of the socialists so we must do everything in our power to increase their fury'.[49] The resumption of party politics in mid-1945 had prompted a vigorous debate concerning both rationing policy and the maintenance of expensive food information campaigns. The MoF chose to focus its money and energy on Food Facts newspaper advertisements, a series that was effective only if a reader was proactive and chose to engage with the Ministry's publicity; the *Flashes*, which addressed a captive and potentially hostile audience, were cancelled.

During the autumn and winter of 1946 it became clear to the MoF that the *Food Flashes* were no longer a cost-effective means of communicating with the British public. Although cinema attendance remained high, 'the public was losing interest in this form of direct propaganda', and the decision was taken to terminate the *Flashes*. Although plans were mooted to revise and reintroduce regular MoF cinematic publicity in the guise of a longer monthly film, little seems to have come of this.[50]

Charlie Chester was recruited to front the last five *Flashes*, screened during consecutive weeks from 7 October to 4 November 1946, but by this time the MoF appeared to have already lost faith in both the films' ability to communicate food information and the *Flash* format. Chester was a popular comedian and dominated the *Flashes* in which he appeared, bringing about notable presentational changes. The self-consciously comic opening of these last films, in which the standard cymbal crash was replaced by the sound of a glockenspiel followed in sequence by a drum being hit, the flatulent 'parp' of an old-fashioned car horn and the bursting of a balloon, is entirely in keeping with their content. Not only does the humorous aural montage anticipate Chester's amiable, rambling style, the less insistent feel the sounds lend to the opening sequence prepares the viewer for the longer films that follow. Whereas most of the earlier *Flashes* last for less than thirty seconds, Chester's films ran for more than forty, with one, dealing with the best way to cook a cabbage ('Charlie Chester No. 2', week of 14 October 1946), clocking in at a very leisurely 57 seconds.

While occasionally amusing, the length of the Charlie Chester films militated against the tautness and brevity that had contributed to the impact of the earlier *Flashes*, with each piece of food information struggling for attention amid the thick comic padding provided by the comedian and his gang. Whereas in previous *Flashes* humour had most often arisen from the subject under consideration, the Chester films had to work hard to adapt a subject to Chester's patter, lending the films a somewhat contrived tone. That is not to say that the films are entirely ineffective but, when compared with the tight, deftly constructed earlier films, they seem vaguely self-indulgent, promoting Chester as star as much as the policies of the MoF.

For many years, however, the typical *Flash* format – the cymbal crash opening followed by a short message – had made the *Flashes* both a familiar and memorable part of the weekly cinema programme. In a survey carried out between December 1942 and January 1943, more than 40 per cent of cinema-goers said that they seen a *Food Flash* (a figure which approximates to the proportion of cinemas showing the films at the time), and of these, nearly 60 per cent could accurately remember the subject of the last such film they had seen. When compared with figures for the slides and non-*Food Flash* publicity the MoF exhibited in cinemas, such numbers suggest that the *Food Flashes* were the most effective form of cinematic publicity at the Ministry's disposal.[51]

The MoF's filmed publicity of course, needs to be considered alongside the publicity it issued via the radio and the press. However, the MoF's very obvious presence on British cinema screens meant that even during their precious leisure hours wartime cinema-goers were encouraged to acknowledge the political and social influence of the Ministry and found themselves positioned as a distinct gastronomic-cultural entity.

Notes

1 'Potato Resolution' was exhibited in British cinemas in the week of 28 December 1942. 'Potato Pete Fair' was shown in London in the week of 21 December 1942. For a full list of *Food Flash* films, see Appendix.

2 The National Archives (TNA) MAF 156/195: Monthly Report of the Public Relations Division, December 1942; *The Economist*, 26 December 1942, p. 809; *The Times*, 17 December 1942, p. 2.

3 'Letter from London', 27 December 1942, in William Shawn (ed.), *London War Notes, 1939–1945* (London: Longman, 1972), p. 256.

4 *Advertiser's Weekly*, 21 October 1943, p. 43.

5 *The Times*, 18 April 1942, p. 2.

6 Annette Kuhn, '*Desert Victory* and the People's War', *Screen*, 22:2 (1981), p. 56.

7 Much of the information in this chapter relating to the structure, function and personnel of NSS is taken from Denis Gifford's interview with Esther Harris, recorded in January 2000. Harris worked at the British arm of NSS from its formation until the 1960s, eventually attaining the position of director. BFI Special Collections: BECTU Oral History Project – Tape 465: Esther Harris.

8 By 1943, NSS was producing trailers for 28 different film producers in Britain, and distributing more than 5,500 trailers each week to nearly 4,000 cinemas. *Documentary News Letter*, 4:3, March 1943, p. 194.

9 NSS publicity in *Kinematograph Weekly*, 13 January 1944, p. 184.

10 TNA MAF 75/67: 'General Account of the Work of the Public Relations Division, 1939–1950', p. 4.

11 *Daily Film Renter*, 4 November 1943, p. 3.

12 *Daily Express*, 12 August 1946, p. 3; Cecil Hepworth, *Came the Dawn: Memories of a Film Pioneer* (London: Phoenix House, 1951), pp. 160–1.

13 The MoF appears to have followed the MoI in taking advantage of NSS's distribution capability. See James Chapman, *The British at War: Cinema, State and Propaganda, 1939–1945* (London: I. B. Tauris, 1998), pp. 93–4.

14 TNA MAF 138/161: 'Notes for the use of the Accounting Officer on the Ministry's Vote Appropriation Account for 1942–43', p. 24; *The Times*, 18 April 1942, p. 2. In September 1942 there were 4,714 registered cinemas in Britain. Central Statistical Office, *Annual Abstract of Statistics, No. 84: 1935–1946* (London: HMSO, 1948), p. 72.

15 TNA MAF 75/67: 'General Account, 1939–50', p. 5.

16 TNA MAF 138/161: 'Notes for the use of the Accounting Officer, 1942–43', pp. 22, 24. The advent of the *Food Flash* campaign led to a reduction in expenditure on cinema slides: £1,242 was spent in 1942–43.

17 *Kinematograph Weekly*, 9 April 1942, p. 12. The programme that concerned J. M. Cannon of Gaumont-British featured '"The March of Time", a M. of I. film, a "Prunes six points a lb." film [probably the *Food Flash* 'Prunes and Dates', week of 30 March 1942], and then at last … the feature'.

18 *Kinematograph Weekly*, 6 July 1944, p. 4.

19 *Kinematograph Weekly*, 8 January 1942, pp. 45, 9. By 1945 it was estimated that the

government had enjoyed 200,000 hours of screen-time for free, a figure equating to £3,000,000 if charged at commercial rates. *Kinematograph Weekly*, 5 April 1945, p. 5.

20 See, for example, *Kinematograph Weekly*, 8 January 1942, p. 3.

21 For more on quota films, made after the Cinematograph Films Act came into force in April 1928, see Steve Chibnall, *Quota Quickies: The Birth of the British 'B' Film* (London: BFI, 2007).

22 *Kinematograph Weekly*, 21 December 1944, p. 4; *Advertiser's Weekly*, 4 February 1943, p. 94.

23 TNA MAF 138/163: 'Notes for the use of the Accounting Officer on the Ministry's Vote Appropriation Account for 1946–47', p. 21.

24 *Kinematograph Weekly*, 21 December 1944, p. 4.

25 TNA MAF 129/110: Letter from R. Stanhope-Palmer to R. Gray, 9 February 1945. 1944 *Food Flash* expenditure: £12,072; initial 1945 *Food Flash* budget: £25,000.

26 TNA MAF 138/163: 'Notes for the use of the Accounting Officer, 1946–47', p. 21.

27 TNA MAF 129/110: Letter from R. Stanhope-Palmer to E. R. Copleston, 4 September 1945. The MoF's initial 1945 allocation of 5,000,000 feet was increased to 6,000,000; the *Food Flash* budget rose from £25,000 to £30,000.

28 TNA MAF 138/161: 'Notes for the use of the Accounting Officer, 1942–43', p. 22; MAF 138/163: 'Notes for the use of the Accounting Officer, 1946–47', p. 18.

29 See Paul Swann, *The British Documentary Film Movement, 1926–1946* (Cambridge: Cambridge University Press, 1989), pp. 167–8

30 *Kinematograph Weekly*, 5 April 1945, p. 26.

31 *Kinematograph Weekly*, 5 April 1945, p. 5. It was estimated that although the total amount of film stock processed had risen from 320,000,000 ft in 1939 to 450,000,000 ft in 1945, the amount of stock made available to commercial producers had declined by some 40,000,000 ft.

32 *Kinematograph Weekly*, 21 December 1944, p. 18.

33 *Kinematograph Weekly*, 20 November 1941, p. 11. The MoF also issued numerous print advertisements that informed consumers that details of the rationing system were available from cinemas. See, for example, Food Facts No. 255, week of 28 May 1945.

34 'Ration Book "B"' from the week of 18 May 1942 features a location shot of a cinema advertising *Dancing on a Dime* (1940) and a British Paramount Newsreel (probably No. 1168, released 11 May 1942), whilst in 'New Ration Book No. 3' (12 July 1943) promotional material for *Thunder Birds* (1942) is clearly visible.

35 TNA: MAF 75/67. 'General Account, 1939–50', p. 5.

36 In some later *Flashes* an alternate, more sinuous MoF logo was used.

37 A female voice does appear in 'Help the Grocer', week of 5 April 1943. In the film, a woman – with a faux refined voice à la Joyce Carey in *Brief Encounter* – asks a shopkeeper 'how many points would I have left if I took one each of these and a few of those?' The male narrator introduces her as an irritant, and explains how she can help the shopkeeper in future.

38 Woolton claimed that 25 per cent of British merchant sailors were engaged in shipping wheat to Britain. *The Economist*, 16 January 1943, p. 68.

39 *Advertiser's Weekly*, 21 January 1943, p. 52; *Ministry of Food Bulletin*, No. 213, 22 October 1943, p. 1. The survey from which this statistic was taken was carried out between May and June 1943. The 'ship saving' motive was somewhat disingenuous; ships that were not laden with wheat would simply import other cargoes.

40 MoF report quoted in R. J. Hammond, *Food: Vol. II – Studies in Administration and Control* (London: HMSO, 1956), pp. 146–7.

41 TNA RG 23/46: Gertrude Wagner, '"Eat More Potatoes": An enquiry into the effect of a publicity campaign', July 1943, p. 1.

42 Food Facts No. 178, week of 29 November 1943.

43 *Time*, 17 November 1947, p. 26.

44 Charles Hill, *Behind the Screen: The Broadcasting Memoirs of Lord Hill of Luton* (London: Sidgwick & Jackson, 1974), p. 16. After suggesting that women be honest with their children about where babies came from, Hill was criticised by Carlisle alderman C. H. Cant: 'Anything more blunt and tactless I have never heard'. *Daily Mirror*, 1 April 1943, p. 4. Reader responses can be found in *Daily Mirror*, 9 April 1943, p. 6.

45 *Time*, 17 November 1947, p. 26.

46 Food Facts No. 292, week of 11 February 1946.

47 For more on bread rationing, see Ina Zweiniger-Bargielowska, 'Bread rationing in Britain, July 1946–July 1948', *Twentieth Century British History*, 4:1 (1993).

48 *The Times*, 20 July 1946, p. 3.

49 Quoted in John Ramsden, *The Age of Churchill and Eden, 1940–1957* (Harlow: Longman, 1995), p. 169.

50 TNA MAF 138/163: 'Notes for the use of the Accounting Officer, 1946–47', p. 21.

51 TNA RG 23/18: Wartime Social Survey, 'Food: 1) Food Schemes, 2) Publicity, 3) Shopping and Shortages' (May 1942–March 1943), pp. 64, 58, 67.

3

Laying a table for a family of 45 million: celebrating and contesting communal consumption

In *The Myth of the Blitz*, Angus Calder makes clear that the 'Blitz spirit' exhibited by Londoners in the face of German air-raids came not from any innate or atavistic resilience, but from the population's desire to conform to an idealised image of how the typical Briton was expected to act in difficult circumstances.[1] In short, Londoners (and other Britons) were able to endure the horrors of the Blitz because they were told, and believed, that, as the title of a celebrated wartime documentary put it, *London Can Take It!* (1940). American journalist Quentin Reynolds's commentary for the film declared that:

> Today the morale of the people is higher than ever before. They are fused together, not by fear, but by a surging spirit of courage the like of which the world has never known. They know that thousands of them will die, but they would rather stand up and face death, than kneel down and face the kind of existence the conqueror would impose upon them.

Reynolds's later claim that there was 'no panic, no fear, no despair in London town' is demonstrated by Calder to have been untrue, but it appears that very few Londoners were prepared to publicly admit as much: a consensus emerged in which these emotions were considered shameful, abhorrent and even unpatriotic. Eric Sevareid, a compatriot and colleague of Reynolds, suggested that the panic felt by many could not be expressed openly for fear of how others would react. His wry conclusion was that 'the British were afraid of one another'[2] – more so, at any rate, than they were of the Germans.

When discussing the power of national myths, George Orwell observed that those that are believed tend to become true 'because they set up a type, or "persona", which the average person will do his best to resemble'.[3] To Orwell, the importance of emulation in the construction of national identity is such that behaviour can in certain circumstances be conditioned by the presentation of an idealised model. During the war, the British persona came to be identified with, among other things, resolution, communality and a phlegmatic approach. Though it is possible to debate just how widespread these character traits actually were, it is necessary, and perhaps more important, to understand them to have been frequently *presented* as the apotheoses of Britishness.

The Conservative MP Lord Hinchingbrooke was certainly aware of the importance of the group dynamic in influencing public attitudes. In 1944 he voiced concerns that the emergence during the war of state-sponsored communal institutions that favoured the masses might, if permitted to continue unchecked, represent the triumph of 'equality over quality' and thereby undermine the foundations of Britain's 'dynamic economic democracy'. First on Hinchingbrooke's list of potentially disruptive institutions were British Restaurants, a chain of state-subsidised refectories that provided cheap, off-the-ration meals to the public and to urban workers whose place of employment did not have a canteen of its own. Hinchingbrooke was concerned that such was the authority of the state – and so great was the population's faith in 'the handiwork of a supposedly all-seeing Government' – that its attempts to promote such institutions had invested them with 'a kind of moral superiority' which, in turn, created an institutional persona which the average Briton was expected to celebrate.[4]

If we understand communal consumption to represent not only the act of eating in factory canteens, British Restaurants, cafés, pubs and the like, but also an acceptance of a rationing system that attempted to distribute food equally, gastronomy emerges as an important aspect of the shared national experience, and one that was frequently mobilised to advance a consensual and corporate agenda. Talking to the nation on the Home Service on 13 June 1941, Lord Woolton declared his intention to instil in Britons 'a public and a personal conscience about food – a national "Food Code"'.[5]

Short propaganda films presented cinema-goers with idealised images of different aspects of food policy, and the presence in the cinema programme of, for example, the Ministry of Food's (MoF's) *Food Flashes* reminded patrons of the importance that the government ascribed to food in wartime and so helped shape a patron's recognition of, and responsiveness to, food imagery in feature films. The high profile of British Restaurants and the MoF's Herculean publicity campaigns encouraged those who ate at communal feeding establishments to recognise and celebrate the importance of food as a cornerstone of a shared national experience. From these experiences emerged an identity informed by the state's right to dictate consumption.

Further, just as the works canteen – both in propaganda shorts and commercial features – was frequently presented as the principal (and principled) site of consumption for the nation at work, so the pub was often shown to fulfil a similar function for the British during their leisure hours. Within such spaces, the positive images of dutiful, responsible and communal consumption found a contrast with more negative portrayals of solitary consumption (most often excessive drinking), in order that the desirability of certain dietary norms could be more clearly demonstrated.

However, despite numerous attempts to create a communal gustatory paradigm, not all films adhered to the stereotypical representation of wartime Britain as selfless and straight-laced. Food imagery was also used to present alternate visions of Britain which critiqued the promotion of the idea of 'food as duty' or 'food as site of community'. Just as Britons were able both to utilise British Restaurants and to maintain a certain degree of ambivalence towards them, so were they also able to enjoy films which both praised and contested dutiful gastronomic communality. Food was one of several themes used to challenge the prioritisation of duty over pleasure, and the lavish narrative and visual style of historical or melodramatic films such as *Champagne Charlie* (1944), *Madonna of the Seven Moons* (1944) and *The Wicked Lady* (1945) glorified excess and suggested the continued appeal of sensual self-indulgence. In contrast to the more sober approach of films such as *In Which We Serve* (1942) and *Millions Like Us* (1943), food was used in these melodramas in ways that can be understood as a challenge to the supposed dietary consensus. It is, however, perhaps more useful to recognise this challenge not in terms of an absolute rejection of the rationing system per se, but instead a rejection of the rigid, arithmetical formulas which could appear to make it ignore the validity and significance of both individuality and the pleasures of the flesh.

Such was the significance of food in wartime British culture that it is possible to see distinct visions of British society in cinematic representations of, and attitudes towards, consumption. The MoF's attempts to convince the British people that they constituted a single 'family of 45,000,000' led to the promotion of communal institutions.[6] Yet food's continued sensual appeal meant that it could still be used to communicate ideas of pleasure, individuality and indulgence.

The paradigm of communal consumption

There is an irony in the fact that a war waged against the tyrannical excesses of Hitler's dictatorial regime saw the British state significantly extend its influence over the lives of the British people. Justifying such enforced regimentation through appeals to community, shared experience and common sacrifice, Britain was mobilised at the national level, and visions were expounded of a shared cultural, political and ideological heritage and a future that the national community might enjoy as a reward for wartime toil.

While it should come as little surprise that the army, navy and air force were presented as functioning in a collective manner, with service personnel both integral to, and defined by, a larger whole, the significance of the Home Front meant that the civilians who fought the war out of uniform were also presented as being mutually dependent. Films which centred on the services demonstrated the cohesiveness of their uniformed characters through montages of drill, target practice or group training; they also demonstrated the bond that existed between individuals by setting scenes in the mess (*The Next of Kin*, 1942), or at a NAAFI canteen (*The Way Ahead*, 1944). Using food in this way reminded viewers of the corporeality of the servicemen's bodies while simultaneously positioning them within the Britannic body corporate. Films dealing with non-military subjects utilised similar strategies to foreground communal themes, many of which dealt with shared participation in community activities. Eating was one such theme, and consumption was presented in a number of Home Front films in order to stress the importance of community in wartime Britain.

Margaret Butler has suggested that the idea of community was 'intrinsic to British wartime culture' and described how it became a 'ubiquitous and highly successful conduit for the transmission of ideas about harmony and consensus'.[7] Other film historians have noted the presence of such themes in British wartime cinema, with James Chapman, for instance, stating that 'the images of the British at war presented through the cinema were a powerful and dramatic means of constructing the people as united in their common struggle'.[8]

While it is certainly possible to debate the extent to which wartime Britain actually manifested such communality, it is obvious that communal images are very much in evidence in British wartime films and in wartime culture more generally. Further, such imagery tended to be presented very positively. In his first radio *Postscript*, broadcast on 16 June 1940, just days after the British retreat from Dunkirk, J. B. Priestley talked of the evacuation as producing in him a 'powerful and rewarding sense of community; and with it too a feeling of deep continuity'.[9] By positioning the collective wartime present as an extension of the British past, Priestley advances the idea that the thread of communality that he saw as running through British society and history might, if celebrated and mobilised, help bring the war to a successful conclusion.

The communality which so appealed to Priestley was clearly also popular with British filmmakers. To take but a few examples, cinema-goers were presented with scenes of communal singing in *Fires Were Started* (1943), *San Demetrio, London* (1943) and *Two Thousand Women* (1944), dancing in *The Demi-Paradise* (1943) and *The Way to the Stars* (1945) and concert-going in *Listen to Britain* (1942) and *Millions Like Us*. While many of these are included in a canon of 'quality films' (more often than not made in a documentary-realist style) lauded by sections of the British critical establishment during and after the war, films from very different cinematic traditions were also willing to glorify the communal ideal, although perhaps in a less reverential manner.[10] The Arthur Askey comedy *Back Room Boy* (1942), for instance, celebrates the pleasures of the dance hall, while George Formby, then at the height of his popularity, spends a night at a variety theatre in *Spare a Copper* (1940).[11]

Sites of communal entertainment were considered to be powerful metaphors for the communities they served. Several films produced during the war introduced the threat of closure or redevelopment of such places, prompting the community to come together to save these institution in question and simultaneously celebrate local spirit and pride. In *Let the People Sing* (1942), adapted from a story by J. B. Priestley, a town saves its local music hall. The Flanagan and Allen vehicle *Theatre Royal* (1943) revolves around the eventually successful attempt of theatre staff to save their workplace from closure, while *Battle for Music* (1943) sees an orchestra face down both bankruptcy and the disruptions caused by the war. More peripatetic forms of entertainment also got in on the act; in *Old Mother Riley's Circus* (1941) audiences could enjoy the performers' struggle to keep both their show on the road and the public entertained.

Those who sought shelter from the Blitz in London Underground stations were shown, in films such as *I Thank You* (1941) and *Gert and Daisy's Weekend* (1941), to have banded together in close-knit communities, enduring hardships and meeting the challenges of the war with a smile and a song. Indeed, the power of such scenes allowed the American-made *A Yank in the RAF* (1941) to use them to epitomise the ways in which the war had affected the lives of ordinary Britons. More bucolic settings were also mobilised, and films like *This*

England (1941), *Tawny Pipit* (1944) and *Great Day* (1945) all dealt with varying aspects of communality in rural British locations.

It is clear, then, that many British films contained images of community and mass-participation activities. It is within such a context that films which feature communal consumption practices need to be understood, for although such portrayals are often brief they served both practical and ideological functions. For if we are what we eat, then we are surely also *where* we eat; and in wartime, Britons were eating in public and with other people, as never before.

Films which contained scenes set in canteens and other communal eating establishments represented, and perhaps helped to reinforce, a wartime reality in which the number of meals eaten outside the home rose dramatically after the introduction of canteens and British Restaurants.[12] While the practical benefits of canteen-style eating were obvious (especially in terms of savings of food, time and fuel), the ideological benefits were also significant. In 1946, the National Council of Social Service (NCSS) declared the 'development of social life' to be a 'very important by-product' of communal eating spaces, and quoted a report produced by the London Council for Social Service which described such establishments as 'essentially democratic in price and clientele' and thus able to bring about a 'fusion of class types'.[13]

This fusion of different types of people, brought together for a shared gastronomic ritual, helped further promote a communal ethos in wartime Britain. While it should be remembered that many if not most meals were still eaten in the home (a fact acknowledged in wartime cinema), and that not all consumers approved unquestioningly of wartime changes, the government's desire to promote 'eating out' resulted in a situation where a paradigmatic sense of communality was presented as an ideal for those who consumed meals at canteens and British Restaurants.

Writing about the aspect of display evident in the eating of restaurant meals, Joanne Finkelstein suggests that 'when we are dining out we are aware of an obligation to give a performance in accord with the normative demands of the circumstances'.[14] This has the effect of making meals consumed in the public arena inherently theatrical, and also of rendering them significant in terms of the way in which they express (and contest) ideological and social norms. By accepting that communal consumption in a public space transforms eating into an ensemble performance, it can be suggested that state-sponsored canteens and British Restaurants encouraged patrons to understand food not as a solitary pursuit, but as an exemplar of the resolution and unity of spirit that might contribute to Britain winning the war.

Whether they appear in government propaganda films or feature films, the many representations of mass dining coincide with other displays of communality seemingly intended to promote a nationwide *esprit de corps* among British civilians. Indeed, given that scholars such as Jane Ferry have claimed that shared meals imply 'acceptance … social intimacy' and 'being physically united by the common food in the stomach',[15] the communal eating spaces that sprang up throughout the United Kingdom during the war can be understood as the mess halls of the Home Front, closely linked to the nation's ability to prosecute the war. So keen was the state to promote communal consumption that it produced and exhibited films dedicated to this ideal. *Eating Out with Tommy Trinder* (1941) is discussed in some detail below, but it is worth mentioning briefly other government propaganda films that addressed similar topics.

Although *Eating at Work* (1941) discusses the workings of factory canteens and the ways in which a scientifically approved diet can benefit employees, it is most keen to illustrate the social element of communal dining by linking eating with recreational activities. Films such as *Mrs T. and her Cabbage Patch* (1941) adopt a familiar MoF refrain by arguing for the consumption of fresh vegetables while also demonstrating the cleanliness of factory canteens and other communal feeding spaces. A 1943 episode of *Warwork News*, produced for the Ministry of Supply by British Paramount News and exhibited in factories at special lunchtime screenings, urged factory workers to 'make your main meal of the day the one you get in the canteen'. Careful to remind viewers of the benefits such canteens offered, both to employee and nation, each of the talking heads encouraged by the camera to commend the food served at the canteen is presented as part of the larger factory community, an individual in a sea of similarly well-fed faces. The MoF's own *Food Flashes* were, of course, not averse to promoting communal dining. In 'Potato Pete' (week of 7 September 1942), a shot of a legion of efficient and busy-looking cooks is immediately followed by another of a dining room full of uniformed women tucking into plates of hot food, while in 'Victory Dish' (week of 29 March 1943) a shot of a restaurant shows diners ordering dishes, marked with a 'V', which did not make use of imported foodstuffs, and which could therefore be presented as benefiting the country.

Eating Out with Tommy Trinder promotes the merits of the British Restaurants, and was released six months after a decision was taken to establish the restaurants nationwide, rather than simply on an ad hoc local basis. The film, then, can be understood as an exercise in raising brand awareness as, until this point, the restaurants had been individually named and lumped together under the collective title of 'communal feeding centres'. Winston Churchill contacted Woolton, advising that such terms were 'suggestive of Communism and the workhouse' and requesting that a new name be found.[16] Woolton, via the *Daily Mail*, launched a public appeal for a more suitable name. There were hundreds of responses, many of which are instructive of the public's attitudes towards the institution. Suggestions such as 'Good Companions', 'People's Mess', and 'All Together' flag up the important communal role that the British Restaurants were understood as playing, whereas the name 'Blitz-Ritz' speaks of the small luxuries that they might offer a war-weary public. The most common suggestion was 'The Woolton' – a variant was the 'wooltaurant' – a name that the Minister of Food's 'natural modesty' compelled him to reject.[17] Even so, 'Lord Woolton Restaurants' sprang up all over the country.[18] Eventually, the Prime Minister's suggestion of British Restaurant was adopted, but this name was often adapted to fit local circumstances: for example, in Bristol the British Ambassador Restaurant opened at an Odeon-run cinema, the Ambassador, in August 1942.[19]

In *Eating Out with Tommy Trinder*, the eponymous variety and film star, having dined at the home of the Joneses, his fiancée's parents, and been disappointed by the food they prepared, takes his prospective in-laws to a British Restaurant where he treats them to a tour of the institution, an explanation of how it functions and then, as a reward, a hearty meal. Produced by Strand, the film has a slick, commercial style that was appreciated by *Documentary News Letter*, which noted that its photography was 'a nice piece of work'. The same review also found the film effective as propaganda: 'I am going to go out of my way to find one and try [its food] for myself.'[20]

The modernity and convenience of the British Restaurants are made evident within the film. In contrast to the tight, static shots that dominate the sequences set in the Jones's house, the British Restaurant is constructed in wider, more expansive shots by a more mobile camera, communicating notions of space, energy and purpose. In a montage sequence, the industrial scale and nature of food preparation is shown, with spotless machines operated by uniformed (and equally spotless) staff. Each shot in the sequence shows only a single worker, pointing to the modernity of the mechanical process and demonstrating the savings gained when individuals utilise efficient modern methods to cook for hundreds. Such modernity was praised by Barbara Drake of the left-leaning Fabian Society, which described the British Restaurants as having helped transform domestic service 'from a skilled handicraft to a mechanised and mass-produced industry'.[21]

The low cost of the food and the generous size of the portions led many observers and patrons to praise the British Restaurants. An M-O survey found that 96 per cent of those who had eaten in one had a positive attitude towards the experience, while the affordability of the meals helped create a democratic reputation.[22] That said, British Restaurants also attracted a fair amount of criticism. To some, the mechanical and uniform approach to food, though beneficial to individuals and the nation, risked seeming a little impersonal. The author Edward Blishen claimed that the British Restaurants were 'anonymous' whereas the Conservative MP Sir William Bell delivered his own damning indictment: 'They are brutal in their cooking, brutal in their presentation of food. One needs to be British to "take it" in a British Restaurant.'[23]

The film, and the MoF, worked hard to counter these accusations. Lord Woolton was adamant that he did not want British Restaurants to acquire 'an "institution" atmosphere', and called upon the local authorities who ran the restaurants to create an environment in which eating could be enjoyed rather than a merely endured.[24] J. B. Priestley agreed, suggesting that British Restaurants had 'a real social value of their own' in their ability to bring people together. When Priestley interviewed Woolton for *Picture Post*, he urged the Minister of Food to 'Open [British Restaurants] in the drabbest districts, make them bright and gay, let them have music. Make a civilised social virtue out of war necessity.'[25] In *Eating Out with Tommy Trinder*, the first establishing shot of the inside of the British Restaurant, filmed on location at the Byrom British Restaurant in Liverpool, shows a series of relatively small and homely rooms, each of which has a mural painted on the wall.

The need to create a positive atmosphere was increased by the novelty of the method of service adopted in the British Restaurants. In order to minimise the number of staff employed, counter- rather then table-service was the norm. When conscription of staff resulted in a similar scheme being adopted in some private restaurants, not all patrons were happy: 'some of the more conservative businessmen, it is said, do not like having to help themselves', reported the *Manchester Guardian* of one London establishment.[26] *Eating Out with Tommy Trinder* contains numerous shots that explain how self-service works, with the labour-saving nature of the system demonstrated by a fast-moving line of customers on one side of the counter being served with no small measure of skill and efficiency by just a handful of staff.

Yet for all the demonstrations of modern food preparation visible, the film's trump card is Trinder; the comedian brings his star value to bear on the British Restaurants, investing these fairly prosaic institutions with a touch of West

End glitz. Trinder dominates, and it is clearly his enthusiasm for public dining that is meant to instil a similar sense of eagerness in those who watched the film. The eponymous title sets it apart from the propaganda shorts that other comedians made for the Ministry of Information (MoI) (for example Arthur Askey in *The Nose Has It* or Will Hay in *Go to Blazes!*, both 1942), and within the film Trinder plays himself, not a fictional consumer. Although it starts with a shot of Trinder on stage at a theatre, thus reminding the viewer of his celebrity bona fides, the remainder of the film presents Trinder going about his everyday business, thus making his support of the British Restaurants a good deal more convincing and effective. This is boosted by the clever choice of Trinder as the public face of the film, and thus of the Restaurants, for although as a star he brought with him glamour and fame, his cheeky, working-class, wisecracking image served to remind viewers of his ordinariness.

Trinder's position as an entertainer, and therefore as public property, serves as a convenient bridge between the private space of the family dining table and the more public space of the restaurant: so comfortable does Trinder appear in the British Restaurant that the film leaves the viewer with the impression that patrons of such establishments could reasonably expect to dine alongside a star of stage and/or screen on a regular basis. Indeed, Trinder's final line reinforces this linkage: when he delivers his catchphrase – 'You lucky people!' – straight to camera, the restaurant and the stage become one, the act of consumption undertaken in one nuanced by the other.

Trinder's insistence that the family accompany him to the British Restaurant demonstrates that communal dining need not pose a threat to domestic life. By dining *en famille*, the Joneses seek to disprove, or at least contest, the notion, as quoted in an NCSS report, that communal feeding 'tends to disrupt family life'.[27] It might be suggested, though, that the British Restaurants were in fact a product of disrupted family life, for their success was attributable in part to the number of working men who, following the evacuation or conscription of their wives, chose to frequent these institutions rather than cook for themselves. However, the British Restaurant as presented in *Eating Out with Tommy Trinder* is careful to maintain a prominent family dynamic: the Joneses dine at their own table and, in so doing, retain a sense of their discreteness and distinctiveness. Yet at the same time they are subsumed into a wider national family: as they eat, 'Mr Jones, Mrs Jones and all the other Joneses' are carefully positioned so that unnamed fellow diners are visible in the background of the shot, sharing not only space but also food from a common menu. It was in the British Restaurants and factory canteens the length and breadth of the country that Woolton's proud boast that he felt as if he 'were sitting at the head of a huge dinner table – a *family* dinner table' came closest to being realised in a concrete, as opposed to a purely metaphorical, sense.[28]

However, the positive image of British Restaurants is constructed at the expense of the housewife's ability to provide meals for her family. At one point Trinder claims that he would 'rather starve' than sit through another lacklustre meal *chez* Jones. The reason soon becomes clear. As Mr Jones (Edward Chapman) struggles to carve a tough-looking joint, Mrs Jones (Marjorie Fielding) attempts to excuse the food she places before her family and their guest:

> I'm sorry it's lamb again; it's all I could get at the butchers ... Sorry about there being no greens, I couldn't get to the shops in time – it's just been one of those mornings. Didn't know which way to turn, one thing after the other. And that doorbell! If it went once it went a thousand times. Sorry there's nothing else. We were going to have rice-pudding...[29]

This litany of complaints would no doubt have been familiar to many female viewers (and those they cooked for), and introduces an undercurrent of tension, suggesting that Mrs Jones is no longer able to perform her role as cook in a satisfactory manner. This is especially true given that Trinder's concerns about the quality of the meal are given greater weight than is afforded to the troubles faced by the apologetic and embarrassed Mrs Jones. In addition, *Eating Out with Tommy Trinder* also appears to suggest that the basic rations provided to ordinary Britons by the MoF were insufficient.

Yet to women who had to listen to criticism about their wartime recipes, the sight of the well-fed Joneses sitting happily around a table at a British Restaurant might well have overridden any annoyance they felt about the implication that the primary reason to eat out was to avoid food prepared at home. The fast-moving line that guaranteed (in the film, at least) quick and ready access to food prepared by other people was surely another point of appeal to women tired of spending countless hours in food queues that often proved ultimately unsuccessful.[30] The cheap meals at communal feeding establishments could be enjoyed 'off the ration', and provided families and individuals with a cost-effective way of augmenting the food allocated by the government. Thus the real target in *Eating Out with Tommy Trinder* is not so much Mrs Jones (although jokes, often in the well-established 'mother-in-law' tradition, are certainly made at her expense) as it is those who are too stubborn, too proud or too ignorant to utilise the different avenues of food procurement made available to them by the state.

It is also interesting to note that Trinder's disappointment arises not from his rarefied tastes, but from his desire to eat the simple meat-and-three-veg dinner that Mrs Jones has such difficulty in preparing; in his attempt to impress the family he takes them to a British Restaurant, rather than to the Savoy or the Ritz. The association of simple, wholesome food and the communal nature of the dining experience positions the British Restaurant as a repository for the spirit of, as well as a refectory for, the nation at war. This was especially true following the passing of sumptuary laws that restricted the diners at private restaurants to consumption of a single main course (of meat, fish, game or poultry) – laws that were intended to curtail the excesses of the wealthy just as they were intended to lessen the gap between what might be eaten at home and in public. As Woolton pointed out over a charity lunch (ninepence for tongue, cod or tripe), 'Those who want luxury feeding in these days are outsiders.'[31] Embracing the communal ideal not only provided a tangible benefit to the individual, it also helped organise these same individuals into a national whole.

Films such as *Eating Out with Tommy Trinder* suggest that the government, through the MoI and the MoF, was keen to directly promote communal consumption. The presence in feature films of similar scenes suggests that either the government's message was knowingly adopted by filmmakers (independently or at the state's suggestion) or had become culturally prominent enough to warrant inclusion in privately financed films, or both. After all, both state-sponsored and commercial films were products of, and contributed to, the construction of a similar culture, even if they approached this culture in different ways. Many feature films exhibited during the war contained images of communal consumption. Films made before the war had often utilised the dining table as a method of bringing characters together; those produced during the war were informed by the raised profile of both food in general and group dining in particular.

As its title suggests, *Millions Like Us* is a film centred on the British community at war. For although families are separated and lives lost in battle, the repetitive use of collective and inclusive imagery unites its cast in a filmic metaphor of the nation. In the film, Celia Crowson (Patricia Roc) is recruited to work in a factory which manufactures aeroplane parts. While there, she replaces her biological family with a new one composed of fellow workers. She also finds love with RAF sergeant Fred Blake (Gordon Jackson).

The factory in which Celia is employed has a huge canteen, and this communal eating space is deployed to reinforce the integrated and communal nature of the film's message, normalising the temporary intrusion of extraordinary events into ordinary lives. For if, as Andrew Higson has suggested, the factory becomes the family, then the canteen might be understood to operate as a massive family dining table, providing a nurturing environment in which issues can be discussed, relationships built and emotions publicised.[32]

In the first of two canteen-based scenes, Celia discusses her forthcoming wedding with her colleagues, expressing concern about acquiring enough appropriate clothes for her honeymoon. The references to the outside world help to establish the factory as an integral part of the British nation as a whole, one which is dominated by the war (as witnessed by the building of aeroplanes and clothes rationing, which had been introduced in 1941) but not solely defined by it (the romantic subplot, the honeymoon). Further, the camaraderie evident in this scene is, within the context of the film, quite novel: women previously differentiated by class and regional identity band together to help Celia augment her wardrobe.

The three establishing shots which precede the friends' conversation subtly position the women in relation to each other and the factory as a whole. In the first shot, Celia's co-worker Gwen Price (Megs Jenkins) receives a tray of food and walks into the main space of the canteen. As Gwen moves through the busy environment, she is obscured from view and the sole individual in the shot that the viewer might recognise is lost among a legion of anonymous – but in the context of this scene in particular and the film more generally – equally important co-workers. There follows a cut to a high-angle shot of the canteen in which Gwen is again not identifiable. This second shot not only demonstrates the size of the canteen – the massive space of the machine shop where the women work is communicated in a similar way – but also insists that the viewer understands that our protagonists are elements of a much larger group. During this brief but telling shot, the viewer is obliged to recognise that Gwen and Celia's table is one among many, and that the film might easily have been about characters seated at another table: there are hundreds of stories in this particular canteen, and Celia's is only one of them. In the third shot, Gwen arrives at her table. *Millions Like Us* lives up to its name by framing Gwen's arrival at her destination with the faces of those seated nearby, so that it becomes even clearer that the meal that Gwen takes in the company of her friends is also eaten in the presence of the rest of the canteen and, by extension, Britain as a whole.

The second scene focused on the canteen is the emotional climax of *Millions Like Us* and leaves the viewer in little doubt as to the film's intentions, namely the promotion of the benefits of community. When news of Fred Blake's death during a raid over Germany is received at the factory, Celia moves from the wide, well-populated expanses of the machine shop along narrow corridors to an enclosed, private office where she is informed of her husband's death. In subsequent shots, Celia is shown alone, isolated by her grief. In the film's final scene, however, Celia, who has returned to work, eats an evening meal at the canteen with Gwen and is reintegrated into the factory, and via a dissolve, to the nation's war effort as represented by an image of British bombers flying to Germany.

Having queued alongside unnamed colleagues to receive their food, Gwen and Celia move among the tables, looking for seats and companionship. The pair find their friends at a table which is surrounded on all sides by other workers, placing them at the heart of their community. As the women eat, they listen to, and crucially join in with a singer who entertains them from a stage in the corner of the canteen. When the singer launches into 'Waiting at the Church', a song previously heard at Celia and Fred's wedding reception, Gwen nervously glances at her friend, wondering how she will react to such an emotionally loaded number. However, at Gwen's prompting, Celia joins in the singing, hesitantly at first but soon with growing conviction. The canteen setting adds poignancy to the scene: Celia's private loss and grief are made public, but are tempered by the compassion and support offered her by the other members of her extended factory community. The emotional succour she gains from her friends is mirrored by the physical succour she gains from the canteen meal; the friendship network in which she dines constitutes part of a national whole.

The collectivity inherent in canteen dining was believed to be part of its appeal and its importance. It was, as an M-O report observed, a significant contributor to the morale of the factory:

> A good canteen is something more than a place for the workers to feed in. It is a social focus, a place of friendly informality, probably the only place in the works where there is not a predominant atmosphere of work, machinery, oil, loud noise, or about-to-be-loud-noise.[33]

It should come as no surprise, then, that *Millions Like Us* was not alone in using the works canteen as the setting for a shared cultural act: a similar scene can also be found, for example, in *Old Mother Riley, Detective* (1943). Such sequences are reminiscent of J. B. Priestley's 1940 description of a factory he had recently visited:

> I saw two thousand people push aside what remained of the meat pies and fried plaice and chips they'd had for lunch, lift their eyes and ears towards an orchestra

consisting of four young women in green silk, and then, all two thousand of them, roar out: 'Oh Johnny, Oh Johnny, How Can You Love'. [T]hese two thousand people, who were mostly young and feminine, and very natty in their coloured overalls, [then] returned – much heartened – to another five or six hours' work at their machines.[34]

While not downplaying the significance of 'meat pies and fried plaice and chips' in heartening and re-energising these factory workers, Priestley acknowledged the importance of community, and of participatory community activities, as integral aspects of the war effort.

The star of the canteen concert in *Old Mother Riley, Detective* is Kitty Riley (Kitty McShane), Mother Riley's (Arthur Lucan) daughter. The maternal pride exhibited by Mother Riley as she watches Kitty perform seems to both inspire and be mirrored by the warm and familial attitude which the factory workers demonstrate as they join in the songs. The smaller, darker and more cramped canteen at this factory stands in contrast to the massive, more evenly lit refectory in *Millions Like Us*, but by producing a space akin to a music hall, the film makes explicit the factory's dedication to its employees, for not only are they fed, they are also entertained, for free, in such a space. Long and medium shots of the stage are intercut with group shots of singing workers and medium shots of Mother Riley, thus linking singer, parent and worker in a single choral family.

Further, it is at the canteen concert that Mother Riley's suspicions of a black-marketeer, the apprehension of whom occupies most of the film's narrative, are confirmed: Mr Popplethwaite (H. F. Maltby) adopts a hypocritical attitude, encouraging others to sing without doing so himself, and appealing for the considered consumption of food supplies while being notably overweight. By failing to partake in the shared rituals of the canteen – communal consumption and group singing – Popplethwaite demonstrates the cohesive nature of a group from which he stands apart.

A canteen concert can also be seen in *The Lamp Still Burns* (1943). The film, made with the assistance of the Ministry of Health, details the sacrifices made by the Queen Eleanor Hospital's nurses as they pursue their vocation. The women are shown to be dedicated to the service of others, putting the needs of the community before their own desires. In the film, scenes set in the nurses' refectory are contrasted with a sequence in a factory canteen, and while the latter is positively portrayed and is not necessarily judged in relation to the hospital refectory, its less regimented seating plan serves to reinforce the orderliness, discipline and exclusivity of the nurses.

When Hilary Clarke (Rosamund John) leaves her family's architectural practice to become a nurse, she is first made aware of the reality of the disciplined, almost militaristic life of service during her first meal in the nurses' canteen. Long rows of tables seat hundreds of uniformed nurses according to a strict hierarchy. Although such images might appear to portray the hospital as an elitist environment, the representation of the canteen as a space where the nursing staff comes together in its entirety undermines such claims: hierarchy here stands for discipline rather than divisiveness. This is especially true when we learn that senior nurses have set aside many of their own freedoms in order to serve the public. While the film does not shy away from confronting the unfairness of a system which forces young women to choose between a career inside the hospital and a private life outside it, it salutes those older nurses who have chosen to make such sacrifices.

As the uniformed nurses sit neatly in regular formations, their discipline and their collectivity are underlined, marking the canteen and the hospital more generally as places of dedication and purpose. It is interesting, then, that one of the few spaces we see in *The Lamp Still Burns*' secondary setting, a factory, is its canteen. The film visits the canteen during a lunchtime violin and piano recital, and we see the workers sitting rapt and contented while they listen to a classical duet. A slow tracking shot moves towards the musicians, and the factory workers' more haphazard, less disciplined seating arrangements are contrasted with the nurses' canteen at the hospital. The flowing, dreamlike music introduces an oneiric feel to the sequence, transporting the workers beyond the factory walls, providing respite from their labours and reminding them of the beauties and freedoms for which Britain was fighting.[35] However, despite the differences from the nurses' refectory, a similar feeling of collectivity is evinced, made all the more noticeable by the medical treatment of a worker, which takes place concurrently in the factory's first-aid room. Separated from the mass of his colleagues, the injured worker's isolation seems at first to be compounded by the communal experience of the concert taking place nearby. However, by acting as a counterpoint to his medically enforced solitude, the concert serves to direct attention to the importance of the individual as an aspect of the communal, strengthening the bond that a workplace accident has temporarily broken.

Listen to Britain, an MoI production, is a poetic and evocative meditation on Britain's wartime experience. It juxtaposes two types of musical entertainment, following shots of Flanagan and Allen performing 'Round the Back of the Arches' in a factory canteen with a sequence showing Myra Hess playing a Mozart piano concerto at a lunchtime concert at the National Gallery. Together, these two sequences account for approximately a quarter of the film's running time. Humphrey Jennings, who co-directed the film with Stewart McAllister, was fully aware of the power of these interlinking sequences, describing them as 'highspots' of the film.[36] Indeed, so brilliantly do the sequences interact to establish a common sense of purpose and resolve that they might be productively understood as two sides of the same coin. For although the juxtaposition on one level serves to remind the viewer of the divisions inherent within British culture, it seems rather more effective in collapsing the distance between the elite (both the Queen and Sir Kenneth Clark, director of the National Gallery and one-time head of the MoI's film division, are shown appreciating Hess) and the masses. The transition between the two sequences occurs with a cut on a shared chord, effortlessly linking two musical styles, two sites of consumption and two groups of consumers. The result is the construction of a coherent, if pluralistic, national whole in which neither high nor popular culture is privileged.

In addition, Flanagan and Allen are established by the film as being intended, like the food that justifies the canteen's existence, for public consumption. Wall-mounted signs introduce both the menu and the performers, playfully associating Bud and Ches – available 'in the canteen today' – with the 'Fried Cod and Chips' and 'Damson and Custard' on offer. The concert at the National Gallery is no less gastronomically informed, and shots of women in uniform eating sandwiches and drinking tea are intercut with those of seamen examining paintings in the war artists' exhibition and members of the audience listening to Hess at the piano. It is thus suggested, as Jennings himself made clear in an early outline of the film, that food and culture come together to 'invigorate' those in attendance, and that spiritual, cultural and physical sustenance all had important roles to play in the winning of the war.[37]

The factory canteen provided filmmakers with a convenient site where the seemingly contradictory processes of production and consumption could be simultaneously feted. That scenes set in these locations frequently used song to transform them from mundane refectories into spectacular, sensational environments shows the pains taken to celebrate the vitality of British communal activities. Filmmakers were not alone in recognising the importance of the factory canteen, and might well have taken their lead from the BBC in this matter, for the live transmission of canteen concerts was the focus of *Workers' Playtime*, first broadcast in May 1941.[38] These concerts acted to both celebrate and inspire the workers who participated in them, with songs lifting spirits as food filled stomachs. The radio show ran until 1964, but its immediate impact was such that in 1943 a film was made which aimed to capture the energy of the canteen concerts and put faces to the performers' familiar voices. *Playtime for Workers* was hamstrung by its studio setting, however, and *Kinematograph Weekly* claimed that there was 'more showmanship in its title than in its stage-craft'.[39] Divorced from a live canteen audience, the symbiosis of entertainer and community, which provided the foundation of the radio transmissions, was lost, and with it disappeared the show's *raison d'être*. For what was the point of celebrating the community if that community was not there?

Listen to Britain: pubs, community and the selfishness of solitary consumption

Because of their link to war production, canteens and British Restaurants were effective ways of demonstrating the collective spirit of a nation at work, and as modern, state-sponsored wartime institutions, such places were perfectly suited to the task of linking the collective to the national war effort. However, other spaces were mobilised to extend this communality beyond the factory gate to show that even after clocking off British society was strongest, and British identity most powerful, when understood in communal terms. The pub was a common feature of many British films, and its long-standing importance within British culture not only provided filmmakers with a ready-made environment in which characters could be gathered together with minimal contrivance, but also with a space which, because it pre-dated the social upheavals of the war, was removed from the immediate concerns of the conflict and could therefore be used to comment on it.

Within British wartime cinema, there is an interesting contrast between the positively coded convivial, social associations of the pub with infrequent but telling images of the solitary drinker – individuals whose willingness to isolate themselves within a typically communal space epitomised the asocial otherness of the dietary outlaw. The rejection of the citizen's obligations to the food-based community was most often shown as resulting in exclusion from the protection and solace this community was able to offer.

The fact that the pub is a contested space which can both reject and celebrate community, both ostracise and integrate an individual, is a consequence of the significant degree of ambivalence with which many Britons view alcohol. Sociologists have established that although it is a social lubricant without equal, alcohol is in Britain also associated with abhorrent behaviour and, *in extremis*, the rejection of the social contract.[40] However, despite such concerns, alcohol and the pub (its most common point of sale within the United Kingdom during the war) play crucial roles in the social life of the nation, providing a common meeting ground, a neutral social space in which, according to Quentin Reynolds, 'you hear England talking'.[41]

If, as Reynolds suggests, it is possible in the pub to hear the nation talking, many films were keen to quote from this conversation. Several short films were made during the war which took as their subject the importance of the pub as a social centre, and such was the institution's significance that American GIs arriving in the United Kingdom were instructed in how to conduct themselves in a pub in *A Welcome to Britain* (1943). Films produced for domestic consumption, however, took it as read that patrons would know how they were expected to behave, and so focused instead on the activities which might be enjoyed therein. For example, *Sport at the Local* (1940) examined traditional games such as darts, skittles and bar billiards that were played in pubs and, in so doing, subtly linked British heritage with notions of fair play and the right to leisure as a reward for work. The film can also be understood to have celebrated the free-spirited and voluntarily communal nature of Britishness, a characteristic altogether more genuine, worthy and positive than the regimentation that exemplified the leisure pursuits popularly understood to embody aspects of totalitarian social policy.[42]

Indeed, such was the pub's symbolic importance that it was chosen as the subject of a film intended to remind British soldiers fighting in East Asia of what awaited them upon their return to Britain and, thus, of what they were fighting for. Produced for the Army Welfare Film Unit, *Down at the Local* (1945) is a paean to the joys of the different types of pubs found in the British regions, and suggests that the community evinced by an individual pub can be understood to operate at the national level, as if each hostelry is a tiny part of a much larger whole. The film adopts a conversational style, directly addressing its uniformed audience during its initial commentary: 'Half-past five in merrie England, and [the pub's] open. Any of you boys feel like having one?' This line breaks the silence of the film's first minutes, during which time a brewer's dray delivers beer to a country pub. The mute unloading of the barrels skilfully introduces a frisson of expectant tension; the wait for the commentary to begin mirroring the anticipation of the opening of the pub and the vocal, social function it performs. Once the pub opens, a group of soldiers, representing 'the boys' mentioned in the commentary, move from inn to tavern to bar in an innocently boisterous (but never drunken) crawl.

The soldiers are drawn from different parts of Britain – London, Scotland, Norfolk, Cornwall and Lancashire – and a pub is visited in each locality. In each, the native pays for the drinks. However, in order to encourage greater identification between the on-screen drinkers and the audience (from whom they are supposedly drawn), the soldiers are heard but not seen and many sequences are filmed from the pub-goers' point of view. There is, for example, a startling shot of a pint being drunk as if by the camera. Such subjectivity has the effect of incorporating all those who watch into the drinking circle, transporting them from the front line to the local and facilitating their participation in the shared social rituals of Britain. Indeed, at the Wymondham Inn the regulars discuss the Asian war, the conflict in which the film's audience were actively engaged, in a conversation that aimed to give the lie to the idea that this was a 'forgotten army'. That the soldiers were not only fighting for, but are also included in, such rituals is an idea reinforced in *Down at the Local*'s final sequence, which shows a wall of a London pub covered with photographs of regulars who are now in uniform, reminding the servicemen that the distance between Britain and Asia was felt as keenly at home as it was at the front line.

Wartime filmmakers inserted references to pubs in many feature films, understanding that to do so might give greater credibility to the fictions of Britain they created. Pubs often stood as focal points within cinematic communities, as witnessed by the chipper East End boozer, the Hopvine, in *The Bells Go Down* (1943), the ancient and sinister Hand of Glory in *A Canterbury Tale* (1944),[43] and the eponymous spectral tavern in *The Halfway House* (1944). In *Old Mother Riley MP* (1939) an unscrupulous developer intends to pull down The Rose and Crown, an establishment described as the community's 'spiritual home', prompting Mother Riley to successfully stand for Parliament in order to protect the pub and the neighbourhood it serves.

In Ealing's *Saloon Bar* (1940), the regulars of the Cap and Bells in Soho band together to prove that the barmaid's boyfriend, Eddie Graves (Alec Clunes), is not guilty of the murder of which he is accused, and for which he is due to be hanged. Based on a play by Frank Harvey, and not entirely able to escape its theatrical origins, the film presents the pub as being integral to its environment, part of the essential infrastructure of urban living. So central is the pub to the viewer's understanding of the film that great pains were taken to create an appropriately convincing set: the Cap and Bells was designed as a composite of more than twenty hostelries and was described by *Kinematograph Weekly* as 'Britain's most perfect pub'.[44] By having the characters share a leisure space, the film celebrates the spirit of voluntarily aligned individuals as the foundation of British society and musters a wider range of types than would perhaps have been possible had the film been centred on the concerns of a particular workplace or family.

It is discovered that one of the regulars, Harry Small (Cyril Raymond), is the actual murderer, but the other patrons' common resolve and desire for justice epitomise the pub's character better than the criminal acts of a solitary murderer. In the film, Small attempts to leave the pub without paying, while in Harvey's play one of the factors which initially arouses the regulars' suspicion is Small's refusal to buy a round of drinks for his fellow regulars. The effect of both non-payment and non-treating is the same, positioning Small outside the pub community: although he might drink with others, by failing to participate in an appropriate manner, he drinks alone.

Sally: In all the time I've been coming here, I've never known him stand
            anyone a drink.
Harris: That's bad.
Sally: Well, have you, Charlie?
Wickers: Can't say I 'ave.
Harris: Then that's right enough. Charlie's an elephant where a drink's
            concerned.
Wickers: Who are you calling an elephant?
Harris: I mean you never forget.[45]

This exchange is just one of many which demonstrates the centrality of good-natured banter to the regulars' understanding of the pub as social space.[46] Quentin Reynolds observed that pubs were one of the 'symbols of what England is fighting to maintain. The pub ... is the place where men gather together to speak their minds. The pub is the symbol of free speech in England.'[47]

Reynolds's contention that the national conversation took place in the pub suggests that inter-personal relations are integral to the social dynamic of such establishments. Further, it offers an explanation as to why those people who chose to drink alone were most often judged negatively. Unable to enter into the national conversation, solitary drinkers were compelled to engage in nothing more than marginalised soliloquies. An M-O study of pubs in 'Worktown' advanced a similar idea, stating that the pub was popular for its social connotations rather than just for the alcohol it served, and that it acted as a participatory environment in which a drinker could bond with others in a common and culturally regulated social space.[48]

Individualistic consumption was anathema to the communal ideal, and to reinforce this message positive portrayals of communal drinking were juxta-posed with negative representations of solitary alcoholic indulgence. A number of wartime films made use of lone drinkers to condemn those who chose to exempt themselves from the food-based community and, therefore, the national struggle.

In a letter to *The Times*, Tom Harrisson, co-founder of Mass-Observation, defended the pub against those who sought to present it as a space defined exclusively by the drinks it sold: 'The pub … serves alcohol among many other things. The biggest other thing is company, comradeship, and good cheer.' Further, Harrisson contended that while boisterousness was a common (and, in his opinion, largely positive) feature of crowded pubs, the nation should be more concerned by those who drank alone:

> The solitary drinker goes more slowly and quietly, [and] there is much to suggest that he or she is the one who, chatterless, anchorless and private, carries on into the area of extremism – drunkenness. [49]

The concerns that Harrisson expressed about those who consumed alone were shared by both *In Which We Serve* and *We Dive at Dawn* (1943), films which use images of the solitary drinker to make points concerning community, rejection and the possibility and desirability of reintegration.

In Which We Serve is a naval drama which promotes HMS *Torrin*, the destroyer on which much of the film takes place, as a microcosm of British society, using the adventures of the ship and the reminiscences of her crew, told in a series of interweaving flashbacks, to investigate aspects of the British national experience. Consensus and duty are such central aspects of the preternaturally happy and efficient *Torrin*'s community so that when Richard Attenborough's Young Stoker abandons his post during battle the sense of shock is palpable. Having, in the words of Captain Kinross (Noel Coward), put his 'own skin first and [his] ship and shipmates second', the Young Stoker is presented as an embodiment of all that the *Torrin*, and the nation, is opposed to: selfishness, cowardice and irresolution.

Attenborough's appearance, although brief, is therefore extremely significant. The Young Stoker's abhorrent actions are linked to, and commented upon by, a trip to the pub which follows his upbraiding. The selfishness he demonstrated on the *Torrin* is compounded by his wilful isolation; his failure to function as an element of the crew revisited by his failure to consume as part of a wider community: his solitary, morbid ritual at the bar furthers his disgrace.

Once ashore, the Young Stoker wanders morose and alone around the docks, strikingly silhouetted against rain-soaked streets. Made anonymous by backlighting, yet, at the same time, made prominent for much of the shot by dint of being the only character on screen, the Young Stoker has lost his individuality but gained infamy. The camera, angled down from the deck of the *Torrin* and slightly canted, passes judgement on his misdemeanour, condemning him to the shadows with a slow pan, a piteous and dismissive movement akin to a disappointed shake of the head. The shot changes to one of the interior of a pub, designated as a naval haunt by its nautical décor, caged parrot and maritime paintings. The public bar, though, resembles nothing so much as the *Mary Celeste*, for it is abandoned, but for the Young Stoker and the barmaid (see figure 12). The absence of other customers accentuates the solitary drinker's isolation, branding him an outsider, rejected by his colleagues and, indeed, by himself.

This being a film about the importance of community, however, the Young Stoker is given the chance to make amends, and to gain absolution from his previous transgressions. Having remained until closing time, the sailor attempts to prolong his stay by putting a penny into the automated piano. His reward is 'Run, Rabbit, Run', a song that forces him to recognise his drunken self-pity as little more than an extension of his cowardice at sea. So perfectly

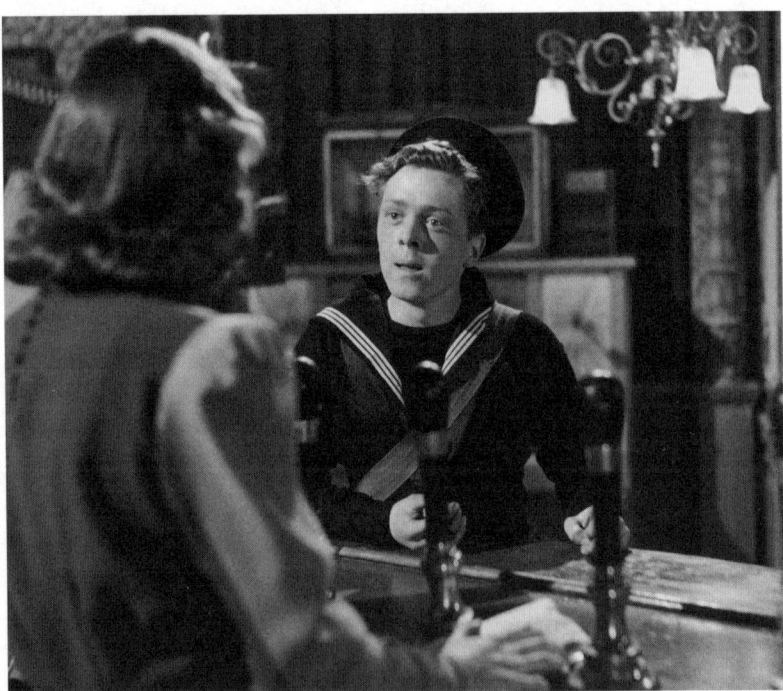

12   The Young Stoker (Richard Attenborough) drinks alone in *In Which We Serve* (1942).

does the song describe his state of mind that on hearing its opening bars, the Young Stoker looks towards the piano as if accusing it of mocking him.

Listening to the music, the Young Stoker becomes sufficiently emotional to admit to the barmaid that 'judging by all I've had tonight I ought to be drunk. I want to be drunk. I want to be drunk more than I've ever wanted anything in my whole life!' However, his continued sobriety exacerbates his feelings of shame, and the scene is therefore able to function as a Damascene moment (as well, perhaps, as slyly commenting on the weakness of wartime beer).[50] By failing to drown his sorrows, the Young Stoker avoids an irrevocable renunciation of the communal ideal, and is thus offered hope of eventual salvation. As he leaves the bar, 'Run, Rabbit, Run' continues to play, chasing him into the street. Yet for all its ironic tones, the song acts as the segue that prepares the viewer for the Young Stoker's rehabilitation. The song continues to play as the scene in the pub dissolves to one on an open lifeboat, with the sailors, accompanied by a harmonica, singing as they drift in the Mediterranean following the sinking of the *Torrin*. The Young Stoker is shown clinging wretchedly to the side of the lifeboat before his crewmates notice his pitiful condition and drag him into the raft. Once back in the boat, and at his request, the sailors launch into a more spirited rendition of 'Roll Out the Barrel'. This second song celebrates the crew's reintegration and also demonstrates the importance of, and emotional succour provided by, the community, quickly dissolving into another flashback, this time of the audience at a packed theatre lustily joining in the chorus. The Young Stoker thereby rejoins the crew, British society and the battle that both are fighting, allowing his eventual death to be presented as a heroic sacrifice rather than a damning judgement of his temporary cowardice.

In Which We Serve was not the only film to use solitary consumption to demonstrate a character's otherness. In *We Dive at Dawn* the image of the solitary drinker is contrasted with the group drinking enjoyed by members of the crew of the British submarine *Sea Tiger*. On leave before the mission that will eventually see them sink a German battleship, the *Sea Tiger's* crew visit various pubs, and the different ways in which these images are presented offer a commentary on how viewers are encouraged to understand the crew's different characters.

Jim Hobson (Eric Portman) is a working-class submariner whose career and private life have been undermined by his borderline alcoholism. Surly, aggressive and cynical, Hobson spends large periods of his shore leave drunk, and his unwillingness to curb his drinking has brought about the problems which blight both his professional and his domestic lives. The film therefore shows

Hobson's selfish, solitary consumption practices as threatening the nation in the present (by not realising his full potential as a submariner, he is effectively short-changing the war effort), and the future (through his inability to maintain or provide for his family and, particularly, his son).

It is implied that Hobson's drinking is the only thing hindering his naval career. The same issue also threatens his marriage. When Alice Hobson (Josephine Wilson) applies for a separation, Hobson blames the influence of her teetotal brother, and angrily insists that he'll 'not join the band of hope' just to please his 'hymn-singing' in-laws. Indeed, when Hobson returns home to find his house empty, instead of looking for Alice and attempting a reconciliation, he walks with no little determination to the Trafalgar public house. The name of this establishment comments ironically on Seaman Hobson's lack of heroism and his unwillingness to join, let alone win, the battle against his demons.

Indeed, so isolated is Hobson that *We Dive at Dawn* abandons him as he opens the door of the Trafalgar, unprepared to let the audience share, and become complicit in, his drunkenness. Hobson's solitary consumption is contrasted with the communal spirit upon which the safety and success of the *Sea Tiger* depends, and serves to isolate him from his family, his crewmates and the wider community. Inebriated, Hobson confronts his wife in the Regent Fish Buffet, the restaurant owned by his brother-in-law. The Regent is a busy concern and functions as a de facto social centre; old and young, male and female customers all patiently wait in line for chips served from a common fryer. Hobson demonstrates his asociality by insulting customers and fighting with the proprietor. It seems fitting that Hobson confronts his wife in this locale, for his aggressive drunkenness distances him from his family and the otherwise stable community in which they live.

Fish and chips have been described as 'a great and quintessentially British institution'. Hobson's inappropriate behaviour in the Regent Fish Buffet, although initially comic, serves to reinforce the idea that he has rejected the social contract, an idea first mooted by his solitary drinking in the pub. Indeed, so important were fish and chips considered to be to the diet of the British working class that, at various points during the war, the government safeguarded oil and fat supplies to the trade while also controlling fish and subsidising potato prices.[51] The linkage of the fish and chip shop and the pub as important local landmarks can also be seen in *The Bells Go Down*, where both Ma Turk's (Beatrice Varley) frying shop and the Hopvine are presented as important signifiers of a functioning local community.

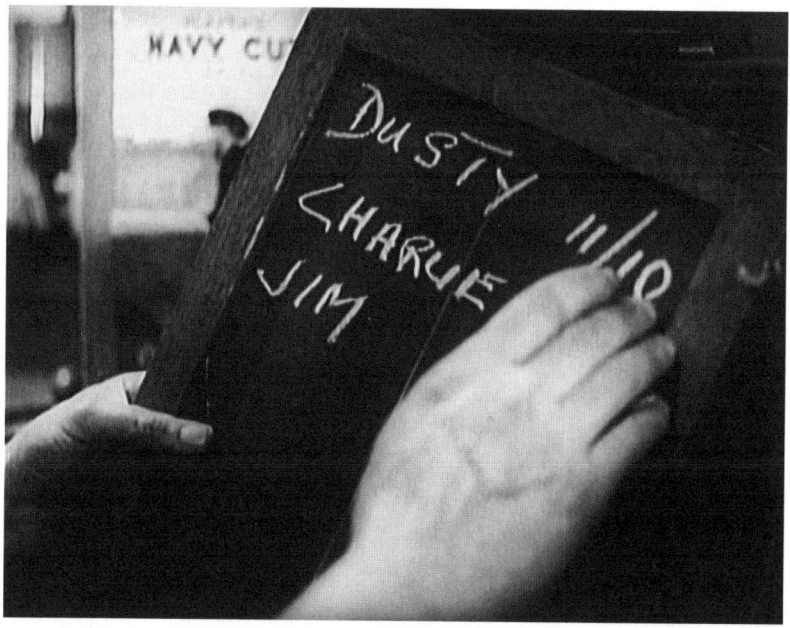

Dusty's name is wiped off the slate in *We Dive at Dawn* (1943).   **13**

Reserving its disapproval only for excessive drinking, *We Dive at Dawn* should not be considered a pro-temperance film. Hobson's humourless brother-in-law is presented as a pompous busybody, and bilge water is described as being a fitting drink for him and his abstemious friends. Furthermore, Hobson's ignominious and lonely drunkenness is contrasted with the convivial social drinking of other members of the *Sea Tiger*'s crew in a different pub. Having disembarked from the *Sea Tiger*, three submariners head to a dockside tavern to relax and enjoy their leave. One of them, Dusty is obviously a regular, well-enough known to have run up a debt of 11*s*. 10*d*. on the slate – significantly more than any other name on the list. Two of Dusty's crewmates accompany him to the pub, and their easy camaraderie on land acts as an expression of their interdependency at sea. Later in the film, after the *Sea Tiger* has (wrongly) been reported lost, the pub's landlord rubs Dusty's name off his list, the movement of his hand across the slate a gentle wave of farewell (see figure 13). Dusty's removal from the pub's register of debit is a simple and affecting tribute to the sailor's significance within in his community, and also of the pub's centrality to the submariners' lives when they are on leave.

Just as an example was made of the Young Stoker, seemingly so that his rehabilitation could inspire others, Hobson is excluded from the naval community in order that he might re-enter its embrace. Whereas at the start of the narrative Hobson's selfishness had threatened his career, his family and his community, his eventual salvation allows him to appreciate the communal ideal and take inspiration and comfort from it. Onboard the *Sea Tiger*, Hobson initially maintains his sour attitude, but is brought back into a more sociable orbit by drinking his daily tot of rum with his shipmates. Hobson's participation in this significant communal ritual is the first step in his reintegration. When the submarine runs low on food and petrol, it is Hobson who leads a raid on a German supply depot, and his heroism in reprovisioning the *Sea Tiger*, in providing fuel for both boat and crew, finally re-establishes his position within the British community. By saving his shipmates, Hobson also salvages his relationship with his wife and infant son; by contributing to the communal wartime present, Hobson creates a better future for his child.

Both Hobson and the Young Stoker fulfil important roles in the films in which they feature: unable to control their selfish impulses – impulses clearly resulting both from, and in, feelings of shame and weakness – they are established in opposition to the close-knit groups from which they are so painstakingly excluded. Their dietary habits epitomise more general failings, and by having their gastronomic otherness so publicly recognised, condemned and overcome, these two characters serve to demonstrate the righteousness and moral power of the British community in wartime, thereby reinforcing the positive images of gustatory collectivity found in films such as *Millions Like Us* and *The Lamp Still Burns*. Food, as an integral part of the war effort, linked Britons to each other and to the state. Indeed, it might be suggested that these films hoped to establish the idea that the nation which eats together, defeats (the enemy) together. Such an idea, although laudable, did no go uncontested.

'Dull, respectable, commonplace. I loathe it!' The fantasy of unrestricted consumption

The line of dialogue from which this section takes its title is spoken in *The Wicked Lady* and might be understood as an expression of the costume melodrama's artistic manifesto as much as it is 'bold, bad' Barbara's (Margaret Lockwood) description of her upbringing. Eschewing the emotional and aesthetic restraint that characterised many of the films that would come to be defined and celebrated as 'quality' British cinema,[52] Gainsborough's melodramas sought to provide the viewer with visual, narrative and emotional excess, a glimpse of an opulent world divorced from the war-torn present and also from an uncertain (and most likely impoverished) post-war future and the potential disappointments that such a time might bring.

Having damned *The Wicked Lady* as 'inept to a point of exasperation' in his review in *Tribune*, Simon Harcourt-Smith conceded that he understood the appeal that historical settings had for cinema-goers:

> The tedium, the grey ruin of modern life have obviously turned the costume picture into, perhaps, the most promising film gamble of today … By all means let us escape on the wings of the movies to less troubled epochs than the present.[53]

Setting aside the success or otherwise of *The Wicked Lady* at facilitating such an escape, Harcourt-Smith was offended by the liberties the film took with its Restoration setting – liberties which wilfully transformed history from a place of instruction where verisimilitude was key into a site of sensual fantasy where sensation was paramount. Speaking soon after the release of *The Wicked Lady*, and having noted the public's recent 'full-blooded pursuit' of the film and other 'costume spectacles' like it, a contributor to *Kinematograph Weekly* offered an explanation for the film's success: 'Costume melodramas pack the box-office. I suggest that this is an escape from the drabness of this present-day world of clothes coupons and austerity.'[54] Images of unrestrained consumption offered similar pleasures to cinema-goers increasingly tired of rationing and food control.

The excessive aesthetic approach adopted by Gainsborough proved commercially very lucrative, and suggests that British cinema-goers were happy to be entertained by visions of worlds unfettered by governmental interference, where stoical self-control was sidelined in favour of impassioned dialogue.[55] Although *The Man in Grey* (1943), the first of the Gainsborough melodramas, is told in an extended flashback from a contemporary setting, it is most satisfying when representing a past shown as a site of flamboyance and sensuality. The success of *The Man in Grey* suggested that an audience existed for films which used historical settings as an escape from the concerns of the present. Such films afforded their audience an opportunity to indulge their sensual desires, an experience which, in refusing to adhere to contemporary social norms, instead operated as an implicit critique of them.

Not needing to manoeuvre within the framework of contemporary events – events which could impose upon even escapist representations of wartime Britain the need to mention rationing, shortages and queues – films with historical settings potentially had greater freedom in the ways in which they could use food to discuss society. Three films from the latter years of the war – Gainsborough's *The Wicked Lady* and *Madonna of the Seven Moons* and

Ealing's *Champagne Charlie* – will be explored to demonstrate how gastro-nomic themes could be used to challenge the idea of wartime Britain as a consensual food-based community.

Many of Gainsborough's costume films proved popular with British cinema-goers, but not all British films saw the past as a different and fantastical country where the travails of the modern world could be ignored. In wartime Britain, the past was a contested space where contemporary issues could be debated, celebrated and problematised. Food, so significant in 1940s Britain, was mobilised in historical films not just to add 'authenticity' to recreations of past eras, but also to comment upon society as experienced by contemporary audiences. Films like *The Wicked Lady* stand in obvious contrast to more sober historical films such as *The Young Mr Pitt* (1942), which viewed the past as significant because of its relevance to modern issues. Using similar events to draw parallels between the past and the present not only provided precedents for wartime campaigns but also allowed for positive resolutions: if Britain endured and triumphed before, then she could do so again.

The designers of the promotional campaign which accompanied the release of *The Young Mr Pitt* were keen to promote the 'timeliness' of a film which presented the Napoleonic threat to Britain as a precursor to that posed by the Nazis. Further, the pre-Pitt Georgian era is established as a site of moral and political degeneracy saved from its degradation only by the efforts of William Pitt the Younger, 'the Georgian Churchill'.[56] Early in the film, a montage – part of a wider 'newsreel' technique employed to contextualise the film's narrative[57] – contrasts the sensual pleasures available to the wealthy with the wretched lives of the poor. A narrator informs the viewer that Georgian Britain was a place of

> highly-polished manners and rather low behaviour, of gay satins and miserable rags. The aristocracy get mellow on delicate wines, the poor dead drunk on gin at a penny a pint. Men are hanged for stealing a sheep while others grow fat on the proceeds of corruption … the country sprawls aimlessly on a multi-coloured quilt of feckless folly.

In contrast to Gainsborough's later visualisation of excess as a method of escape, *The Young Mr Pitt* clearly condemns aristocratic self-indulgence and proletarian debauchery as physical/sensual representations of a more generally corrupt system. By contrast, William Pitt (Robert Donat) eats and drinks in order to fulfil his duties to Britain, not for pleasure. Compared to the venal gluttony of his rival Charles James Fox (Robert Morley), Pitt is shown as having almost unnatural self-restraint, sacrificing corporeal pleasure and well-being in order to serve his country, consuming only, and not always even, that which is necessary for survival.

The sacrifices Pitt demanded of himself and others are shown to be vital components of the war effort, an idea that would no doubt chime with cinema-goers familiar with MoF publicity. The need for controlled consumption is made explicit, and although not always popular with Pitt's constituents, is shown to contribute to Britain's eventual triumph over tyranny. Further, the film's 'newsreel' sections serve to convey the past in a style that intentionally presents it through a medium relevant and knowable to contemporary audiences, allowing the lessons drawn from Pitt's resolute fight against the French to inform the current fight against the Germans.

The reviewers found much to praise in *The Young Mr Pitt*'s measured use of history. Having noted the historical parallels between Georgian and contemporary Britain, *Monthly Film Bulletin* felt relief that a tale with such modern relevance and resonance was told with 'only minor historical faults'.[58] The film's historical accuracy was also praised by Evelyn Russell who in *Sight and Sound* proclaimed *The Young Mr. Pitt* as 'the finest historical film we have made', a piece of hyperbole justified by reference to an 'impeccable' use of period detail.[59] Further, historian Dr Rachel Reid, asked to report on the film for *Sight and Sound*, was impressed by *Pitt*'s 'quite unusual excellence' and declared that

> It remains very greatly to [the filmmakers'] credit that they have resisted so well the temptation to 'improve' on the facts. The result is a film of very great interest and real value, which should be very popular with the general public as well as with schools.[60]

British cinema-goers responded positively to the film; good reviews and the presence of Robert Donat (in his first role following his Oscar-winning performance of 1939 in *Goodbye, Mr Chips*) helping it into fourth place in R. H. 'Josh' Billings' list of British box-office winners for 1942.[61]

It is interesting to note that, according to Billings, one of the films to have done better business than *The Young Mr Pitt* was another film with a historical setting – *Hatter's Castle* (1941) – a tale of brutality, insanity and millinery set in Victorian Scotland. *Kinematograph Weekly* praised *Hatter's Castle*, describing it as the tale of

> an arrogant, dictatorial and vicious Scottish tradesman who becomes a tragic victim of his own evil mind, selfish pride and colossal egoism. Before nemesis overtakes him, his wife dies, his young son commits suicide and his daughter is sullied.[62]

So far, so melodramatic. But beyond the obvious differences in narrative (family history vs political reconstruction, prurient exposé vs hagiography), where *Hatter's Castle* most differs from *The Young Mr Pitt* is in its unashamed use of history as spectacle. Despite the darkness of its plot, *Hatter's Castle* was described by one reviewer as 'a skilfully planned entertainment edifice',[63] while other critics regarded the film's reconstruction of the Tay Bridge disaster and the burning of a castle as being worthy of special mention.[64]

The presence of *Hatter's Castle* on Billings's list suggests that the film-going public liked its history dramatic, passionate (often violently so) and sensual. This suggestion is strengthened by figures from the Regent cinema in Portsmouth. When *The Young Mr Pitt* was exhibited in the week of 20 November 1942 it attracted 10,401 paying customers, the eighth lowest number that year. By contrast, 17,826 watched *The Man in Grey*, while *The Wicked Lady's* tally of 28,615 admissions made it the most successful British film exhibited at the Regent between 1939 and 1948. *Madonna of the Seven Moons*, said by *Kinematograph Weekly* to have 'delighted film fans everywhere', attracted 21,545 patrons despite being 'dismissed in presumptuous paragraphs by more than one lay Press critic'.[65]

The pleasures offered by films set outside wartime Britain, whether they have historical settings (*The Wicked Lady, Champagne Charlie*) and/or foreign locations (*Madonna of the Seven Moons*), are manifold. The rejection of realism in these films and the pleasures offered to, in particular, female spectators, have been discussed in some detail elsewhere, often in terms of the films' escapist aesthetic. Costumes have rightly received critical attention, offering, as they do, visions of an alternative world at odds with the contemporary British reality of clothes rationing and 'make do and mend'.[66] Sets and décor are similarly noteworthy, especially when one considers the testing material circumstances under which they were constructed.[67] Indeed, Harcourt-Smith took a break from excoriating *The Wicked Lady* to express his 'every sympathy' for art departments whose work on historical films was 'hampered by problems of coupons'.[68] These sympathies, it should be noted, were not extended to audience members, particularly women, affected by very similar problems. The failure to recognise the value and appeal of a world where coupons were no longer a problem perhaps goes some way to explaining the differences in opinion between this particular reviewer and millions of cinema-goers.

This is especially true if we bear in mind the idea that the Gainsborough melodramas have often been understood as women's films, successfully targeted at a female audience and constructed to appeal to female desires.[69] Sue Harper has argued convincingly that 'the appeal of garments in the [wartime and immediate post-war] costume melodramas is predicated upon what was *not* available under contemporary clothing conditions'.[70] But if we are to recognise the visual allure of costumes, for example, then we might also pay attention to the ways in which the films present acts of consumption, for gastronomy was equally as affected by government regulation. It does not seem much of a stretch to suggest that food might contribute to the escapist aesthetic, for shortages, queues and complaints are most notable by their absence from the fantasies conjured by the Gainsborough melodramas. And although food might be less dominant an element of the *mise-en-scène* than either costume or set, it functions in a similar way, offering a view of a world unhampered by coupons, offering the illusion of escape from the harsher elements of the MoF's regulation of consumption, just as Elizabeth Haffenden's dress designs offered a temporary escape from clothes coupons, utility blouses and War Office-approved corsets.[71]

Released a few months after the end of the war, *The Wicked Lady* offered an escape from the austerity which followed VE and VJ Days. Based on Magdalen King-Hall's 1944 novel *Life and Death of the Wicked Lady Skelton*, the film retains a largely similar narrative, despite introducing some significant new characters (most notably that of Caroline, played by Patricia Roc). Headstrong Barbara Worth (Margaret Lockwood) enters into a loveless marriage with Sir Ralph Skelton (Griffith Jones), but comes to feel trapped by his dull and worthy ways. Her quest for sensation results in her leading a double life: bored, respectable wife by day, cross-dressing highwayman and adulteress by night. Although Barbara eventually pays for her transgressions and is killed by the man she loves (and therefore, the film suggests, the only man capable of saving her), her wilful wickedness makes her the film's most compelling character. *Today's Cinema* recognised as much:

> It is the perfidious Lady Skelton who dominates the finely crafted canvas, and her talent with a pistol – she would rather shoot a man than a horse – her candid passion for the handsome Captain [Jackson (James Mason)], and her neat hand with a poison phial, all these are pleasantries which must endear her to the pleasure-seeking patron.[72]

The passion mentioned here, the adulterous affair between a married woman and a highwayman, is presented in the film as irresistible and is one of *The Wicked Lady*'s principal attractions.

Indeed, so natural is the lovers' passion that the film introduces it through the commingling of two essential pleasures of the flesh: food and sex. Having met during a robbery, Barbara and fellow highwayman Jackson dine and then consummate their relationship at the Leaping Stag, a country inn whose name carries none-too-subtle suggestions of mating and the hunt. The location is important, for in the film the Leaping Stag acts as a sensual environment catering to the corporeal desires of its patrons, where consumption is hedonistically celebrated rather than endured as mere necessity. The dialogue between Barbara and Jackson crackles with sexual tension and innuendo, with Jackson, for example, introducing the landlady of the tavern in the following manner: 'I've told my friend that there are two things you do better than most women. One of them is cooking…' Raymond Durgnat, writing in *A Mirror for England*, was surely not alone in relishing such sexually loaded dialogue.[73] Further, the couple prepare for dinner by removing their masks, thus introducing an element of erotic display into their pre-prandial routine. The frequent verbal correlation of acts both sexual and gastronomic presents them as virtually analogous within the context of the lovers' affair, and does so in a way that presents both as practices worthy of celebration.

Indeed, when Jackson talks of his relationship with Barbara he uses food as a metaphor for his sexual obsession:

> When I'm with you it's like enjoying a meal prepared by the Gods. I eat and eat until I can't face another morsel. Then I look at you again and before I know it I'm clamouring for another helping.

Barbara's ambrosial qualities aside, describing wanton and unrepentant sexual freedom in terms of overeating takes on additional meanings when it is remembered that food was still heavily regulated in Britain when *The Wicked Lady* was released. The film therefore offers not only a coded critique of rationing but also an alternative to conventional modes of morality, presenting these twin acts of consumption as pleasures in which contemporary British society was unable or unwilling to (openly) indulge. The emphasis on sex, however euphemistic, helps to establish *The Wicked Lady* as a film which celebrates the physical aspects of human existence, prioritising sensual experientialism above the rote-learned, dutiful catechisms of 'conventional' state-regulated asceticism. The (relatively) explicit sexual themes in *The Wicked Lady* helped to establish the film's desire to discuss the pleasures, and costs, of physical sensuality (as opposed to, say, *The Young Mr Pitt*, which sublimated all physical pleasure to an overwhelming ideal of duty). They also mirrored the social changes which had led the Archbishop of Canterbury to claim in 1945 that recent moral developments in Britain were becoming so ingrained that 'people are not conscious of injuring the war effort by dishonesty or sexual indulgence'.[74]

Although *The Wicked Lady* makes it very clear that the relationship between

Barbara and Jackson is sexual in nature, it presents the physical aspect of their liaison in a comparatively chaste manner. And just as sex is left off the screen, so too is much of the food discussed in the narrative. Absent from the film is the magnificent wedding feast Lord Skelton lays on in King-Hall's novel in order to integrate his new bride into his aristocratic circle. Having already detailed the food consumed at the Worth family home, King-Hall describes a second meal taken at the Skeltons' ancestral residence:

> Maryiot Cells, always renowned for its hospitality, lived up to its highest standards that wedding night. There were the wines of France, Spain, the Rhineland and the Orient, as well as homely ale, for the thirsty, and for the hungry a bewildering display of eatables, from the solid toothsomeness of collard pig and stewed carps, to the more refined tastiness of marchpanes, pistaches and chocolate amandes.[75]

The exotic unfamiliarity of some of these foodstuffs does little to detract from the splendour of the meal, and the unavailability of the wines described, the rationing of meat and the long queues associated with fishmongers all directs attention to the fantastic spectacle presented by this literary feast. This banquet has been excised from the film, while the meal served to the lovers at the Leaping Stag – 'stewed carp, pigeon pie, a dish of neat's [ox's] tongues and cheese' – is discussed but never seen. Perhaps for fear of detracting from the primary, sexual, act of consumption which dominates Barbara and Jackson's visit to the Leaping Stag, the viewer's hungry imagination is left to focus on more kinetic and auditory forms of entertainment: dancing, talking, singing and seduction.

Indeed, most of the food actually shown to viewers in *The Wicked Lady* has restrictive, workaday connotations. Drinks are taken both at a meeting of local nobles convened to discuss legal matters, and at the christening of a tenant's child. The remnants of breakfast are seen at the house of Barbara's hated in-laws. There is little pleasure to be taken from these dutiful acts of on-screen consumption, and the miserable breakfast endured by Barbara epitomises her loveless marriage and contrasts with the sexual freedom, passion and feasting enjoyed, mostly off-screen, with Jackson.

However, the fact that the food in *The Wicked Lady* is discussed but not seen, presented as a fantasy, a spectral presence frequently referred to yet remaining just beyond the viewer's vision, only serves to add to its signifi cance. Within the escapist framework of *The Wicked Lady*, food functions as just one of the many unrealisable pleasures offered, but is no less enjoyable for that. By displacing food and, indeed, sex into the virtual world of fantasy, it could not frustrate, for pleasure enjoyed in the imagination is unlikely to disappoint. In *The Wicked Lady* the idea of food is linked to the idea of sex, and the entrancing way in which both are positioned, as representations of freedom, individualism and unapologetic indulgence, provides the film with much of its sensuality.

This is not to say that such representations are unproblematic, for Jackson and Barbara pay for their transgressions with their lives before the film ends, both of their deaths the result of the actions of the ones they love. However, the film suggests that freedom (to love, to eat, to move and to act independently) is positive, and both Barbara's and Jackson's deaths result from their criminality rather than their sensuality: Jackson is hanged as a highwayman (and, falsely, as a murderer), while Barbara is killed attempting a final, violent hold-up. While the film condemns the pair for their lawlessness, viewers are left to make their own judgement about their sexual and gastronomic indulgences. Functioning as a symbol of more than simple criminality, the outlaw here represents unrestrained consumption. It is not surprising that Lockwood and Mason, the actors who brought these sensation-seeking characters to the screen, were so popular in 1945.[76]

Gainsborough's *Madonna of the Seven Moons*, set in Italy and based on Margery Lawrence's 1931 novel *The Madonna of Seven Moons*, also uses food in a way designed to distinguish between 'normality' and 'fantasy'. The film examines the two, diametrically opposed personalities which emerge after a schoolgirl is attacked, and possibly raped. The first half of the film details the life of Maddalena Labardi (Phyllis Calvert) – respectable wife of Giuseppe (John Stuart) and mother of Angela (Patricia Roc) – a woman whose largely ascetic life in Rome is defined by these roles and her commitment to the church. However, a stressful incident triggers a change and Maddalena becomes Rosanna, thief, free spirit and lover of Florentine criminal Nino Barucci (Stewart Granger). Unable to resolve the conflict between self-restraint and free-spirited sensuality, Maddalena/Rosanna dies in a conclusion which proposes that if they are to live happily, individuals (and by implication nations) need to negotiate a position between these extremes rather than destructively embracing just one.

Set before the war, and therefore ignoring the devastation caused by the conflict, *Madonna of the Seven Moons* presents Italy as a sensual playground, a nation where consumption is regulated not so much by the state as by the whims of the individual. Within the film, the Florentine world within which Rosanna operates is contrasted with Maddalena's Roman existence: the former is full of life, noise, chaotic movement and, tellingly, food, while the latter is characterised by respectable behaviour and self-control. Food is just one of the ways (along with costume, locale and conduct) in which the Florentine fantasy space is constructed and explored.

The film, therefore, operates as a double fantasy: within what to viewers might have appeared to be an already exotic foreign locale, a second and yet more exotic space exists. But for their names and their Italianate villa, the Labardis' existence is so markedly and familiarly British – in terms of lifestyle and attitudes – that it is effectively from a representation of Britain, and its regulated wartime society, that Maddalena flees when she escapes to Florence. Behind the imposing walls of their residence, the family is divorced from the wider world and is able to live however – and, in effect, *wherever* – it wishes. It seems that the Larbardis crave the security of the Home Counties, for they live as if Giuseppe is a stockbroker with a commuter's season ticket and a job in the city. Indeed, the idea of the Anglophile Italian appears in Lawrence's novel:

> [Giuseppe Labardi] had been educated in England and was frankly proud of the fact that he was often taken for an Englishman – it had been his insistence on the necessity that his young daughter should speak English, should learn to love England and English ways as well as he did, that had … been the reason for [her] spending … practically the whole of her educational life in England.[77]

The Britishness demonstrated by many of the actors was recognised by *Monthly Film Bulletin* which sniffily declared that 'the players … fail to give convincing studies of the Italian characters they are meant to portray'.[78] This respectable family also prefers British company: Giuseppe's friend and confidante is Dr Charles Ackroyd (Reginald Tate) – they share both membership of the same club and endless polite little cocktails – while Angela, educated in Britain, has fallen for Evelyn (Alan Haines), a young British diplomat. Further, Maddalena's prized possession is a prayer book in which she records, in English, the important dates in her life. The choice to have Maddalena write in English would not in itself be significant if the film's Florentine milieu were similarly inscribed, but all the signs in the Quartiere di San Gimiano where Nino lives and runs the Seven Moons café-bar are in Italian, highlighting the foreign-ness of the location and its inhabitants. Indeed, when Maddalena becomes Rosanna and leaves Rome, she is unable to overcome the linguistic and cultural disjunction between her two personalities and leaves behind her a hieroglyph representing the Seven Moons, written in lipstick on a mirror, to let Giuseppe know where she has gone.

The lavishly staged Quartiere di San Gimiano is introduced with a high-angle pan along a street market in which a laden greengrocer's stall groans under the weight of its wares, a demonstration that in this environment the body's satisfaction is paramount. The explicit gastronomic display serves no obvious narrative purpose: the food is simply *there*; it is a spectacle, an attraction to be enjoyed and consumed by the audience. In addition, the food is immediately available; no queues snake away from the grocer's cart, no points coupons are exchanged, no one looks as if they will return home empty-handed (one woman's shopping basket is so heavy that she is forced to carry it with both hands). To British housewives, this must have looked like paradise, a place where the petty and time-consuming restrictions of a heavily rationed lifestyle were thrillingly, if temporarily, absent. Not for the residents of this bounteous neighbourhood the experience of getting home to find a note saying:

> there is no honey, no sultanas, currants or raisins, no mixed fruits, no saccharine at present, no spaghetti, no sage, no herrings, kippers or sprats (smoked or plain), … no fat or dripping, no tins of celery, tomato soup or salmon. I have bought three pounds of parsnips.[79]

San Gimiano is not a locale that marginalises the importance of food or forces cooking into the private, domestic space of the house. Women are shown sitting on chairs peeling vegetables and plucking chickens, their presence in the street reinforcing the gastronomic motif of the neighbourhood, but also making public – and thus allowing the public, both in San Gimiano and the cinema – to recognise the contribution that women make to the well-being of the community.

The idea that sensual gratification is the defining characteristic of this community is also advanced by set design: narrow streets force an already voluble population to engage with each other amid drying washing and flower stalls. Further, the peeling plaster on external walls suggests that the immediate issues and pleasures of existence, the transient but ever renewable now, are prioritised: domestic life focuses on the living.[80] The soundtrack reinforces these points, with the loud chatter, arguments and playful shouts of children acting as spontaneous choral accompaniment to an (unseen) accordion.

It is this unthinking celebration of life that British artist Jimmy Logan (Peter Murray Hill) finds irresistible. Soon after setting up his easel on a busy Florentine street, Logan is informed that in San Gimiano 'Nino is the law', but the legal system he embodies does not feature ration books, queues or self-denial. Although, before his first appearance, Nino is described in unflattering terms, the first shot of him in his fiefdom shows him redistributing fruit from the greengrocer's stall, encouraging others to consume without guilt, restraint or thought of consequence. The Seven Moons is a front for Nino's unlawful activities and a base for his underworld associates, and although he is more sympathetically represented in the film than in Lawrence's novel, his criminality is less romanticised than that of the highway robbers in *The Wicked Lady*, released a year later when public attitudes regarding the state's right to determine an individual's lifestyle had undergone further changes. Granger's Nino, purportedly so vicious, is described by *Kinematograph Weekly* as 'handsome, if somewhat genteel',[81] and the otherness characterised by his sensual consumerism – of women, of clothes (Granger appears in a series of costumes designed to accentuate his physique) and of food – is more appealing, and better conceived, than his criminality. Further, the casting of the popular Granger, and the vitality with which his surroundings are presented, suggest that audiences were encouraged to empathise with Maddalena's desire to escape to San Gimiano and with Rosanna's desire to stay there.

At the Labardis' house in Rome, pre-dinner drinks anticipate a meal that never materialises; at one point the family's cook asserts that 'the only meal anybody's likely to get in this house is a piece of my mind'. This feast is described by Angela as 'indigestible'. Food in San Gimiano, by contrast, although basic, is an immediate pleasure, an essential part of the rich *mise-en-scène* of the Seven

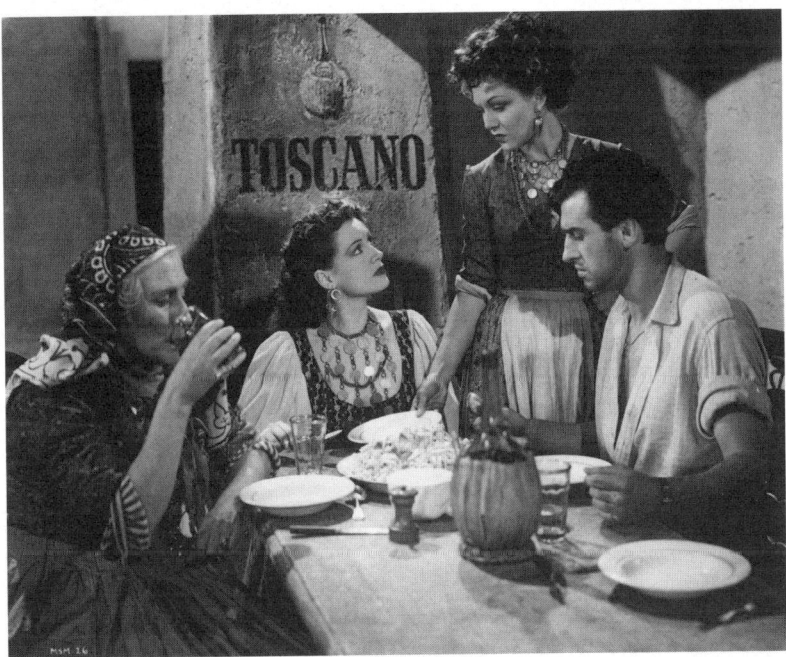

Rosanna (Phyllis Calvert) enjoys some Florentine hospitality in *Madonna of the Seven Moons* (1944).

Moons. One scene, for example, begins with a close-up of a mountainous platter of tagliatelle, its size indicating the abundance of food within this fantastic environment. Rosanna is shown as a voracious and unapologetic consumer – of food *and* of Nino – but she does not cook: food is prepared for her. Indeed, her freedom to enjoy a highly-charged, and satisfying, sexual affair with Nino stems from her not having to use her time procuring or organising the production of food. The relish with which Rosanna eats mirrors her enthusiasm for her sexual relationship with Nino: the pleasure gained from both physically gratifying acts is the result of the absence of Anglo-Roman propriety and the onerous regulations of wartime Britain.

The Florence of *Madonna of the Seven Moons* is a locale defined by the freedom to consume, and since the Seven Moons falls outside the MoF's control, the spectacle provided by the meals proclaims the opportunity to eat without regulation or fear of prosecution. The use of characteristically Italian foods adds to the exoticism of the image, whose appeal to the appetite is located in its otherness: the presentation of foreign food in a similarly foreign location helps *Madonna of the Seven Moons* conjure a fantasy of unrestricted consumption. The gusto with which Rosanna shovels forkfuls of pasta into her mouth provides the viewer with a measure of vicarious pleasure, for although many filmmakers use food as a prop it is relatively unusual for it actually to be eaten on-screen (see figure 14). While this may relate to perceptions about the inelegance of the act of eating or difficulties associated with continuity and multiple takes, during the war, further problems arose from the unavailability of food. In February 1943, a cartoon appeared in the *Evening News* in which an aspiring star was hired to work as an extra in a banqueting scene, but only on the understanding that she hand over her ration book to a producer (see figure 15).

To combat shortages, filmmakers resorted to using fake food and drinks. This had always been the case to some extent, but the practice became ever more widespread during the war. One thirsty studio employee complained of the Three Feathers in *Perfect Strangers* (1945), 'Studio pubs my foot; the drinks are all phoney.'[82] The *Evening Standard* described a feast in *The Peterville Diamond* (1942):

> Three day banquet of turkeys, joints, pineapples, bananas and all the trimmings is being thrown ... But everything is made of papier-mâché. Even the old vintages served are merely water, not even ginger ale.[83]

Similarly, ersatz bananas were created for *Men of Two Worlds* (1946);[84] the 'mountainous heaps' of food at a Roman orgy in *Fiddlers Three* (1944) were made of paper, wax or plaster;[85] and the tables shown to 'groan with food' in

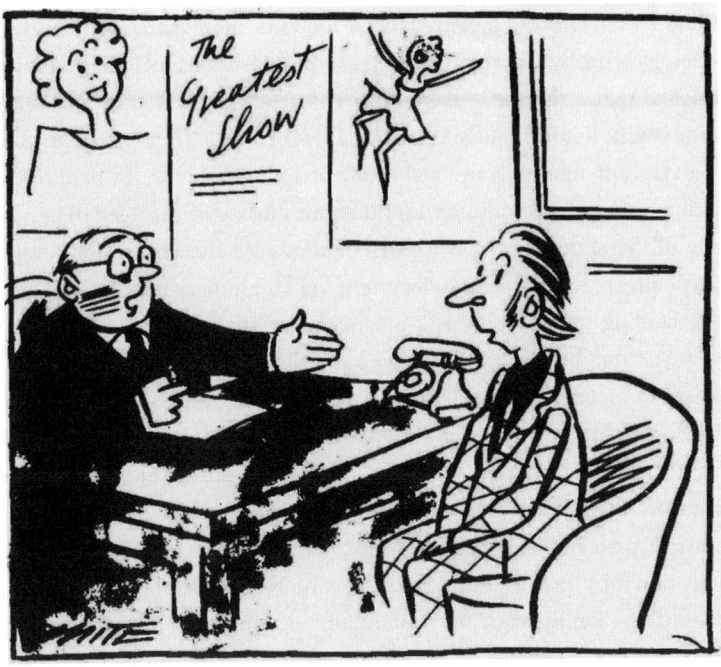

'OK, I'll engage you for the banqueting scene. Where's your ration book?'
White in the *Evening News*, 22 February 1943.

Johnny Frenchman (1945) held only 'plaster food in these days of rationing'. Despite its inedibility, *Kinematograph Weekly* loyally insisted that this last spread was 'none the less appetising to look at!'[86]

Madonna of the Seven Moons' explicit displays of consumption served to foreground the gastronomic elements of the film in such a way as to encourage the viewer to recognise and take pleasure in both the prospect and the act of eating. For by allowing the viewer to see Rosanna eat (rather than cutting away at the moment the fork touches her lips), the viewer is made aware that the food on the screen is edible, that the indexical nature of cinema meant that the actress shown to be eating *really was* eating, and that the pleasure she took from the food might also be genuine. By allowing – in fact, encouraging – the viewer to take pleasure in Rosanna's own enjoyment, the film elicits an almost physical response. An alimentary link is established in which the audience has the chance to vicariously enjoy the food being consumed, for it exists on-screen at this moment with an almost tangible reality. The simplicity of the meal makes it all the more knowable, all the more real, and lends the food a presence it might otherwise have lacked.

Such a haptical use of food is found in relatively few films of the period, which as a whole instead preferred to use food in a more metaphorical way, for its ideological utility and ability to help communicate ideas of a shared national experience rather than as a method of constructing a concrete and sensual diegetic reality. It is intriguing, then, that *Eating Out with Tommy Trinder*, a film with a very different objective and mode of address, also works hard to draw attention to the act of consumption. It seems likely that the need to persuade people of the appeal of the British Restaurants led the film to focus on the sensory allure that the food on offer might hold for hungry Britons, rather than simply lauding the economy and practicality of the institutions. High-angle shots are used in both the private home and the public canteen to contrast, in a subjective manner, the small and unappetising portions a consumer might find before them in the former (see figure 16) with the much more satisfying meals available in the latter (see figure 17). Indeed, the act of consumption is absent from the Jones' house: although food is shown, it is presented in a very negative manner and no attempt is made to eat it. It does, though, serve to build anticipation for a meal to come. The hunger hinted at in the family home is not sated until the family reach the Restaurant, with the film's documentary-style explanatory sequences and Trinder's own antics delaying yet further the final, cathartic shot of the film which shows Trinder, for himself, for the Joneses and for the audience more generally, finally getting to eat.

The recognition and reproduction of the physical aspect of consumption in *Madonna of the Seven Moons* is revisited when Rosanna eats a freshly picked apple during a picnic that she shares with Nino in a deserted and overgrown garden. Rosanna describes the garden as 'wild', adding approvingly that 'it's broken the shackles that once made it neat and tidy'. Such a description might also apply to the couple's rejection of conformity, for they offer an alternative to contemporary British attitudes to both sexual and gustatory norms. Their disorderly, unconventional passion for each other, and for life and sensation

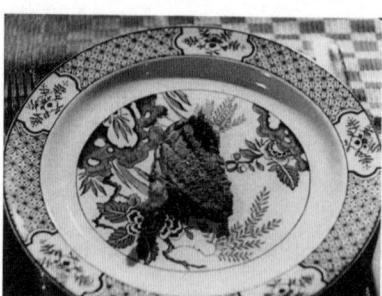 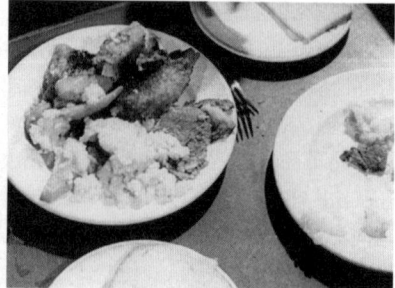

16–17   Spot the difference. Subjective shots of the meals available in the private home and a British Restaurant in *Eating Out with Tommy Trinder* (1941).

more generally, is celebrated, but shown as coming at a cost: Rosanna can only be free when she rejects her alter-ego and the familial responsibilities associated with it, while Nino has to endure the death of the woman he loves following her ultimate failure to reconcile the two halves of her personality.

Madonna of the Seven Moons does, however, offer an alternative to the seemingly irreconcilable conflict between Maddalena and Rosanna, suggesting that by combining the positive aspects of each personality, personal happiness and fulfilment can be achieved. The middle ground between the two extremes is found in the form of two young couples: artist Jimmy Logan and his wife Nesta (Dulcie Gray), and Angela and her fiancé Evelyn. Both couples combine the instinctive sensuality of Rosanna with the loyalty and integrity demonstrated by Maddalena, and both are aware of the need to enjoy, but not overindulge in, the sensual pleasures their lives offer them. The couples are shown cooking, eating and drinking, but their stable relationships allow this to happen within a true union rather than a schizophrenic dichotomy, thus encouraging them to create and nurture intimacy rather than destroy it. To wartime viewers, the realisation that responsibility and sensuality need not be mutually exclusive might well have been extremely satisfying.

It was not only Gainsborough who produced films that can be understood as being critical of government regulation of food and society. At Ealing, Alberto Cavalcanti directed *Champagne Charlie*, a film which celebrates consumption through its recreation of the Victorian-era music hall, and acts as a critique of the government's (seemingly) unnecessary celebration of self-restraint and also, in a more muted way, of rationing. In 1860, rival singers George Leybourne (Tommy Trinder) and the Great Vance (Stanley Holloway) seek pre-eminence in the London music halls and the title of Lion Comique. Having secured his first engagement by singing 'A Half of Half and Half', a paean to beer, Leybourne trades songs with Vance, each successive routine taking as its subject an increasingly expensive and exclusive drink:

Leybourne:	'Ale, Old Ale'
The Great Vance:	'I Do Like a Little Drop of Gin'
Leybourne:	'Burgundy, Claret and Port'
The Great Vance:	'Rum, Rum, Rum'
Leybourne:	'I'm One of the Brandy and Seltzer Boys'
The Great Vance:	'A Glass of Sherry Wine'
Leybourne:	'Champagne Charlie' (see figure 18)

While the title song is inspired by an 1860s number of the same name, many of the other songs were written specifically for the film. The film's writers appear to have found Leybourne's reputation as 'Champagne Charlie' irresistible,

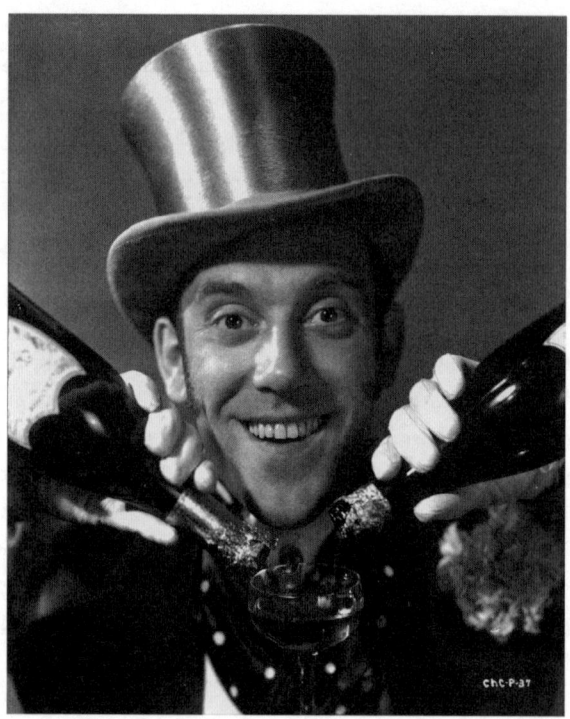

18   Tommy Trinder as George Leybourne in *Champagne Charlie* (1944).

allowing them to celebrate unrestrained consumption through the drinking associated with such choral one-upmanship. The songs dismiss the notion of moderation, and the two singers are as intent on out-drinking each other off the stage as they are in out-performing each other on it. The rivals' songs are inter-cut in such a way as to anticipate the massive binge they indulge in after reconciling their differences, while also perhaps anticipating the hoped-for 'peace brings plenty' celebrations that might accompany the end of the war.

The songs are also clearly intended to encourage and orchestrate consumption, for each has a particular dance routine and costume associated with it, and each is described as 'going down' very well, a phrase applicable to both the song and the drink it promotes. Reaction shots of the crowd singing and drinking associate the two activities in a feast of conspicuous consumption, not just of alcohol, but of performance and of life more generally. There is no utility boozing here – the film's motto seems to be 'more is better', and this applies equally to quantity and quality. As such, the film offers a very different vision of communal consumption to the canteen concerts of films such as *Millions Like Us*.

While the alcoholic arms race positions champagne as the apotheosis of sophisticated, 'swell' (that is, upper class) culture, it also serves to satirise the upper classes, with the Great Vance in particular adopting an ostentatiously fake accent to mock the mannerisms and speech of the well-to-do. The ambivalent attitude that Vance, Leybourne and other music hall artists adopt towards the nobility in their songs is replicated in the film more generally as a distrust of the political institutions which the aristocracy dominate. At one point, a Board of Enquiry, populated by members of the House of Lords and led by the Duke of Petworth (Austin Trevor), investigates whether the music halls are sites of violence and debauchery. The Board sits in a long committee room – a dull and moribund space. The establishing shot of the room recalls a long shot of the Mogador music hall, the chairman sitting where the artists perform, spotlighting the performative aspect of the parliamentary process. However, where at the Mogador there is light and life, in the committee room there is only restraint and sombreness. The room is insufficiently populated to justify its large size, a comment on the relative popularity of the music halls, the political process and the 'legitimate' theatres that have agitated for the enquiry they hope will destroy their rivals. Further, in a scene set at the Duke of Petworth's home, the working class owner of the Mogador, Bessie Bellwood (Betty Warren), introduces an almost anarchic energy into the staid library of her former aristocratic lover. In the library, books, paintings and coin and stamp collections are all kept behind glass, preserved exhibits in a museum of what *Champagne Charlie* presents as an ossified aristocratic culture in need of revivification.

By contrast, the music halls' vitality focuses on the immediate pleasures available to those who wish to experience the world sensually rather than intellectually. The music halls are energetic places where the patrons' alcohol consumption in the auditorium is mirrored, and encouraged, by the songs performed with such relish on the stage. Although Cavalcanti struggles to capture the excitement and vitality of live performance (and it should be noted that the rather static nature of many music hall acts does not help him in this respect), he does create, in the words of the review in *Today's Cinema*, a

> roistering atmosphere of beer-swilling patrons, voluptuous barmaids, stage-door Johnnies and raucous crowd vocalism – these are gaudy commentaries on the masses at play which prove entirely compensatory.[87]

With the focus on crowd involvement in drinking and singing, the music halls represent a world of action and participation where pleasure need not be rationed and indulgence need not be frowned upon. The Board of

Enquiry stands accused of attempting to prohibit such joyous behaviour for, as Leybourne says, 'There are a whole lot of busybodies in this country who are set on stopping the ordinary folk enjoying themselves.' It is not difficult to see in this line a critique of certain government actions during the war.

Indeed, the one song in the film of which the busybodies might have approved is singularly unpopular with the Mogador's audience. Acting as a temperance manifesto, 'Don't Bring Shame on the Old Folks Back Home' condemns alcohol and drunkenness and is at odds with the more indulgent ethos of the music halls. The keening song has a moralising tone and judges rather than embraces the joyfulness and energy of what the film presents as music hall entertainment norms.

The busybodies are also attacked in 'Everything Will Be Lovely', a song that satirises those who make promises they never find the time to fulfil. Leybourne uses food imagery to convey 'the people's' frustrations at this situation:

> Everyone will be wealthy, living like a lord,
> Eating plenty of all the things today they can't afford …
> Everyone will be happy, no-one will complain
> Every house will have beer laid on, like water from the main
> But when's that going to happen? When is by and by?
> Oh everything will be lovely when the pigs begin to fly!

Given the theme of many of the previous songs, we should perhaps not be surprised that *Champagne Charlie* chooses to associate societal progress with the freedom to consume, and gives voice to some of the frustrations that Britons felt regarding the shortages of luxury foodstuffs and the continuation of rationing. By mocking the empty promises of Victorian politicians, the film insists that people have the right to protest *and* to consume, and so suggests that the consensus which dominated much of British wartime society might break down if the busybodies retained too much control in the post-war political landscape.

Champagne Charlie, *The Wicked Lady* and *Madonna of the Seven Moons* are products of the latter years of the war, or the early months of the peace, and need to be understood in this context. As it became increasingly apparent that the Allies would eventually triumph, public attitudes towards rationing in particular, and government control of society in general, became less tolerant: the fruits of victory were demanded by consumers increasingly unwilling to further postpone gratification. That these three films all emphasise the emotive and sensual importance of food suggests that, rather than understanding food in terms of one's duty to the nation, some Britons preferred to celebrate it – and sensual indulgence – either in terms of a fantastic contrast to a limited wartime diet, as a symbol of the physical pleasures available to the individual, or as an escape from the government strictures imposed on so many aspects of wartime life. By presenting alternative visions and strategies regarding consumption, these films glorify excess and remind viewers that although British Restaurants and factory canteens were all well and good, they failed to satisfy the sensual appetites of the British population.

Different tastes

When Lord Hinchingbrooke expressed his concerns about the 'moral superiority' enjoyed by state-run communal institutions that favoured the masses, he implied that it was the middle- and upper-classes who would suffer most as a result. It is somewhat ironic, then, that many of the 'quality films' with the most pronounced tendencies to lionise the communal were often more popular with middle- and high-brow critics than they were with cinema audiences. Conversely, films which promoted individual indulgence and aesthetic excess, and which therefore joined Hinchingbrooke in challenging the communal foundations of institutions perceived as representing the triumph of 'equality over quality', were often box-office successes and critical failures. A contributor to *Kinematograph Weekly* acknowledged that the closer a film stuck to the documentary realist aesthetic, the more it was likely to give the public 'precisely what it does not want', whatever 'pseudo-intellectuals' might claim:

> When the proprietor of a little chain of provincial kinemas shakes a gloomy head over the star 'documentary,' declines to enthuse about its artistic qualities, or its real, raw life sequences, and moodily turns away to see a Hollywood musical, they ['earnest people with serious minds, educative tendencies, and artistic souls'] damn him with fluency, fervour and zeal for a soulless moron.[88]

That high-brow critical opinion and popular taste should so often diverge will come as little surprise, for each ascribes value and pleasure to different aspects of the cinema-going experience.[89] What is more intriguing is that films from either side of this divide often used food in different ways to explore the nature of British society in wartime, and to position the individual consumer in relation to the state.

Many of the feature films influenced by the British documentary movement promoted 'realistic' images of the communal and the consensual, and presented a very particular image of Britain. The documentary realist school was not alone in this, and films from other generic and aesthetic traditions also helped to advance this cause. Such films are often replete with portrayals of consumption organised at group level – be it the platoon, the crew, the family or the factory. These images not only provided a convincing rationale for gathering characters in the same place and so were useful in terms of narrative development, but also took their power from, and helped to reinforce, a communalist dietary paradigm. By presenting cinema-goers with positive representations of group consumption, these films can be understood as chiming with the ideals of the food-based community, thus furthering the appeal of the gastronomic collective.

Other films chose to explore the sensual and physical pleasures afforded by individual gratification. Many of these films chose to construct their gastronomically transgressive narratives in the relative safety of the past or overseas, away from the world of official rationing. Through this strategy, fantasies of unrestricted consumption could critique regulated wartime society without necessarily having to either come into direct conflict with its realities or explicitly renounce the 'moral superiority' of the food-based community. The importance of the temporal settings of films like *The Wicked Lady* or *Champagne Charlie*, which used period sets, costumes and feasts to produce a luxuriantly excessive visual and narrative style, is further demonstrated by a series of films which addressed gastronomic transgression in contemporary settings. The next chapter investigates the representation of the black market in such films, which by condemning rather than celebrating self-indulgence attempted to paper over the gap existing between the restrictions and enforced asceticism of everyday wartime reality and the sensual desires of individualistic fantasy. Films like *The Wicked Lady* adopted a different approach, and suggested to British cinema audiences that escapism was both acceptable and pleasurable. It was also necessary; the appeal of the food-based community was limited, and although this community was generally successful in feeding the British people, it was not always so adept at fulfilling their emotional needs.

Notes

1 Angus Calder, *The Myth of the Blitz* (London: Jonathan Cape, 1991).

2 Eric Sevareid, *Not So Wild a Dream* (New York: Alfred A. Knopf, 1946), p. 173.

3 George Orwell, 'The English People', in Sonia Orwell and Ian Angus (eds), *The Collected Essays, Journalism and Letters of George Orwell: Vol. 2 – As I Please* (London: Secker & Warburg, 1968), p. 6.

4 *The Times*, 23 September 1944, p. 2. From 1940, all workplaces employing more than 250 people were required to provide a canteen.

5 Bodleian Library, Oxford: MS Woolton 12: Broadcast talk on the Home Service by the Minister of Food, 13 June 1941.

6 Food Facts No. 72, week of 1 December 1941.

7 Margaret Butler, *Film and Community in Britain and France: From* La Regle du Jeu *to* Room at the Top (London: I. B. Tauris, 2004), pp. 11, 180.

8 James Chapman, *The British at War: Cinema, State and Propaganda, 1939–1945* (London: I. B. Tauris, 1998), p. 254. See also Andrew Higson, *Waving the Flag: Constructing a National Cinema in Britain* (Oxford: Clarendon Press, 1995), pp. 176–271; Charles Barr, *Ealing Studios* (London: University of California Press, 3rd edn, 1998), pp. 13–38.

9 The talk is reprinted in J. B. Priestley, *Postscripts* (London: Heinemann, 1940), pp. 9–13.

10 For more on the development of the idea of the 'quality film', see John Ellis, 'The quality film adventure: British critics and the cinema, 1942–48', in Andrew Higson (ed.), *Dissolving Views: Key Writings on British Cinema* (London: Cassell, 1996).

11 Formby was declared the most popular British male film star by the *Motion Picture Herald* each year between 1939 and 1943. Anthony Aldgate and Jeffrey Richards, *Britain Can Take It: The British Cinema in the Second World War* (Edinburgh: Edinburgh University Press, 2nd edn, 1994), p. 59.

12 See *The Times*, 22 August 1942, p. 5; 7 March 1946, p. 6.

13 National Council of Social Service, *British Restaurants: An Inquiry* (London: Oxford University Press, 1946), p. 73.

14 Joanne Finkelstein, *Dining Out: A Sociology of Modern Manners* (Oxford: Polity Press, 1989), p. 53. A similar argument is advanced in Gaye Poole, *Reel Meals, Set Meals: Food in Film and Theatre* (Sydney: Currency Press, 1999), p. 123.

15 Jane F. Ferry, *Food in Film: A Culinary Performance of Communication* (London: Routledge, 2003), p. 23.

16 Memo from Churchill to Woolton, 21 March 1941. Reprinted in Winston Churchill, *The Second World War: Vol. III – The Grand Alliance* (London: Cassell, 1950), p. 663.

17 *Daily Mail*, 4 April 1941, p. 3; H. L. Mencken, 'War words in England', *American Speech*, 19:1 (1944), pp. 3–15.

18 Vere Hodgson, diary entry, 24 August 1941, in *Few Eggs and No Oranges: A Diary Showing How Unimportant People in London and Birmingham Lived Through the War Years, 1940–1945* (London: Dennis Dobson, 1976), pp. 176–7. See also *Cambridge Daily News*, 27 December 1940, p. 4.

19 *Kinematograph Weekly*, 3 September 1942, p. 23.

20 *Documentary News Letter*, 2:6, June 1941, p. 107.

21 Barbara Drake, *Community Feeding in Wartime* (London: The Fabian Society and Victor Gollancz, 1942), p. 28.

22 Mass-Observation, *People in Production: An Enquiry into British War Production, Part 1* (London: John Murray, 1942), p. 273.

23 Edward Blishen, *A Cackhanded War* (London: Thames & Hudson, 1972), p. 184; Bell quoted in Philip Ziegler, *London at War, 1939–1945* (London: Sinclair-Stevenson, 1995), p. 251.

24 Diary entry, 7 May 1942. MS Woolton 2.

25 *Picture Post*, 12 July 1941, p. 27.

26 *Manchester Guardian*, 27 March 1942, p. 4. It was not only wealthy business-men who objected. Midlands housewife Clara Milburn stated quite categorically that 'Even wartime difficulties did not make me enjoy this method of serving oneself.' Diary entry, 30 April 1943, in Peter Donnelly (ed.), *Mrs Milburn's Diaries: An Englishwoman's Day-to-Day Reflections, 1939–1945* (London: Abacus, 1995), p. 176. Among the highest profile casualties of the move to counter service were the Nippies, the waitresses employed at Lyons' Corner Houses. Peter Bird, *The First Food Empire: A History of J Lyons & Co.* (Chichester: Phillimore, 2000), pp. 120–2.

27 NCSS, *British Restaurants*, p. 19.

28 MS Woolton 13: *Postscript*, 2 August 1942.

29 Readers concerned for Trinder's stomach will be relieved to learn that there are, naturally, plenty of potatoes on offer. 'They're awfully good for you', insists the soon-to-be-Mrs Trinder.

30 For more on queuing see Nella Last's diary entry, 29 August 1945, in Sandra Koa Wing (ed.), *Our Longest Days: A People's History of the Second World War* (London: Profile, 2008), p. 266.

31 E. S. Turner, *The Phoney War on the Home Front* (London: Michael Joseph, 1961), pp. 265–6; Woolton is quoted in Philip Ziegler, *London at War*, p. 90. BBC employee and diarist Anthony Weymouth admitted to 'a feeling of shame' when presented with smoked salmon and white wine in early 1941. He did not let this feeling stop him from indulging in these luxuries though. Diary entry, 9 February 1941, in *Plague Year, March 1940–February 1941* (London: George G. Harrap, 1942), pp. 240–1.

32 Higson, *Waving the Flag*, pp. 227–9.

33 Mass-Observation, *People in Production*, p. 274.

34 *Postscript*, 11 August 1940. Reprinted in Priestley, *Postscripts*, pp. 49–53.

35 Classical concerts were not staged purely for the benefit of film audiences. In November 1941, a factory welfare manager from Birmingham noted his satisfaction at seeing 'rows of grimy men sitting rapt and motionless listening to classical and operatic music … It's a profound mistake to play down to factory audiences. Good taste doesn't go with higher incomes necessarily.' Quoted in Mass-Observation, *People in Production*, p. 276.

36 Letter from Humphrey to Cicely Jennings, 3 December 1941. In Kevin Jackson (ed.), *The Humphrey Jennings Film Reader* (Manchester: Carcanet, 1993), p. 36.

37 Humphrey Jennings, treatment for 'National Gallery 1941', 28 April 1941. In Anthony W. Hodgkinson and Rodney E. Sheratsky, *Humphrey Jennings – More Than a Maker of Films* (Hanover and London: University Press of New England, 1982), p. 58.

38 Kitty Riley is described as singing for *Workers' Playtime* in the Press Book for *Old Mother Riley, Detective*. BFI Microfiche Collection: Press Book – *Old Mother Riley, Detective*. 'Calling All Workers', the theme from *Workers' Playtime*, features in both *Millions Like Us* and *Listen to Britain*.

39 *Kinematograph Weekly*, 8 April 1943, p. 32.

40 See, for example, Social Issues Research Centre, *Social and Cultural Aspects of Drinking: A Report to the Amsterdam Group* (A report presented to the European Commission on 29 November 2000).

41 Quentin Reynolds, *The Wounded Don't Cry* (London: Cassell, 1941), p. 183. Reynolds, like many contemporary commentators (both American and British) used England and Britain almost interchangeably.

42 See the short film *Germany Calling* (1941) in which footage of Nazi soldiers marching is edited to a soundtrack of the Lambeth Walk. Jo Fox discusses *The Lion Has Wings* (1939) in terms of its contrasting visions of Britons and Germans at play in *Film Propaganda in Britain and Nazi Germany: World War II Cinema* (Oxford: Berg, 2007), pp. 64–5.

43 Michael Powell hoped to enhance the sinister feel of the opening scenes by naming the pub the Hand of Glory. 'In English witchcraft a "hand of glory" was the severed and pickled right hand of a hanged murderer, which robbers believed would act as a charm and stupefy their victims.' Paul Tritton, A Canterbury Tale: *Memories of a Classic Wartime Movie* (Maidstone: Tritton Publications, 2000), p. 39.

44 *Kinematograph Weekly*, 1 February 1940, p. 27.

45 Frank Harvey, *Saloon Bar: A Play in Three Acts* (London: Year Book Press, 1942), p. 40.

46 The importance of such conversation in social bonding is discussed in Kate Fox, *Watching the English: The Hidden Rules of English Behaviour* (London: Hodder & Stoughton, 2004), pp. 98–108.

47 Reynolds, *Wounded Don't Cry*, p. 227.

48 Mass-Observation, *The Pub and the People: A Worktown Study* (London: Victor Gollancz, 1943), pp. 17, 42–3. 'Worktown' was the name given by Mass-Observation to Bolton, Lancashire.

49 *The Times*, 5 April 1944, p. 5.

50 George Orwell noted that during the war 'beer has doubled in price and been heavily diluted'. Review of Mass-Observation, *The Pub and the People*, in the *Listener* (21 January 1943), in Orwell and Angus (eds), *The Collected Essays, Journalism and Letters of George Orwell: Vol. 2*, p. 43.

51 John K. Walton, *Fish and Chips and the British Working Class, 1870–1940* (Leicester: Leicester University Press, 1992), p. 1. On the wartime fish and chip trade, see pp. 19–20.

52 Ellis, 'The quality film adventure'. See also Pam Cook's discussion of many melodramas' 'decorative excesses' in 'Neither here nor there: national identity in Gainsborough costume drama', in Higson (ed.), *Dissolving Views*, p. 54.

53 *Tribune*, 23 November 1945, p. 10.

54 Mark Ostrer in *Kinematograph Weekly*, 20 December 1945, p. 64.

55 *Fanny By Gaslight* (1944) cost £90,000 to make and grossed approximately £300,000, and *Madonna of the Seven Moons* cost £125,000 and grossed well in excess of £300,000. *Kinematograph Weekly*, 9 April 1945, p. 5.

56 BFI Microfiche Collection: Press Book – *The Young Mr Pitt*.

57 *Kinematograph Weekly*, 27 November 1941, p. 41.

58 *Monthly Film Bulletin*, July 1942, p. 84.

59 *Sight and Sound*, 11:42 (Autumn 1942), p. 42.

60 *Sight and Sound*, 11:42 (Autumn 1942), p. 50.

61 *Kinematograph Weekly*, 14 January 1943, pp. 46–8.

62 *Kinematograph Weekly*, 20 November 1941, p. 20.

63 *Today's Cinema*, 14 November 1941, p. 19.

64 *Daily Mirror*, 14 November 1941, p. 7; *Kinematograph Weekly*, 20 November 1941, p. 20.

65 Sue Harper, 'Fragmentation and crisis: 1940s admission figures at the Regent cinema, Portsmouth, UK', *Historical Journal of Film, Radio and Television*, 26:3 (2006), pp. 385–91; *Kinematograph Weekly*, 26 April 1945, p. 5. Of the British films exhibited as first features at the Regent in 1942, only *The Common Touch* (1941) attracted fewer customers than *The Young Mr Pitt*.

66 See Sue Aspinall and Robert Murphy (eds), *BFI Dossier Number 18: Gainsborough Melodrama* (London: BFI, 1983); Pam Cook, *Fashioning the Nation: Costume and Identity in British Cinema* (London: BFI, 1996), p. 96.

67 Sue Harper, *Picturing the Past: The Rise and Fall of the British Costume Film* (London: BFI, 1994), p. 127.

68 *Tribune*, 23 November 1945, p. 10.

69 For contemporary recognition of the gendered appeal of the Gainsborough films, see J. P. Mayer, *British Cinemas and their Audiences* (London: Dennis Dobson, 1948).

70 Sue Harper, 'Historical pleasures: Gainsborough costume melodramas', in Christine Gledhill (ed.), *Home Is Where The Heart Is: Studies in Melodrama and the Woman's Film* (London: BFI, 1987), p. 187. Emphasis in original.

71 Antonia Lant, *Blackout: Reinventing Women for Wartime British Cinema* (Princeton, NJ: Princeton University Press, 1991), pp. 109–10.

72 *Today's Cinema*, 16 November 1945, p. 9.

73 Raymond Durgnat, *A Mirror for England: British Movies from Austerity to Affluence* (London: Faber & Faber, 1970), p. 215.

74 John Costello sees in the Second World War the beginnings of 'a profound sexual revolution'. *Love, Sex and War: Changing Values, 1939–45* (London: Collins, 1985), pp. 356, 372.

75 Magdalen King-Hall, *Life and Death of the Wicked Lady Skelton* (London: Peter Davies, 1974), pp. 77–8.

76 In a *Daily Mail* poll to establish the most popular film stars of the war, James Mason topped the male list, and Margaret Lockwood the female. *Daily Mail*, 25 April 1946, pp. 1–2.

77 Margery Lawrence, *The Madonna of Seven Moons* (London: Hurst and Blackett, 1931), p. 25.

78 *Monthly Film Bulletin*, December 1944, p. 140.

79 Rosemary Black, diary entry, in Leonard Mosley, *Backs to the Wall: London Under Fire, 1939–45* (London: Weidenfeld & Nicolson, 1971), p. 206.

80 The press book which accompanied the release of the film was keen to point out the authenticity of the San Gimiano set. BFI Microfiche Collection: Press Book – *Madonna of the Seven Moons*.

81 *Kinematograph Weekly*, 14 December 1944, p. 31.

82 *Kinematograph Weekly*, 20 July 1944, p. 36.

83 *Evening Standard*, 15 April 1942, p. 6.

84 *Kinematograph Weekly*, 10 May 1945, p. 40. Shooting in Technicolor made the manufacture of convincing bananas more difficult.

85 *Kinematograph Weekly*, 25 November 1943, p. 39.

86 *Kinematograph Weekly*, 30 November 1944, p. 38B. Clothes became so hard to come by that many of the period hats seen in *This Happy Breed* (1944) had to be made from paper; *Daily Mirror*, 28 May 1943, p. 7. Antiques and props were also in short supply, as the art designer of *Gert and Daisy Clean Up* (1942) found when attempting to dress the film's set. See *Kinematograph Weekly*, 5 March 1942, p. 28.

87 *Today's Cinema*, 25 August 1944, p. 21.

88 *Kinematograph Weekly*, 11 January 1945, p. 90.

89 See *Kinematograph Weekly*, 26 April 1945, p. 5. 'Josh' Billings begged his fellow critics to 'be humble for a bit and admit that good notices don't necessarily mean [commercially] successful films' and that 'frequently the critics delight in wiping the floor with films that have obvious popular appeal'.

4

The rat in England's storehouse: the black market in wartime cinema

The fact that, in spite of all the scarcity of supplies and the rigidity of rationing, there was little or no black market in Britain was a tribute to the British people which I hope the historians of this period will proudly record. It was, of course, nothing more than the normal operation of the British people, their attitude to the law of their land, and their sense of fair dealing with one another.[1]

So declares Lord Woolton in his memoirs, retrospectively downplaying the extent of the black market. Looking back on his tenure as Minister of Food, Woolton chooses to remember the consensual nature of British society in wartime, the righteousness of the government's actions and the success of the rationing system. In so doing, he conveniently ignores a reality of which he, as administrator of the rationing system, was well aware. Although hindsight afforded him the opportunity to compare the extent and influence of the British black market favourably with the more organised and widespread American and German versions,[2] the knowledge that the food rackets never posed a serious threat to the state's right to control food distribution would not have been so obvious during the war itself, as a number of recent histories of the period have shown.[3] Contemporary consumers were just as aware of the existence of the black market, with more than 70 per cent of those questioned in a Gallup poll in July 1943 testifying to the existence of food rackets in Britain.[4] Woolton, deploying the selective recall common to memoirists, obscures the seriousness of the problem in Britain behind the phrase 'there was little or no black market', which concedes that, although the black market *did* exist, it was barely worthy of mention; its existence served predominantly to demonstrate the virtuous, communal, law-abiding nature of the vast majority of British consumers who took no part in it.

This chapter examines a series of films made during the war, which adopted the black market as a central narrative theme, analysing the way in which the illicit trade in food was presented in three relatively low-budget comedies (*Gert and Daisy Clean Up*, 1942, *Old Mother Riley, Detective* and *Up With the Lark*, both 1943) and one thriller (*The Hundred Pound Window*, 1943).[5] These films were not particularly successful in commercial terms (they do not feature, for example, in Josh Billing's end of year list of box-office winners) and this may explain why neither *Gert and Daisy Clean Up* nor *Up With the Lark* are available for viewing at the National Film and Television Archive, and why they have received so little critical attention. They are, however, extremely intriguing, speaking of wartime attitudes towards criminality, rationing and the 'food-based community'. While they do not have the polish or élan of more celebrated films, they are no less historically interesting. As products of the wartime British production industry that would most likely be screened in what *Kinematograph Weekly* habitually called 'lower-class halls', these films suggest that common concerns, arising from shared experiences at the national level, are visible in many of the seemingly disparate films that were made in Britain between 1939 and 1945.

The four films contain many similarities. In each, for instance, female volunteers are recruited from the ranks of the 'ordinary' citizenry and given the task of catching black marketeers and defending the well-being of the individual, the family and the state. The criminals, on the other hand, are presented as mocking both the war and the idea of equality on which the rationing system was founded. That four such similar films were made in so short a time suggests that, despite Woolton's claims, the black market was a recognisable enough social phenomenon to enter popular culture and popular consciousness.

Additionally, the films seek to reinforce the idea of the food-based community by mobilising consumers to oppose those who would undermine it. The films all feature female protagonists who might be described as active consumers, people who recognise the value and essential fairness of the rationing system and who are prepared to fight to preserve it. By establishing these honest, active consumers in opposition to the racketeers, the films had the effect of clearly delineating a community of food companions while demonstrating the principles that underpinned it, presenting consumption as a shared national experience which bonded the individual to the state. Further, by painting a very negative picture of the racketeers, and establishing them as operating outside the boundaries of the food-based community, the films also provided exemplars of how and how not to act in wartime.

Although these criminals were described in one film as the 'rat in England's storehouse', they also fulfilled a more controversial, and perhaps unintentional, function. Black marketeers occupied the liminal space at the edge of the population's acceptance of the rationing system, and as such manifested many of the tensions inherent in the heavily regulated society of wartime Britain. Their presence, although condemned in these films, acknowledges the conflict that many British citizens felt between personal desire and corporate sacrifice, between the feasting of the cinematic racketeers and the ascetic approach advocated by the *Food Flashes*, between the 'under-the-counter' gluttony on the screen and coupon exchange in the shops.

Consequently, it might be suggested that scenes of illicit consumption offered audiences a degree of transgressive pleasure. Foodstuffs that were hard to come by were shown being consumed by those who chose to operate outside the law. Such scenes, often set in glamorous locales, highlighted the stresses that existed within British attitudes to rationing. Narratives set in the present, which demonstrated the possible rewards accruing to those who broke the law, were potentially more damaging to the idea of the food-based community than were stories based in a fantastical past which made evident the pleasures of unregulated consumption. Filmmakers adopting black market themes thus utilised a strategy of displacement in order to attempt to resolve the tensions inherent in wartime representations of food racketeering. Audiences were permitted the thrill of gastronomic voyeurism, but were encouraged to defer gratification until after the conclusion of the war, while wrongdoers were prosecuted with a thoroughness that spoke of the community's frustration with both wartime regulations and those that ignored them for personal gratification or exploited them for personal gain.

In the immediate post-war era, with the government still unable to satiate the British public's desire for consumer goods, films began to adopt a different line. The black market, which had grown slowly throughout the war, attained full maturity in the age of austerity that followed the defeat of the Axis. Most scholarship on British black market films has analysed the post-war period and a series of films that have come to be known as the Spiv Cycle.[6] The ambiguous moral stances of the spiv films mirror the increasingly hostile attitudes that many British consumers adopted towards rationing in the years following the war. The chapter concludes with an analysis of *Waterloo Road* (1945), a film released in the last months of the war but which anticipates many of the themes of the Spiv Cycle, acting as a link between the wartime black market films, and those made in the second half of the 1940s.

'Parasites preying on the body of a community at war'

Described by one government minister as a 'form of sabotage [that] should be ended by a firing squad', the black market in wartime Britain was evidently a serious enough problem to attract the attention of government publicists.[7] Lord Woolton, so dismissive of the problem in his memoirs was, during the war, far more concerned about the issue, and he discusses the problem in an interview in *World of Plenty* (1943). Cabinet-level involvement lent the film the full weight of government authority, so that Britons watching the film were left in little doubt as to the state's hostility towards the black market. Woolton was questioned about the trade of food 'on the side' and insisted that:

> My ministry is getting on to that, and getting on top of it. And while I'm on the subject, I might say that there is a small section of the public that isn't making things any too easy for us. We must remember that it takes two to make a black bargain.

Woolton was evidently frustrated by the scale and tenacity of the food rackets, publicly describing them as 'a thorn in our side' and privately expressing doubt that 'anything short of penal servitude with the threat of flogging will frighten those people engaged in the Black Market'.[8]

Although Woolton publicly distanced himself from those who called for corporal or capital punishment to be meted out to racketeers, he maintained that the state should reserve the right to impose severe sanctions in order to 'frighten the malefactors' and so limit the extent of the black market:

> For the operation of Governmental control of food we depend as much on public co-operation as on law; and our plans work because the public believes that they are fair for everybody; once they believe that the black market people can operate outside of the law then we shall lose their respect and their confidence.[9]

Woolton's desire to punish black market activity should therefore be understood not only as a response to those who would wilfully defy the rule of law, but also, and perhaps more significantly, as a method of negating the threat that racketeering posed to both public confidence in, and therefore the integrity of, the rationing system. For, as Woolton himself explained, any 'persistent undermining' of that confidence could produce 'tragic results' if the food situation were to suddenly take a turn for the worse.[10]

But one might also argue that the strict and comprehensive nature of the Ministry of Food's (MoF) rationing policy, operating alongside rationing systems administered by other government departments and the drastic reduction of the manufacture of luxury goods, can be considered catalysts of black market growth. Although it is unlikely that the amount of black market activity in Britain will ever be accurately established – it was a secretive business and only careless or unsuccessful racketeers faced prosecution – one can assert that illicit merchandise became increasingly desirable as consumer goods became scarcer.

Given the existence of the black market, it comes as no surprise to learn that the government was keen to combat the rackets. Despite the limited size of most individual black market transactions, the state could not condone, or be seen to be condoning, illegal or immoral acts, especially as the aggregate of these small-scale transactions constituted a significant amount of criminal activity. However, although the black market posed a threat to the integrity of the rationing system, the Prime Minister feared that a disproportionate response to those involved in low-level racketeering might result in a loss of public sympathy.[11] Winston Churchill therefore advised the MoF to tread carefully, warning that if it were to gain a reputation for securing draconian punishments of individuals guilty of minor (or, in some cases, unintentional) breaches of the food regulations, it might become popularly associated with 'bureaucracy in its most pettifogging and tyrannical aspect'. This in turn might 'bring [the] Ministry into disrepute', undermine popular support for rationing and thus reduce food's value as an emotionally and culturally significant resource.[12] For the rationing system to succeed, public cooperation with the MoF and its agents was essential, and such cooperation was predicated on sympathy for a scheme that most consumers believed to be equitable and necessary.[13]

The black market threatened the rationing system by offering a rival to the state's monolithic food distribution programme. By competing with the MoF, the racketeers had the potential to render ineffective a system that relied largely on its exclusivity for its success; when all were getting the same, rationing fulfilled its function. The black market was a direct challenge to the spirit of communal solidarity that the policy of 'fair shares for all' hoped to instil. Consequently, the government went to great lengths to remind Britons that only by purchasing their foodstuffs through legal channels could equality, and hence the food-based community, be maintained.

Britons were encouraged to obey the law, through appeals to their personal identification with the objectives of rationing as much as through fear of the consequences of breaching food regulations. Wartime publicity attempted to establish that the greed and selfishness inherent in the black market were alien to the British way of life, and that purchasing goods from the black market was unfair and therefore fundamentally un-British. When M-O diarist Nella Last condemned her sister-in-law's use of the black market, she couched her criticisms in the language of fair shares: 'If you take someone else's share they will have to do without.'[14] A similar attitude is also evident in an exchange in *Old Mother Riley, Detective* when Mother Riley (Arthur Lucan) discusses food with a neighbour. When asked if she has ever been tempted to take 'a little extra' the woman replies, 'No, never. I mean, after all, it wouldn't be right. It's the same for us all, isn't it?'

Inherent in such lofty ideals, though, is the admission both of the existence of the black market and the desirability of the goods it offered. This necessitated a change in tactics with regard to publicity, as the government attempted to drive a wedge between consumers and the racketeers. The illegality of the black market was stressed, and those who opted to make use of it were forced to acknowledge their complicity in a criminal enterprise. Further, the threat that the racketeers posed to the nation's ability to prosecute the war provided government publicists with a ready-made other, a type against whom the food-based community could rail in order to define itself more coherently. By presenting the racketeers as the bogeymen against whom the nation was fighting, government propaganda not only positioned such criminals outside the national community, but also placed them in league with the enemy.

The issue of an individual's complicity in black market criminality was the theme of the Ministry of Information (MoI) film *Partners in Crime*, released nationwide in the week of 1 June 1942. Written and directed by Frank Launder and Sydney Gilliat, the film attempts to force black market consumers to acknowledge the illegality of their actions by likening housewives who buy black market food to criminals who receive stolen goods.[15]

Partners in Crime achieves this effect by establishing, and equating, parallel stories: in the first, stolen jewels pass from burglar to fence, in the second, stolen meat is passed from thief to retailer to consumer. The former storyline is concluded with a trial in which the fence is condemned by a judge (Robert Morley):

> If you refused to buy the goods, the thief would find no point in stealing them. The law recognises this truth by laying down heavier penalties for the receiver, as the instigator of the crime ... You create the demand, you offer the market. You are the real criminal.

As this speech ends, the film returns to its second narrative. A close-up of the judge's face dissolves to a shot of a middle-class housewife, Mrs Wilson (Irene Handl), placing a joint of off-the-ration meat in her shopping basket. The implication is clear: a housewife who knowingly buys black market food is no better than a fence who receives stolen goods.

The film having made its point, the words 'The End' are superimposed over the familiar MoI logo. Toying with audience expectations, though, the shot pulls back to reveal that the stolen jewels narrative, and therefore the trial and condemnation of the fence, is part of an MoI short being watched in a cinema by Mrs Wilson. The judge reappears on the cinema screen and directly addresses Mrs Wilson, asking her whether she, and others like her are 'any better than common criminals; parasites, preying on the body of a community at war'. In this instance, the judge stands not only for the law, but also for Britain more generally. His anachronistic judicial finery brings the full weight of the supposedly common and established British traits of decency and honesty to bear on modern criminality, and suggests that the black market poses a direct threat to centuries of tradition. The abrupt and surreal interruption also comes as a rude shock. By picking out a single face in the crowd and forcefully scrutinising their actions, the judge encourages soul-searching among other members of the audience.

Partners in Crime is especially damning of those who participate in the black market but who deny their actions' illegality because they do not consider themselves to be criminals. Although Mrs Wilson's actions equate her with the fence – as the final destination of the illicit goods – the film implies that the actions of this selfish housewife are also akin to those of the burglar. Played by Charles Victor, a recognisable character actor, the burglar is presented as a stereotypical cinematic criminal: male, swarthy, nocturnal and working class. In establishing a moral framework in which the illegal actions of the middle-class consumer are presented as morally equivalent to those of more obviously villainous types, Launder and Gilliat skilfully counter the argument that purchasing food on the black market was a victimless crime.

In September 1941, the MoF published a Food Facts column which, under a picture of a telescope, had the heading: 'Not with the blind eye, please'. This attempt to get British consumers to acknowledge the presence of (and, perhaps, their involvement in) the black market also served to recognise the danger that the rackets posed in wartime. The government thus admitted that the black market existed, and insisted that it arose from selfishness and greed. Those who knowingly undermined the efficacy of the rationing system were accused of 'play[ing] Hitler's game'.[16]

Collusion with the enemy was a theme returned to in later Food Facts columns which addressed the issue of the black market. In April 1942, one column carried the following poem:

> Food obtained
> By methods shifty
> Is shared with Hitler
> Fifty-fifty. [17]

In a similar vein, a cartoon by Strube, published in the *Daily Express* in May 1941, shows a black marketeer shaking hands with a U-boat captain. In the drawing, the racketeer emerges from a can of food and shakes hands with a German submariner emerging from his vessel's conning tower. The caption of the cartoon, 'Brothers under the skin', leaves little doubt as to the cartoonist's opinion of those involved in illegal food transactions.[18]

The black market, then, was a very real concern for the MoF during the war. The Ministry's efforts to dissuade consumers from partaking in illicit transactions had brought the racketeers into the spotlight, and it is no surprise that British producers, casting around for topical ideas, adopted a black market theme in some of their feature films.

Black market, silver screen

Gert and Daisy Clean Up, *Old Mother Riley, Detective*, *Up With the Lark* and *The Hundred Pound Window* use the black market as a backdrop to what are otherwise fairly formulaic genre films: music-hall inspired comedies in the first three cases and a comedy-thriller in the fourth. Whereas many genre films produced earlier in the war had employed spies (*Band Waggon*, 1940), fifth columnists (*Cottage to Let*, 1940) or saboteurs (*Spare a Copper*, 1940) as antagonists, the decision to use racketeers as villains speaks of the immediacy of the food and contraband rackets in British society in the middle years of the war. Indeed, *Today's Cinema* suggested of Gert and Daisy's 'rampage' against the black market that 'nothing could be more timely or dear to the hearts of the British public'.[19] The idea that these films were playing a useful social and political role was also noted by other reviewers: the *Daily Film Renter* observed a 'propagandist note' in *Old Mother Riley, Detective*, while the same film was described by *Kinematograph Weekly* as reminding criminals – and presumably cinema audiences, too – that 'the working classes are no easy game'.[20]

Gert and Daisy Clean Up was produced by Butcher's Film Service and released in July 1942. The second feature film to star Elsie and Doris Waters as Cockney sisters Gert and Daisy, the film built on the success of their screen debut, *Gert and Daisy's Weekend* (1941), their music hall act and their radio appearances (some of them on behalf of the MoF, see Chapter 1). *Gert and Daisy Clean Up* sees the sisters foil an attempt by local councillor and businessman Mr Perry (Joss Ambler) to divert a shipment of canned pineapple away from a children's party and into his shop so that he can sell it 'under the counter'. Gert and Daisy are framed for stealing the fruit, but the case against them collapses and they capture the racketeers and deliver the pineapple to the delighted children.

Described by *Monthly Film Bulletin* as a 'good rollicking farce into which a very topical message has been adroitly sandwiched',[21] with the anti-black market stance adopted by the film noted as one of its selling points, *Gert and Daisy Clean Up* was also considered by contemporary reviewers to be aimed squarely at a working-class audience who, it was thought, 'look upon the popular duo almost as personal friends'.[22] The topicality inherent in Gert and Daisy's films lent an immediacy to their actions, while the representative nature of the sisters' characters made their exploits intimate and, potentially, imitable. Positioned as everywomen in a knowable locale, part of Gert and Daisy's appeal was the very ordinariness of their personas. Despite the studied 'literary Cockney'[23] of their stage accents, audiences – especially women – reacted favourably to their self-deprecatory independence and stubborn pride.[24] Additionally, by promoting *Gert and Daisy Clean Up* as coming 'down your street', the film's advertising campaign intentionally positioned the sisters as characters who audiences might come to know outside the cinema, suggesting that the situations in which Gert and Daisy found themselves were intended to allow – to encourage, even – the audience to associate themselves with the narrative.

Despite inhabiting a similarly proletarian world, Arthur Lucan's Mother Riley used a different approach to provoke laughter. Whereas the relatively gentle humour of Gert and Daisy sent up the idiosyncrasies of working-class life, Lucan's manic, anarchic humour frequently arose from a clash of classes (and cultures). A prematurely aged washerwoman, Mother Riley is marginalised by her age, gender and class, but her outsider status, unorthodox syntax and inappropriately kinetic modus operandi functioned, in the words of David Sutton, as a 'critique of both the self-satisfied middle-class world-view and of a middle-class art with its emphasis on restraint and realism'.[25]

As one of Britain's most successful music-hall comedians, Lucan had first brought his irreverent, and frequently incoherent, act to British cinema screens in the summer of 1937.[26] Between August 1937 and the release of *Old Mother Riley, Detective* in January 1943, Lucan and his wife Kitty McShane (who played Mother Riley's daughter Kitty) appeared in a new film, on average, every seven months. Such brief gestation periods encouraged production company

British National to include topical references, and in *Old Mother Riley, Detective* such references centred on the black market. In the film, Mother Riley loses her job after being accused of stealing important documents from the Food Office where she works as a cleaner. After her arrest, and subsequent release, she is recruited by the police and tasked with apprehending the racketeers who have actually stolen the papers. She tracks a shipment of illegal goods from consumer to supplier to wholesaler and, after a hectic chase, arrests the criminal gang's boss, who turns out to be the owner of the building in which the Food Office is located.

Straight-facedly claiming that 'there is more [to Lucan's] performance than meets the eye', *Kinematograph Weekly* described this 'fruity, good-humoured, low-life slapstick' as 'a box-office certainty for the many keen and persistent Old Mother Riley fans'.[27] Knowing that in order to satisfy these fans the film would have to do little more than repackage familiar material in a topical framework, the idea that Mother Riley should take on the racketeers offers not only the necessary novelty but also the chance for Lucan's charlady to demonstrate, as previously, a good degree of proletarian agency.

Many films in the series have as their central motif the inability, or unwillingness, of Mother Riley to adapt to the bourgeois world in which she temporarily finds herself, preferring to have her stay true to her roots. In *Old Mother Riley in Society* (1940), for example, Kitty's engagement to a prosperous suitor allows Mother Riley to bewilder her potential in-laws before eventually winning them over. However, as Sutton notes, Lucan's character is so 'unrepentantly working-class [that] the humour of the films is always on her side in her transgressions of middle-class propriety'.[28]

Whilst Mother Riley appealed to working class audiences in general, it might be understood that the character had particular appeal for women. This address to female viewers, clearly visible in each of the black market comedies analysed here, and only marginally less so in *The Hundred Pound Window*, is most explicit in *Old Mother Riley, Detective*. In a bizarre and self-reflexive moment, a moment even more joyously divorced from the constraints of realism than the rest of the film, Mother Riley speaks directly to the camera for the only time:

> My dear Mrs Cinema, I implore you, I beseech you, turn your husband out of the hall, hide your children under the seat, put your fingers in your ears, for what I'm about to say … would bring a blush to an innocent Sergeant Major. I'm going to put my feet firmly on the ground, I'm going to become as common as muck, I'm going to give myself plenty of rope and let myself go.

Like Gert and Daisy, Mother Riley addresses the viewer as an equal, allowing her fight to become the viewer's fight, her victory to become the viewer's victory. The anger she directs at the black market is righteous and visceral, and transforms her into an avatar of the community's hostility towards the racketeers.

The third film in this comic black-market sequence was *Up With the Lark*, which starred Ethel Revnell and Gracie West, a comedy pairing whose theatre and radio work as 'The Long and the Short of It' (Revnell was tall, West was not) and 'Ethel and Gracie, The Cockney Kids' underlined their predilection for physical humour, their gender and their class. Released in December 1943, the film did not expect to be taken too seriously, for its press book describes it as being 'Made for laughter only' and proudly proclaimed that *Cinema* had declared it 'competent'.[29] Having been mistaken for racketeers during a police raid at the exclusive hotel where they are employed, Ethel and Gracie are recruited by a government food detective, Mr Britt (Anthony Hulme), and set the task of capturing the hotel's manager and other members of his black-market gang. This quest leads to a small country village, where the girls apprehend the criminals and the gang's boss, the local vicar. The methods employed by Ethel and Gracie to apprehend the crooks help to distinguish *Up With the Lark* from *Old Mother Riley, Detective* and *Gert and Daisy Clean Up*: humour is generated by the unswerving incompetence of Revnell and West, as opposed to the anarchic unconventionality of Mother Riley and the dedicated yet amateur approach adopted by Gert and Daisy.

Produced by New Realm, *Up With the Lark* is the least polished of the three comedies. Perhaps with *Gert and Daisy Clean Up* and *Old Mother Riley, Detective* in mind, *Kinematograph Weekly* described the cast as 'fighting a hard battle with a sketchy and unoriginal script' and, casting about for something positive to say, conceded that its 'quota angle' (that is, its British origin) was one of its most significant points of appeal.[30] Other reviewers were less kind: the *Daily Film Renter* claimed that *Up With the Lark* had 'all the defects of the unlamented quota quickie of the pre-war years', while *Monthly Film Bulletin* concluded that: 'Those who do not find [Revnell and West] funny will be inclined to agree with Ethel when she says, "Things might be worse, but I don't see how."'[31]

Despite such poor reviews, *Up With the Lark* was re-released in 1947. The growth of the black market in the years after the war had done little to diminish the relevance of the film's plot. However, as the black market had grown, attitudes had changed, and some of the reviews written at the time of the re-release reflect these changes. Whereas the film was originally criticised by some for not taking the black market seriously enough – 'despite, rather than because of, [Revnell and West's] help, the villains are eventually arrested' – by 1947, reviewers, although not necessarily raising their opinion of the film, were less critical of its willingness to make fun of the black market, and the plot was described as a 'an appropriately light-weight vehicle for the antics of the two comediennes'.[32]

For all its technical shortcomings, *Up With the Lark* is in many ways representative of the numerous cheap, essentially disposable British films that functioned as star vehicles for established music-hall performers. Episodic in nature, each film showcased the talents of its leading players. Hackneyed comic patter, songs and physical routines were attached to a contemporary narrative selected to take advantage of the immediacy of the subject matter as well as the familiarity of the humour. While the best of these films enjoyed greater resources (which translated into higher production values), most attempted to find a topical theme around which gags and tunes could be arranged. In these three films, Gert and Daisy, Mother Riley and Revnell and West all raged against the black market, but previous films in which they starred had used various wartime conditions for narrative inspiration: the plight of evacuees in *Gert and Daisy's Weekend*; women in the services in *Old Mother Riley Joins Up* (1939); and the deployment of dirigibles in *The Balloon Goes Up* (1942).

Indeed, it may be this constant need to refresh their generic narratives that drew working-class comedies to the black market. As novel domestic conditions arose, music hall stars enthusiastically embraced them. Further, as light-hearted films intended primarily, if not exclusively, for domestic consumption, low comedies might have been granted more leeway to explore potentially controversial themes such as the food rackets and the breach of the social contract between individual consumers and the state.

However, for all their comic intentions, these films present a critique of British society absent from many films of the more acclaimed documentary realist tradition. The exuberance and physicality of many comic routines, accompanied by flights of increasingly absurd verbal fancy, lead to the inverted social world of the carnival where even though characters such as Gert and Daisy, Mother Riley or Revnell and West might share an end with certain authority figures, they employ very different means to get there. That food was considered to be a subject worthy of occupying the apex of this inversion is telling, speaking of the politics of consumption and the centrality of a regular food supply to a well-ordered society. By making visible the unfairness of a social system in which the rich can afford more than the poor (through access to high price black-market goods in wartime and through more general societal inequalities in peace time), and the refusal of working class women to passively and unquestioningly accept such a system, these films recognise the energy of working-class culture and point to the significance of a very different British cinematic tradition.

The antagonism between classes present in certain sections of these comedies is intriguing, especially in an era noted for the communal, democratic nature of many of its films. Whereas the realist, middle-class cinema of the mid-war years, influenced by the British documentary movement, looked to portray a Britain united by common ties to a prevailing social order, many working-class comedies preferred to show a more pluralistic Britain, in which different cultures could interact, and maybe occasionally clash, in defence of the British traditions of liberty, eccentricity and bawdy humour. However, although such films acknowledge the tensions present in British society, it should be noted that class differences were most often played for laughs rather than as part of a revolutionary agenda. Working-class protagonists required socially differentiated antagonists to function as the butt of their jokes, and the bourgeois boss, whether a landlord, a factory manager or the leader of a black market gang, was the obvious choice.

This is not to suggest, though, that these black market comedies are toothless hymns to the established social order. Gert and Daisy, for instance, were said by one contemporary observer to be 'possessors of a nice sense of sarcastic humour in their contact with aristocratic shoppers'.[33] Rather, the films stress the willingness of the working class to contribute to the debate concerning what it meant to be British in wartime, and lambast the selfishness of those who chose, or could afford, not to do likewise. Consensus, as presented in these films, is predicated upon *all* sections of society finding common ground and agreeing to make common sacrifices, rather than on the workers meekly following orders sent down from on high. Furthermore, the middle-class cinematic criminals of the war years are a temporally specific phenomenon, for many post-war films dealing with black market crime featured the ubiquitous spiv, a criminal type commonly understood as having emerged from the working class. Thus, the bourgeois racketeers and their presence on British screens is testament to the hostility felt by the majority of Britons towards those who sidestepped rationing.

Although there is ample evidence to suggest that dockers, stevedores and railway workers were not above a spot of pilfering when the opportunity arose, financial clout – as represented by disposable income – was, inevitably, an important factor in determining who could access the black market, and how often. So while the food rackets were as much of a national endeavour as the rationing system they sought to circumvent, populist genre films did not present them as such: the working-class characters were shown *choosing* not to partake in illicit transactions, just as the middle-class villains were shown to be deliberately neglectful of their duties by organising the black market and purchasing food from it.

It is notable, then, that although *The Hundred Pound Window* has much in common with *Gert and Daisy Clean Up*, *Old Mother Riley, Detective* and *Up With the Lark*, its narrative is focused primarily on the middle rather than the working class. The Draper family inhabits a comfortable and relatively affluent suburban world, but is not cocooned from wartime realities: it too is compelled to fight the threat to its domestic security posed by unscrupulous racketeers, demonstrating that the middle classes could be just as committed to the 'fair shares' ideology of wartime Britain as their working-class compatriots. In the film, Ernest Draper (Frederick Leister) loses his job as cashier of the high-profile £100 betting booth at a racecourse after becoming involved with gangsters, and then unknowingly proceeds to accrue massive debts playing roulette at the Cucaracha, a casino-nightclub used by the crooks as a black market outlet. Ernest's daughter Joan (Anne Crawford) works with the police to extricate her father from this difficult position, and the disruption caused by Ernest's unwitting flirtation with the underworld is eventually resolved. While Gert and Daisy, Old Mother Riley and Revnell and West all based a series of 'topical burlesques' on a black market theme, *The Hundred Pound Window* used the black market as just one of many criminal activities engaged in by its gangsters.[34]

Produced by the British arm of Warner Bros, *The Hundred Pound Window* was given its trade show in November 1943 and received generally positive reviews, although conflicting reports in the press as to whether it was a comedy or a suspense-melodrama suggest that it failed to fully convince in either respect.[35] The studio had high hopes for the picture, and its general release, after an initial three-week run at the Warner Theatre in London's West End, was accompanied by 'a top-budget advertising and exploitation campaign'.[36] The film was also carefully promoted by local exhibitors. In Peterborough, the manager of the Princess cinema exploited the horseracing aspects of the film by paying 'a small boy dressed as a jockey' to ride a Shetland pony around a dancehall holding a banner which read 'Back me as a winner at "The Hundred Pound Window" at the Princess.'[37]

Less manic in style than the three comedies, though possessing a storyline that was no more plausible, *The Hundred Pound Window* is the only film of the four under consideration to really explore the viciousness of its criminal characters. In the comedies, very little is seen of the racketeers, who remain, for the most part, spectral and largely absent figures. Indeed, when they are seen they tend to be presented in a somewhat two-dimensional manner. They are greedy, selfish and criminal, but beyond these traits their characters are largely undeveloped and unexplored. Perhaps because of its desire to introduce some tension into its dramatic narrative, *The Hundred Pound Window* presents audiences with more fully fleshed-out criminals. The *Manchester Guardian* spoke of the film's 'blacker gangsters', even though it concluded that, because of the uneasy balance between comedy and suspense, the film as a whole failed to live up to the sinister ambience created by its antagonists.[38] Francis Lister, in particular, was praised for his portrayal of criminality; playing Captain Johnson, the black market boss and manager of the Cucaracha, he was singled out by *Today's Cinema* for his 'menacing' performance.[39]

Even so, the emphasis of the narrative is on the disruption caused to the Drapers' secure domestic environment and their eventual triumph over the racketeers. In this regard, *The Hundred Pound Window* maintains the emphasis on the consumer's reaction to the black market challenge also seen in *Gert and Daisy Clean Up*, *Old Mother Riley, Detective* and *Up With the Lark*. Indeed, the unquestioningly fierce anti-black market stance adopted by the protagonists is one of the most interesting aspects of this sequence of films.

The active consumer

Food during wartime was a symbol of the social and political contract that existed between consumers and the government, an idea paraphrased by the narrator of *World of Plenty* in the following terms: 'The relationship between the individual and the State is clear: an individual's duty to the State is to keep healthy, and the State's duty to the individual is to ensure the means to keep healthy.' When a small minority of unscrupulous individuals threatened to disrupt this relationship by putting personal comfort above the national struggle, the citizenry was mobilised in defence of the state's right (during wartime) to dictate food policy. The black market films counteracted the threat the racketeers posed to the democratic rationing system by transforming a select band of previously passive consumers, the beneficiaries of the system, into active defenders of it and the nation and ideals it represented.

By including the public in the fight against the racketeers, the black market films effectively nationalised the struggle against Woolton's 'malefactors' and reduced the risk of the state being seen as too heavy-handed in its prosecution of small-scale crimes. Because there were so few food control officers, black marketeers operated in the knowledge that the chances of being caught – or entrapped, in some cases – were very small. Indeed, the successes that the MoF did enjoy against the black market were often heavily publicised, leading to a loss of anonymity for the few employees which the Ministry dedicated to investigating the food rackets. These difficulties increased the government's reliance on the individual actions of a few conscientious consumers. As Edward Smithies suggests, such a strategy was not unproblematic:

> People who exposed black-marketeers were exceptional characters: at a time of painful shortages many members of the public who discovered the existence of one must have been tempted to keep the fact a dark secret and pray that he remain at liberty and continue to supply them with otherwise unobtainable goods.[40]

Furthermore, the basic rationing system tied consumers to specific retailers, meaning that many customers were wary of informing on traders from whom they might have to continue to purchase food, especially if they were required to give evidence in court. By engaging consumers in the fight against the unauthorised acquisition, the black market films attempted to inspire a crusading zeal in cinema audiences by showing active consumers

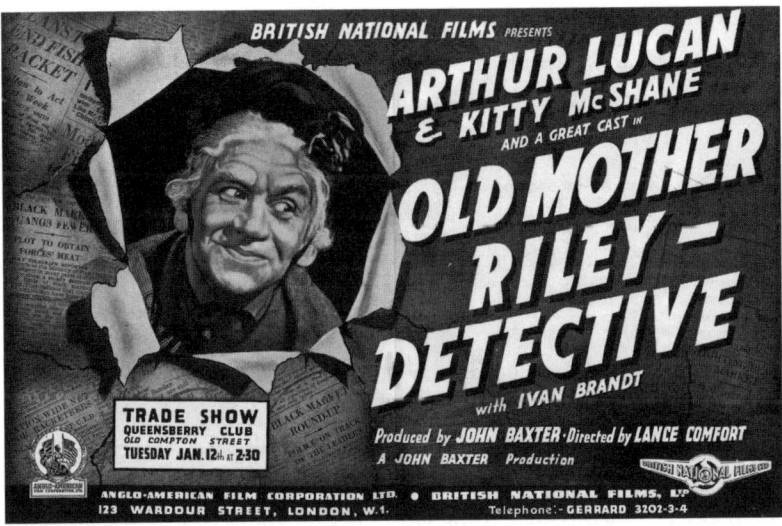

Poster for *Old Mother Riley, Detective* (1943).   **19**

rejecting and opposing the soft living offered by illicit goods, not because they feared the repercussions of breaking the law, but because they believed in the righteousness of the rationing system that the rackets were attempting to bypass.

Active female consumers are central to the black market films. In *Gert and Daisy Clean Up*, the Waters sisters act on their own initiative to bring a criminal to justice, while in *Old Mother Riley, Detective, The Hundred Pound Window* and *Up With the Lark* citizens join with the state in opposing the racketeers. In each film, it is the protagonists' willingness to act against the racketeers which marks them out as special. Indeed, *Old Mother Riley, Detective*'s release was accompanied by a poster campaign (see figure 19) which showed Mother Riley's head bursting through a collage of newspaper cuttings about the black market, suggesting that here was a woman who preferred action to words, who was prepared to move beyond second-hand reports of criminality in order to confront the problem herself.

The use of such strong, principled female characters grew out of a situation in which a significant proportion of Britons engaged in purchasing black market goods were women. The introduction of clothes rationing had helped create a lively and illegal trade in clothing coupons, while the restriction of cosmetics manufacture to just 25 per cent of pre-war levels brought about a thriving black market in make-up.[41] Illegal food sales also tended to involve women. Contemporary reports suggested that racketeers preferred dealing with women rather than men; women became 'indispensable' to many black market transactions.[42] When Woolton expressed a similar view in *Picture Post* in July 1941, he was criticised by Mrs G. Sugden, a Nottingham housewife, who took issue with his assertion that, when it came to food rackets, the women of Britain were especially culpable.

> It's not the housewife who's to blame; she does not know where to find such markets – and if she did, could not afford the prices. The black markets thrive on country hotels, clubs, restaurants, etc., who can afford the exorbitant prices asked and can recoup themselves in their charges to patrons.[43]

The female consumers visible in these black market films, who not only rejected the chance to augment their rations with under-the-counter goods but who also actively worked to destroy the food rackets, might well have met with Mrs Sugden's approval.

While the temporary conscription of untrained citizens into the ranks of the police provided numerous opportunities for comic set-pieces and drama (and so must have appealed to script writers and directors), this narrative development also reinforced the bond that rationing was shown as having produced between the state and the individual. In *Up With the Lark* this dialogue between the consumer and the state is invoked by the name given to Ethel and Gracie's handler: Britt. By working alongside the authorities to bring racketeers to book, these protagonists offered a vision of a mutually supportive system in which consumers were encouraged to claim ownership of, and responsibility for, the success of rationing.

The damage that the black market could do to the national community is made obvious in *The Hundred Pound Window*. When Joan Draper visits the Cucaracha Club, she is informed by Captain Johnson that not only can he help her come into possession of hard-to-come-by goods, but also that 'if you're in any little difficulty over the call up, I can get that fixed too'. Thus the black market is shown as providing an escape not only from the sacrifices necessitated by the war, but also from the fighting itself. Later, Johnson explains to Joan that as far as the war is concerned,

> You've got to make up your mind where you want to stand. You can either clean up out of the war, or be dumb and stand in queues, ride in buses and work for the government. It's a matter of conscience. Personally, I've never let my conscience let me feel broke.

Johnson's attitude very clearly divides Britain into those who work for the government and those who work against it.

While food is closely associated with the stability of society in general, it is also essential to the health and well-being of the individual and is one of the foundations of familial interaction. This meant that the actions of the racketeers were also often shown as threatening the security of the family. Ernest Draper's recklessness in *The Hundred Pound Window* endangers his children's prospects, for in order to repay his debt to the racketeers he risks losing not only the money he has set aside for his son's engineering apprenticeship but also the home he has purchased for Joan as a wedding present. His unwitting involvement with the racketeers thus jeopardises both the industrial and domestic futures of Britain, and it is his desire to make up for this mistake that inspires him to fight back against the gangsters that have so upset his family's prospects.

The threat posed to deserving local children by self-interested racketeers provides motivation for Gert and Daisy in their campaign against the black market, while the threat to the family also lies at the heart of DI Cole's (Ivan Brandt) recruitment of Mother Riley.

Cole:	What would you do if somebody tried to steal the food out of [your daughter's] mouth?
Mother Riley:	If I wasn't a lady, I'd give them a slap in the gob!
Cole:	Exactly! And so would any British mother. Now the Food Controller is, in a way, the mother of the whole nation … His job is to see that everybody gets a fair share of food; that's the idea of rationing … Now certain people are trying to make money by stealing your rations and selling them to others who are willing to pay higher prices for them.
Mother Riley:	The Black Market!
Cole:	That's what it's called and it's working in this district on a pretty big scale. Now what we want to do is, how did you say, 'Give it a slap in the gob.'

Having persuaded Mother Riley to work for the police, Cole concludes by linking individual, family and state in opposition to the black market: 'Will you help me track down this blackguard who's stealing your food, your daughter's food, Great Britain's food, this rat in England's storehouse?'

So motivated is Mother Riley by this appeal to her maternal instinct that once back on the street she immediately questions a pram-pushing neighbour about her experience of rationing, focusing on the impact that government food policy has had on domestic harmony:

Mother Riley:	I see you've got your shopping in. I'm sure that you must find it chronic to try and feed your family on the rations you get.
Neighbour:	I don't complain, and nobody else ought to.

The introduction of children into this discussion not only acts as a very effective form of emotional manipulation, but also posits the success of the MoF's work as determining the fate of the next generation of Britons (and therefore the future of the country itself).

Children and expectant or nursing mothers were often singled out for special attention by the MoF, and the image of the well-fed family as the building block for the nation is a recurring theme in MoF publicity. While many *Food Flashes* and Food Facts columns focus on the health benefits to be gained by a balanced, vegetable-rich diet, the most powerful publicity focuses on the benefits children will enjoy from early access to vitamins and other nutritional supplements.[44] The *Food Flash* 'Milk – Babies only' (week of 20 December 1943) discussed the health benefits that British youngsters could expect to enjoy as the beneficiaries of a regular milk bonus. *The Kitchen Front's* Radio Doctor regularly advocated the health benefits of vitamins, and their abundance in orange juice and cod liver oil was the reason that each child was given a regular allocation of both.

Of course, this was an aspect of a wider strategy of the promotion of a just and healthy society, where all could enjoy access to the foodstuffs necessary for a decent standard of living. The black market threatened this egalitarian vision and British women such as Mother Riley, ineligible for active military service, were mobilised to fight on the Home Front.

That female protagonists are shown working in tandem with the state to defeat the racketeers and restore normal social and familial relationships is not surprising given female domination of shopping, cooking and child-care. By empowering female characters, the films assert that not only were women capable of fighting, but also that their battles were of a similar significance to those fought by the army, navy and air force. In the black market films, women were constructed and addressed as active consumers, as the first line of defence against the black marketeers and criminals who posed a very real threat to the British nation. But rather than merely criticising those who illegally obtained more than their share (as, for example, *Partners in Crime* did), these commercial features show a more assertive, active aspect of femininity, suggesting that, on the Kitchen Front at least, women could engage and defeat the enemy.

During the war, the conscription of husbands, fathers or sons dramatically increased the number of households run single-handedly by women. Such environments were similar to the world inhabited by Gert and Daisy for, after 1931, the sisters' menfolk were discussed but are never actually seen or heard, leaving the pair to their own devices and allowing them to demonstrate the full range of their talents.[45] This gynocentric existence offered special comfort to female audiences, who might have seen something of their own experiences on the screen. In the decade or so before they made their first film appearance in 1941, Gert and Daisy were established as strong and independent characters willing to make jokes at the expense of both authority figures and their absent partners.

> Daisy: [My husband] Bert's ordered the furniture [for the Anderson Shelter].
> Six crates of mild ale. He calls it his ARP nerve tonic.
> Gert: 'e would.
> Daisy: You see, now we can use the crates to sit down on when they're empty.[46]

In *Gert and Daisy's Weekend*, the ordinariness of both the sisters and the neighbourhood in which they live is established in the film's opening seconds. From a shot of a bombed-out building, the camera pans down and tracks at pavement level along a queue of women waiting at a fishmonger's. Thus Gert and Daisy are introduced to the cinema audience not with a shot of their faces, but rather with a close-up of their ankles, which serves to emphasise their anonymity and groundedness as members of their community. The banality of their concerns, allied with their resolutely cheerful good humour, established Gert and Daisy as sympathetic, longsuffering and, most significantly, unaffected. At the fishmonger's, Daisy tries to return a fish purchased the previous day:

> Fishmonger: What do you expect me to do about it?
> Daisy: Change it!
> Fishmonger: Oh, no. I can't change it.
> Daisy: Well if you can't change it, would you like to talk to it? Don't turn your back on an old friend.
> Fishmonger: Old friend! Here, if that's cooked properly it'll go down grand. Curry it, that's what you can do with it.
> Daisy: You wouldn't like us to tell you what *you* can do with it, would you?

Gert and Daisy find humour in the frustrations of everyday wartime life, but their jokes arise from their willingness to participate in the workings of their community rather than their attempts to undermine or escape from it. Indeed, as Gert and Daisy leave the fishmonger's, the street on which it is located is shown in a high-angle shot, which is maintained for six seconds after the sisters have walked offscreen, lending it a reality independent of its most famous inhabitants.

So strong is the sisters' association with the community that they volunteer to defend it and the country of which it is a part, acting as chaperones to evacuees in *Gert and Daisy's Weekend*, before persecuting the black marketeers in *Gert and Daisy Clean Up*. For all that they operate in a world notable for its absence of equally strong male characters, Gert and Daisy – along with Joan Draper, Revnell and West, and Old Mother Riley – are all dedicated to the preservation of their families, their communities, Britain, and in the case of these black market films, the rationing system. Further, the strength that Gert and Daisy *et al.* demonstrated in attacking the racketeers, and their refusal to resort to illicit means to provide for themselves and those around them, can be seen as having offered inspiration to those women who found it difficult to provide as much food for their family as they were used to.[47] The agency that these women demonstrated in their resolute defence of rationing signified an active involvement in, and protectiveness towards, the system, offering an alternative example in how to deal with racketeers, and potentially dissuading some of those who might otherwise have supplemented their weekly allowance with something from under the counter. The protagonists' gang-busting actions are shown to serve both the familial and national interest and, as such, they established these active female consumers as role models: warriors on the Kitchen Front, defenders of the food-based community.

Transgressive pleasure/deferred gratification

For all that wartime films featuring black market themes promoted an idea of active consumerism, the fact that they presented images of the illicit sale and consumption of foodstuffs introduced a degree of tension into their narratives. There is a duality in the presentation of food in these films, since it is at once fetishised and declared off-limits. The locales from which the racketeers operated, and the foodstuffs in which they traded, also provided an element of glamour, setting them at odds with the utilitarian diets and lifestyles that the rationed community was supposed to be championing.

The brightly-lit nightclubs, hotels and restaurants of the criminal demimonde were inhabited by the crooked, the wealthy and, occasionally, the naive, and offered filmmakers an excuse to move away from the drab, blacked-out and theoretically egalitarian world of wartime Britain. Such images operated both as an escape from the daily horror and monotony of the war and as the stylised reward subtly promised for its successful conclusion. However, the pleasure aroused in hungry, frustrated viewers by portrayals of luxury and illicitly obtained comestibles was, by the end of each film, displaced into the swift and inevitable punishments handed down to the wrongdoers.

The exclusive locales appear unaffected by the war and have clearly exempted themselves from sharing in the common sacrifices that all Britons were expected to accept. Gert and Daisy discover that fashionable West End stores are being run by unscrupulous proprietors, while other black market locales have names that smack of privilege or extra-territoriality: the Hotel Royale in *Up With the Lark*, the Bolivia Club in *Old Mother Riley, Detective*, and the Cucaracha in *The Hundred Pound Window*. Names such as the Bolivia and the Cucaracha share a common Latin American influence; given the neutrality of large parts of Central and South America during the war, such names ally their patrons with the languid, exotic luxuries of the New World rather than the rationed diet of war-torn Britain.[48] Indeed, the failure of the war to penetrate these luxurious sanctuaries suggests the irresponsibility of both individuals and nations who fail to recognise and oppose the Nazi threat.

The introduction of the spacious, floodlit Bolivia Club in *Old Mother Riley, Detective* follows directly from a sequence in which Mother Riley and Kitty travel through the blackout to reach the establishment. The darkness of the night makes the cavernous, opulent Bolivia seem even more incongruous and unworldly; light is one of the luxuries made available for consumption by wealthy patrons. The tight, confined sets that characterise Mother Riley's house (situated, we are told, on Ration Row) contrast with the sweeping, open spaces of the Bolivia, a place where music plays and blackout curtains (and the war) are ignored. The shots that comprise these two sequences reinforce these differences: closer, quicker shots in the blackout produce an almost claustrophobic effect, whereas the lengthy, high-angle pans that accompany the Rileys' arrival at the Bolivia serve to emphasise the space and unhurried comfort of the club. The Bolivia, with its suggestion of pre-war gaiety and its lavish restaurant, hints that the war need be but an awkward and temporary intrusion into the world of those selfish enough to ignore the sacrifices needed for the defence of the state.

Woolton was himself suspicious of many exclusive restaurants and clubs, noting that he was 'sure' that the Dorchester was 'one of the places that pays "black market" prices for its food', and linking this refusal to adhere to the principles of rationing to the fact that 'many of the staff are suspected of being foreign agents'.[49] In order to maintain their exclusivity and reputation for fine dining, many restaurants felt obliged to obtain food from dubious sources. In May 1943, the exclusive Grosvenor House on Park Lane was prosecuted for obtaining almost six times its quota of fish – including more than a ton of salmon – for sale to its most favoured (read: wealthy) customers.[50] In response to concerns that public morale was being undermined by apparent inequalities of sacrifice, sumptuary legislation was introduced which limited the price of a restaurant meal to five shillings and allowed only three courses to be served.[51] This move, as newspapers such as the *Daily Express* recognised, was little more than a gesture: there was no limit to the number of meals that a hungry, well-capitalised individual might enjoy.[52] We should not be surprised, then, that the films have their black marketeers operate from lavish establishments.

Mother Riley and Kitty arrive at the Bolivia as guests of Mr Popplethwaite (H. F. Maltby), a man 'whose extreme grossness', the film's press book declares, 'is alone sufficient to arouse suspicion'.[53] Doubts as to Popplethwaite's honesty are confirmed when he boasts that Manoel, a foreign waiter working at the Bolivia, can acquire for him the goods that allow him to maintain his privileged lifestyle in an era when others were making significant sacrifices. Manoel's name, attitudes and unsubtly coded foreignness further reinforce the restaurant's otherness, suggesting that to make use of the illicit services provided by the staff at the Bolivia is fundamentally un-British.

The Cucaracha Club in *The Hundred Pound Window* is presented in a similar manner. The middle-class Draper family are treated to a night at the club by Mr Humphries (Claude Bailey), Ernest Draper's employer, who has won a significant sum at the races and uses this unearned money to finance his guests' consumption. The Drapers are dazzled by the club: they drink champagne (used here, as so often, as shorthand for luxury), they eat, they gamble, they dance. The *Daily Film Renter* was similarly impressed by the Cucaracha, describing it as 'glittering … easy on the eyes and big'.[54] The club seduces the Drapers, encouraging them to leave the reality of the war behind; it encourages decadence and selfishness and, on the brightly illuminated dancefloor, points to their complicity in the individualistic corruption the club promotes.

While the Cucaracha's regular patrons take the plentiful luxuries for granted, the Drapers are shocked to see so many rare and precious foods on offer. Joan Draper, surprised to be plied with champagne and canapés, has the following conversation with Captain Johnson:

Joan: However did you get all these?
Johnson: Well, it's just a matter of knowing how. You mustn't take this war too seriously, you know.
Joan: Some of us can't help it.

As this exchange makes clear, the Cucaracha is not so much ignorant of the realities of the war as wilfully ignoring them. Johnson's refusal to take the war seriously identifies him as a corrupting influence, but his assumption that Joan Draper will concur with his views simply because she is in his club presents the Cucaracha in similarly negative terms.

The willingness of exclusive restaurants to ignore MoF legislation is presented most explicitly at the Bolivia, where Mother Riley orders 'a nice juicy steak, four eggs on the top of one chip, some buttered toast and a cup of cha'. She then asks, with entirely disingenuous naivety, 'Can I have that for five shillings?' However commonplace this fantasy meal might sound, it consists in the main of hard to come by, or rationed, foodstuffs, suggesting the difficulties that many Britons had in acquiring even the most basic ingredients. Although Mother Riley's working-class tastes are seemingly at odds with the exclusivity of the surroundings, she observes that she could 'only order a meal like that in a place like this'. As such, it is perhaps more subversive than the more obviously luxurious champagne and canapés on offer at the Cucaracha Club in *The Hundred Pound Window*, and was certainly enjoyed by *Today's Cinema* which singled out Mother Riley's satirical turn as a 'society dame at a posh restaurant' for special praise.[55]

The films are commendably frank in portraying the pleasures that the black market could offer. Within the spaces of the black market there is a concentration on the inherent sensuality of acts of consumption, and the fetishised presentation of food and drink attracted (not entirely disapproving) comment at the time. One paper noted of *Up With the Lark* that 'There was a certain nostalgic atmosphere about th[e] set on which appeared whole sides of beef and bacon, to say nothing of carcasses of sheep and stacks of various tinned commodities.'[56] Such a description could also be applied to Mr Popplethwaite's larder in *Old Mother Riley, Detective*, a store well stocked to the point of bursting. A wide-eyed Mother Riley is informed that Popplethwaite's wine cellar is similarly plentiful, and reacts by saying that, 'It's been so long since I saw a full bottle of whisky that I've forgotten what a corkscrew looks like.' Shots of Popplethwaite's larder pointedly contrast the illegal smorgasbords available to those who flaunted the law with the more meagre rations of those such as Mother Riley who continued to inhabit (or perhaps could not afford to leave) Ration Row.

Viewers were divided about the value of representing rationed or illicitly obtained goods. Some were angered at the continued portrayals of plenty in American films, insisting that 'Someone *should* tell Hollywood that food is

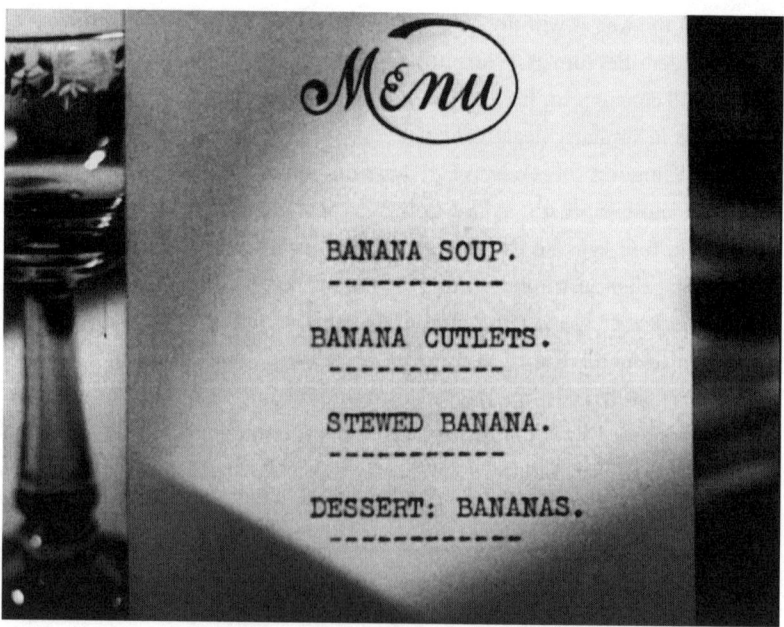

20   Detail of menu in *Sailors Three* (1940).

rationed here – but definitely.'[57] Others, however, welcomed scenes of conspicuous consumption on the screen, observing that:

> It gives *me* the greatest of pleasure to see rationed goods in plenty on the films,
> because I'm reminded that one fine day *my* table will be full of good food ...
> Give us *more* of these pictures that bring into view that glorious tomorrow when
> we can ladle sugar into our tea (if we wish).[58]

The tension that such portrayals evidently introduced into cinema-goers'
experiences suggests a mixture of anger and yearning, a blend of resentment
at those who had more and the hope (indeed, expectation) that all Britons
might soon enjoy such luxuries.

The absence of foodstuffs which before the war had been easily available
lent those films which featured such products a wistful air. Great prominence,
although no direct verbal recognition, was given to an orange – shot in Technicolor – in *This Happy Breed* (1944), where its presence suggests the transient
luxuries of peace and anticipates in an ironic manner the changes that would
be brought about by the war. Actress Celia Johnson described the excitement
she felt upon procuring an orange of her own, noting its exotic appeal:

> Pause for – what do you think – eating an *orange*. I was given one the other day
> by the police and Tish [Johnson's sister-in-law] and I have just shared it ... We
> had such an argument as to the best way of eating it, that we had to toss up and
> I won so we ate it in pigs and now the drawing-room has a lovely old-fashioned
> smell like the gallery of a theatre.[59]

Other fruits were in equally short supply. Following the MoF's decision to
halt importation in December 1940, bananas came to epitomise the imported
luxuries that British consumers had previously taken for granted. Basil
Dearden, director of *My Learned Friend* (1943), described a shot of a young
boy eating a banana as 'the most effective way of suggesting a pre-war theme'.[60]

Bananas also feature prominently in *Sailors Three* (1940), where a trio of
British seamen commandeer the German battleship *Ludendorff* and discover
that the only food on board is a crate of bananas. The three set about the
fruit with some gusto before they come to realise that a diet of 'Banana Soup
– Banana Cutlets – Stewed Bananas – Dessert: Bananas' might soon become
tedious and repetitive (see figure 20).

Given the scarcity of bananas in Britain even before importation stopped,
there is an obvious irony in a select band of British sailors enjoying an
all-banana diet. This irony is compounded by the numerous other goods that
were virtually unobtainable in wartime Britain, for example the champagne
which accompanies many of their meals. However, the price that the sailors

pay for this diet is isolation: onboard a German battleship they are temporarily exiled from the British nation. After a few days on the *Ludendorff* the trio are keen to divest themselves of the remaining fruit and re-enter the British community. When the three sailors are intercepted by a Royal Navy vessel they ask their rescuers, with equal amounts of generosity and desperation, 'Do you want any bananas?'

Indeed, so effectively had food been linked with the war that filmmakers were able to use unrestricted consumption to demonstrate the selfishness of those sections of British society who sought to exempt themselves from the privations of the wartime national community. The hostility the black-market films directed towards characters such as Popplethwaite, Captain Johnson or Martel – the 'oily' manager of the Hotel Royale in *Up With the Lark*[61] – confirms the protagonists' commitment to the ideals of the food-based community, even though the underworld locales and illicit foodstuffs in evidence are continually glamorised. However, the images of criminals in exclusive settings, surrounded by luxury goods, are legitimised by the audience's foreknowledge of their coming disgrace. The momentary guilt that viewers might have experienced as a consequence of the transgressive pleasure of enjoying scenes of bounty and opulence could be alleviated by the satisfaction they could eventually take in the thieves' comeuppance.[62]

Within such a framework, luxury goods and settings are promised as the fruits of victory. The pleasures associated with such images were to be deferred until after the war and, it is suggested, would be Britain's reward for enduring the war and the sacrifices it had demanded. As such, the films criticise not so much the luxury nature of the goods, but the inappropriateness of coveting them, and obtaining them through the black market, in wartime. *Gert and Daisy Clean Up* concludes with an explicit point about what it considers to be the true cost of illicitly obtained goods: 'sweeping aside any offer of thanks' for breaking up the racket, the sisters 'pay tribute to those who had faced danger in order to bring the food to this country – the men of the Merchant Navy'.[63] Such a sentiment was appreciated by those present at the film's trade show, for the audience was reported as 'lustily cheering' the songs which praised the merchant marine.[64]

In films such as *Gert and Daisy Clean Up*, *Old Mother Riley, Detective*, *Up With the Lark* and *The Hundred Pound Window*, volunteer citizens acknowledge the honest consumer's desire for more than wartime rationing could provide, yet simultaneously explain their refusal to take more than their fair share by demonstrating that food obtained illicitly is eaten at the expense of the wider community. The producers of *Old Mother Riley, Detective* realised this, for while the script initially submitted to the British Board of Film Censors is described as showing Mother Riley 'stealing a clutch of eggs she has found in a haystack', the scene was excised from the final version of the film. Having worked hard to establish Mother Riley as a hero of the community, the filmmakers were clearly unwilling to lose sympathy through such an abrupt volte-face.[65] The pleasures offered by oranges, steak, butter and chocolate were not denied by this sequence of films, but enjoyment of these goods was deferred in pursuit of a more immediate and important goal.

This, though, allowed filmmakers to have their cake and eat it, too. For while this sequence of black market films frequently fetishised the possibilities of glamour and wealth (and did so in a visually expansive style), the inclusion of such images was justified by ensuring that those who were seduced by the easy money and lifestyle afforded by involvement in illicit enterprises got their comeuppance and were returned to the monochrome world of the rationed masses. In return, those rationed masses were promised a Technicolor post-war future, a future that would provide them with the same luxuries offered by the black market, but legally obtained.

Waterloo Road and the Spiv Cycle

The war had been the *raison d'être* of the food-based community, but at its conclusion Clement Attlee's newly elected Labour government found itself unable to gratify the pent-up desires of British consumers. Rationing continued; indeed, the system was expanded to include, for a time, both bread and potatoes. As the state begged consumers to further defer pleasure, popular attitudes towards food control changed. Resentment towards the state's dictation of consumption grew and 'sacrifices', as one contemporary commentator put it as early as December 1945, 'were no longer necessary, and had ceased to be fashionable'.[66] Churchill's administration had done such an effective job of linking the need for rationing with the prosecution of the war that Attlee's government found it impossible to maintain public enthusiasm for the scheme after the cessation of hostilities.[67] When peace brought continued penury rather than plenty, the position of food in the state–citizen relationship changed dramatically.

The Attlee government was confronted not only with the unenviable task of reconstruction, but also with the re-emergence of party politics. The coalition government of the war years had faced relatively little press or political criticism of rationing and had used the desperate international situation to dissuade consumers from black market activity. Labour's attempts to explain the continued need for rationing in terms of reconstruction and the trade deficit were inevitably less arresting than the Nazi threat.

The return of electoral politics also saw the return of a partisan media. MoF policies were scrutinised by Fleet Street, and those which offended editorial sensibilities were excoriated. The Public Relations Division at the MoF acknowledged that this made their job considerably more difficult:

> Since the end of the war, the Ministry has been faced with a rising tide of political criticisms, and a largely antagonistic press, also to some extent politically inspired. Under such conditions the most objective Government publicity is suspect and has to break down considerable public resistance before it can achieve any positive results.[68]

During the war, the state had acted as the guarantor of the individual ration, ensuring that each member of the British public was adequately, if unexcitingly, fed. The post-war Labour government was regarded as a body that restricted consumption. Consequently, Britons became increasingly hostile to food control, especially following the reduction of the weekly allowance to *below* wartime levels.[69] As rations shrank, the black market expanded. Increasing numbers of those who could afford the premium supplemented their rations with black market food. The notion of 'fair shares for all' – laudable, democratic and egalitarian during the years of conflict – was reinterpreted in peacetime as meaning 'not enough for anyone'.

It was this expansion of the black market in the immediate post-war years that informed the Spiv Cycle, a group of films which investigated the changing nature of the relationship between the state and the individual-as-consumer. Portraying the greater visibility of the black market and its attendant criminals in the age of austerity, the films of the Spiv Cycle feature anti-heroes whose disenchantment with the conventions of respectability emerges directly from the contested principles and politics of the late 1940s, while their seedy glamour and frequently amoral attitudes spoke to Britons tired of shortages, and longing for the spoils of war after years of scarcity. Rationing doled out the fruits of victory by the segment, and films such as *They Made Me a Fugitive* (1947) and *Noose* (1948) operate within a diegesis defined by the resentment that this caused, producing narratives awash with complex and ambiguous moral stances.

Released in late 1945, *Waterloo Road* is often described as the first film in the Spiv Cycle, and its opaque attitude towards criminality foreshadows

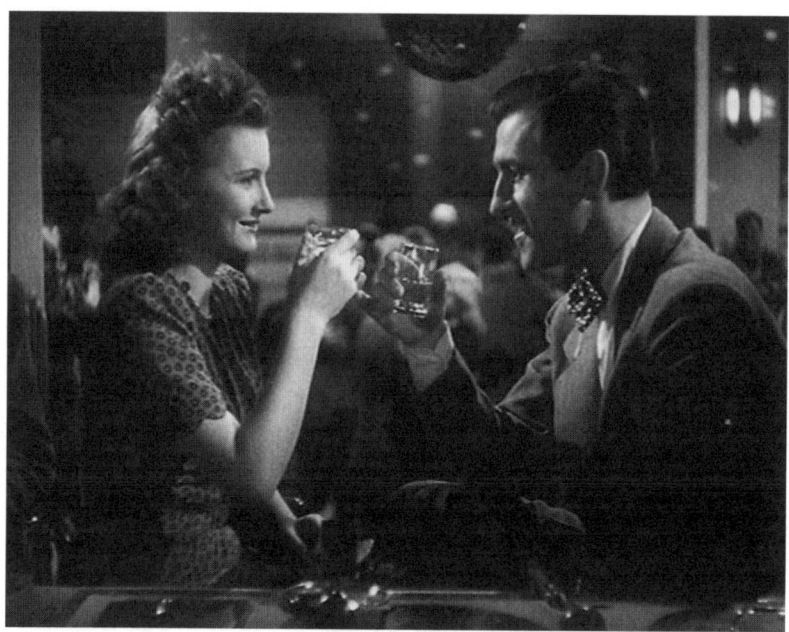

Charismatic consumer, conspicuous consumption. Tillie (Joy Shelton)   **21**
succumbs to Ted's (Stewart Granger) glamorous lifestyle in
Waterloo Road (1945).

themes addressed in subsequent films.[70] The film describes the unsanctioned furlough taken by everyman soldier Jim Colter (John Mills) to rescue his lonely wife Tillie (Joy Shelton) from the clutches of local spiv, Ted Purvis (Stewart Granger). Although by its conclusion *Waterloo Road* has reconciled the Colters, the film seems unwilling to condemn Purvis too harshly. This is, perhaps, because *Waterloo Road*'s main focus and main pleasure is Purvis. Indeed, the film's original portmanteau style, in which a series of interlocking stories focused on Waterloo railway station, was abandoned to concentrate more attention on the charismatic spiv, who is a more richly drawn character than the dogged but bland Private Colter. To Purvis, the pleasures of the flesh are paramount, and, as a dapper ex-boxer, embodied by the glamorous and high-profile Stewart Granger, Purvis's physicality is accentuated, as is his quest for sensation and gratification (see figure 21).

Although the film does not necessarily condone Purvis's selfishness, there is no doubt that his criminal lifestyle is demonstrated as luxurious and exciting when compared to the drab, impoverished world that surrounds him. Purvis is an unapologetic consumer in a world of wartime production, a self-interested individual in an era of consensus and communality. In his attempts to woo Tillie, Purvis takes her from pub, to lunch, to a tea dance, eating and drinking at each stop, before finally purchasing a couple of bottles of liquor to drink at home. Purvis's conspicuous consumption marks him out as a man apart, an illicit epicurean among ill-fed proles. Whereas wartime films such as *Old Mother Riley, Detective* make a point of condemning such consumption, *Waterloo Road*, by making Purvis's most significant crime his attempt to make a cuckold of Jim Colter, merely uses Ted's consumption to demonstrate the options available to those wilful enough to pursue them.

Furthermore, Purvis's single-minded quest for gratification comes at the expense of the war effort. The major part of *Waterloo Road* is set in the winter of 1940–41, and Purvis is free to create his wartime criminal empire and pursue Tillie because he has used spurious medical grounds to avoid conscription. Purvis's contempt for the legitimate authority of the government is indicative of his determination to use his body in pursuit of personal pleasure rather than the aims of the state. Purvis comes closest to corrupting Tillie when the pair visit the Alcazar dance hall:

Tillie: I'd forgotten about places like this, almost. The band. Dancing. Seeing people enjoying themselves.
Ted: You ought to get around more. The best years of your life and you're wasting 'em.
Tillie: I'm beginning to think you're right.
Ted: Sure. All work and no play, you know…

Indeed, even though at the film's conclusion Purvis discovers that the fictional heart condition he had used to avoid the call up is in fact real, his cocky demeanour does not change. Purvis will now be able to legitimately avoid conscription and maintain his avaricious businesses and, although told by his doctor that 'wine, women and song must play an increasingly unimportant part in [his] life', the viewer is left with the suspicion that such advice will do little to change him.

We might, then, understand Jim Colter's breathless and continual pursuit of Ted Purvis – a prolonged chase which constitutes much of the film's running time – as standing for the pursuit of the luxuries that the spiv could provide but which the soldier could not. Further, the AWOL soldier has to avoid the state, in the shape of the Military Police who hunt him down while he searches for the racketeer. *Waterloo Road* thus also critiques the state's continued interference not only in the consumer marketplace, but also in family life. Such an attitude would have been almost unthinkable in the cinema of the early years of the war, but became more noticeable as the conflict drew to a conclusion and attention was turned to peace and reconstruction.

By setting the narrative during the second winter of the conflict, *Waterloo Road* establishes the spiv and resistance to food control as features of British wartime society. By taking the ambiguity that surrounded the black market in 1945 and retrospectively applying it to the entire war, the film suggests that wartime Britain was far from being the cosy, communal place that some films and many commentators would have us believe.[71] For although films from 1942 and 1943 featured black market themes, they were far less subtle in their representations of criminality, which was unequivocally condemned, even though, as seen, such representations introduced a good deal of tension into narratives. *Waterloo Road* abandons the two-dimensional criminal and establishes the black market as a liminal space, a site of contested morality, a product of a world of shortages in which those who took no more than they were entitled to received 'pitying looks'.[72] As such, it suggests that the state's right to dictate consumption might not be absolute and would certainly not be enduring, and acknowledges that the food-based community was a temporary construct bound together by the immediate realities of life in wartime Britain.

'Following the rules, playing the game'

When attempting to negotiate a position for the black market in wartime cinema, filmmakers had to be aware of the risks associated with the excessive glamorisation of their subject, just as they had to take care to demonstrate the very real threat that the rackets posed to the rationing system's ability to assist in the definition of a distinct sense of Britishness. By focusing on protagonists who deferred individual (and national) gratification, *Gert and Daisy Clean Up*, *Old Mother Riley, Detective*, *Up With the Lark* and *The Hundred Pound Window* neatly ostracised criminals and strengthened the collective identity of the food-based community, thereby neutralising some of the tensions arising from government regulation of consumption. Establishing wartime sacrifices as essential and egalitarian, the films suggested that the reward for wartime toil would be a plentiful and similarly democratic future, a future which might be more swiftly realised should British consumers assist in the prosecution of the war by actively participating in, and defending, rationing. The films posited that the defence of the rationing system was one of the duties of those who used and benefited from it, and by demonstrating the proactive, participatory nature of this defence, consumers were encouraged to understand themselves as stakeholders in the communal institutions, which determined so many aspects of their lives. Further, the films united ruler and ruled, provider and consumer, in an alliance against those within Britain who, by illicitly acquiring or distributing food, would undermine national unity and stability and assist those outside the country whose ultimate aim was Britain's defeat.

Directing hostility at the product of food-related tension (the black market and its attendant criminals) rather than at its cause (a rationing system which dictated to a very great degree an individual's ability to consume) the films attempted to channel popular resentment towards an ill-defined and shadowy institution which was therefore able to function as a general purpose gastronomic bogeyman. By focusing attention on the criminals who aimed to circumvent food control, the system of rationing, and the sense of community it hoped to foster, was itself strengthened. While this strategy was effective for much of the war, films from the last phase of the conflict, for example *Waterloo Road*, demonstrate the limitations of such an approach. By continually displacing the rewards for wartime struggle into a future it could not guarantee to provide, the state risked alienating many of the consumers upon whose acceptance of the moral, social and political righteousness of rationing the system was predicated, thereby increasing the number of potential black market customers. In the age of austerity, when it became increasingly clear to British consumers that rationing, queues and shortages were set to continue, the lack of an immediate external threat seems to have undercut the idea that to acquire food through the black market was a form of low level treachery. This meant that although recourse to the rackets was no less illegal after VJ Day than previously, it became easier for consumers to ignore the ethical implications of personal involvement.

During the war, though, the danger posed by enemy action, both to Britons at home and those overseas, justified the existence of a comprehensive rationing system. The external threat made it easier to delineate the boundaries of the British wartime community, not only through an insistence on adherence to the principles of food control, but also through reference to more abstract and traditional notions of Britishness such as fair play. As Woolton told the public, food control was 'a matter of conscience as well as law'.[73] Such an argument made sense in wartime, observed Philip Carr in December 1945:

> we did follow the rules. Then we played the game. But is was not so much from honesty as from patriotism ... Getting around the restrictions was simply not done, even by those who could afford it, which most could not. The King in Buckingham Palace had no more than his rations, and we all stood together to win the war.[74]

In May 1943, a senior MoF official made a similar claim, stating that the food rackets would only ever be a minor problem in Britain because 'to buy on the black market in this country today is not merely an offence, it is worse – it is bad form'.[75] The use of such language appropriates almost stereotypical conceptions of British identity to promote the idea of the food-based community; it is not difficult to imagine Charters (Basil Radford) and Caldicott (Naunton Wayne) using similar phrases to condemn spivs and racketeers. The ideas of fairness and equality operated as ideological constructs, which allowed Britons to define their own relationship with compatriots and the state.

They also, through their appeal to national exclusivity, helped British consumers to understand and position Britain in relation to the rest of the world.

Notes

1 Lord Woolton, *The Memoirs of the Rt. Hon. The Earl of Woolton* (London: Cassell, 1959), p. 231.

2 Edward Smithies, *The Black Economy in England Since 1914* (Dublin: Gill & Macmillan, 1984), p. 84.

3 See, for example, Edward Smithies, *Crime in Wartime: A Social History of Crime in World War II* (London: George Allen & Unwin, 1982), esp. pp. 59–91; Ina Zweiniger-Bargielowska, *Austerity in Britain: Rationing, Controls, and Consumption, 1939–1955* (Oxford: Oxford University Press, 2000), pp. 150–202; Donald Thomas, *An Underworld at War: Spivs, Deserters, Racketeers and Civilians in the Second World War* (London: John Murray, 2003).

4 *The Gallup International Public Opinion Poll: Great Britain 1937–1975: Vol. 1 – 1937–1964* (New York: Random House, 1976), p. 78.

5 These films are not unique in presenting images of the black market, although they are unusual in adopting it as a dominant narrative theme. While films such as *The Bells Go Down* (1943) also feature racketeering, such behaviour is detailed in secondary storylines.

6 See: Robert Murphy, *Realism and Tinsel: Cinema and Society in Britain, 1939–49* (London: Routledge, 1989), pp. 146–67, and 'Riff-raff: British cinema and the underworld', in Charles Barr (ed.), *All Our Yesterdays: 90 Years of British Cinema* (London: BFI, 1986); Peter Wollen, 'Riff-raff realism', *Sight and Sound*, 8:4 (1998); and Tim Pulleine, 'Spin a dark web', in Steve Chibnall and Robert Murphy (eds), *British Crime Cinema* (London: Routledge, 1999).

7 The unnamed minister was quoted in *The Times*, 18 February 1942, p. 2.

8 Woolton broadcast quoted in *The Times*, 20 September 1941, p. 4; The National Archives (TNA) MAF 286/19: Lord Woolton quoted in memo M60/2 by Winston Churchill, 28 February 1942.

9 TNA MAF 286/19: Memo from Lord Woolton to Winston Churchill, 5 March 1942. A maximum penalty of 14 years penal servitude could be handed down for

black market offences.

10 *Picture Post*, 12 July 1941, p. 27.

11 TNA MAF 286/19: Memo M60/2, 28 February 1942.

12 TNA MAF 286/19: Memo from Churchill to John Llewellin, 26 February 1944.

13 TNA RG 23/9a: Gertrude Wagner, 'Food During the War: A Summary of Studies on the subject of Food made by the Wartime Social Survey between February 1942 and October 1943', pp. 2–4.

14 Diary entry, 28 April 1942, in Richard Broad and Suzie Fleming (eds), *Nella Last's War: The Second World War Diaries of Housewife, 49* (London: Profile, 2006), p. 193.

15 The film was condemned by one MP for casting an 'unjustifiable slur' on pawnbrokers. 8 July 1942. *Parliamentary Debates: House of Commons*, 5th Series, vol. 381, cols. 778–79. Further, 'Scotland Yard complained – because a pound note had been photographed during the film's making, something which was highly illegal. Edward Black [the film's producer] was then asked if the note was real or genuine; he told Scotland Yard to deal with the people they received the note from – the Treasury. The Treasury then complained'. Geoff Brown, *Launder and Gilliat* (London: BFI, 1977), p. 105.

16 Food Facts No. 59, week of 15 September 1941. See also Food Facts No. 46, week of 16 June 1941, which equated the black market with looting.

17 Food Facts No. 89, week of 1 April 1942.

18 *Daily Express*, 12 May 1941.

19 *Today's Cinema*, 19 June 1942, p. 7.

20 *Daily Film Renter*, 13 January 1943, pp. 6, 9; *Kinematograph Weekly*, 14 January 1943, p. 22.

21 *Monthly Film Bulletin,* June 1942, p. 69.

22 *Daily Film Renter*, 17 June 1942, p. 9.

23 Paul Matthew St Pierre, *Song and Sketch Transcripts of British Music Hall Performers Elsie and Doris Waters* (Lewiston, NY: Edwin Mellen Press, 2003), p. 7.

24 Morwenna Banks and Amanda Swift discuss this point in *The Joke's On Us: Women in Comedy from Music Hall to the Present Day* (London: Pandora, 1987), p. 59.

25 David Sutton, *A Chorus of Raspberries: British Film Comedy 1929–39* (Exeter: University of Exeter Press, 2000), p. 151.

26 Lucan regularly earned in excess of £40,000 a year through a combination of radio, film and music-hall bookings. Steve King, *As Long As I Know, It'll Be Quite Alright: The Life Stories of Lucan and McShane* (Blackpool: Lancastrian Transport Publications, 1999), p. 93.

27 *Kinematograph Weekly*, 14 January 1943, p. 22.

28 Sutton, *A Chorus of Raspberries*, p. 150.

29 BFI Microfiche Collection: Press Book – *Up With the Lark*.

30 *Kinematograph Weekly*, 25 November 1943, p. 34.

31 *Daily Film Renter*, 24 November 1943, p. 17; *Monthly Film Bulletin*, December 1943, p. 134.

32 *Monthly Film Bulletin*, December 1943, p. 134; *Today's Cinema*, 22 October 1947, p. 10.

33 *Kinematograph Weekly*, 26 February 1942, p. 32D.

34 *Daily Film Renter*, 17 June 1942, p. 9.

35 *Today's Cinema*, 19 November 1943, pp. 9–10; *Monthly Film Bulletin*, November 1943, p. 121; *The Times*, 28 February 1944, p. 8.

36 *Kinematograph Weekly*, 13 January 1944, p. 123; *Today's Cinema*, 19 November 1943, pp. 9–10

37 *Kinematograph Weekly*, 31 August 1944, p. 50.

38 *Manchester Guardian*, 25 February 1944, p. 6.

39 *Today's Cinema*, 19 November 1943, pp. 9–10.

40 Smithies, *Crime in Wartime*, p. 68.

41 Zweiniger-Bargielowska, *Austerity in Britain*, pp. 177–91; Antonia Lant, *Blackout: Reinventing Women for Wartime British Cinema* (Princeton, NJ: Princeton University Press, 1991), pp. 68–72.

42 *Spectator*, 28 December 1945, p. 617.

43 *Picture Post*, 12 July 1941, p. 26; letter from G. Sugden, Nottingham, in *Picture Post*, 9 August 1941, p. 5.

44 Food Facts No. 148, week of 3 May 1943, was aimed at pregnant women; Food Facts No. 171, week of 11 October 1943, found the Radio Doctor discussing the need for good child health under the heading 'Nations out of Nurseries'.

45 St Pierre, *Song and Sketch Transcripts of Elsie and Doris Waters*, p. 68.

46 Quoted in St Pierre, *Song and Sketch Transcripts of Elsie and Doris Waters*, p. 94.

47 See also Andy Medhurst, 'Music hall and British cinema', in Barr (ed.), *All Our Yesterdays*, p. 178.

48 The Cucaracha, taking its name from a popular Mexican song, translates from Spanish as 'cockroach'.

49 Woolton diary entry, quoted in Philip Ziegler, *London at War, 1939–1945* (London: Sinclair-Stevenson, 1995), p. 250.

50 Thomas, *An Underworld at War*, pp. 115–16.

51 Robert Mackay, *Half the Battle: Civilian Morale in Britain During the Second World War* (Manchester: Manchester University Press, 2002), p. 200.

52 *Daily Express*, 13 May 1942, p. 2. The *Express* did not welcome the scheme, proposing that it was 'the outcome of the austerity mood which many classes of the community seek to impose on their fellow-beings'.

53 BFI Microfiche Collection: Press Book – *Old Mother Riley, Detective*.

54 *Daily Film Renter*, 18 November 1943, p. 6.

55 *Today's Cinema*, 15 January 1943, pp. 9–10.

56 *Kinematograph Weekly*, 18 March 1943, p. 3.

57 Letter from 'Housewife', Blaina. *Picturegoer*, 4 October 1941, pp. 9, 15.

58 Letter from Mrs M. Fleming, Ramsey. *Picturegoer*, 15 November 1941, p. 15.

59 Letter to husband, January 1944. Reproduced in Kate Fleming, *Celia Johnson: A Biography* (London: Weidenfeld & Nicolson, 1991), p. 126. The introductory voice-over in *Millions Like Us* (1943) refers to an orange, only for a caption to appear explaining what an orange actually *was*.

60 *Kinematograph Weekly*, 3 June 1943, p. 35. In late 1941, the Capitol cinema in Winchmore Hill, Buckinghamshire, raised £89 by twice auctioning a bunch of bananas that had been grown in the area. A third auction for the fruit had been

planned, but 'the bananas began to feel the strain'. *Kinematograph Weekly*, 1 January 1942, p. 23.

61 *Kinematograph Weekly*, 25 November 1943, p. 34.

62 *The Hundred Pound Window* was described by *Kinematograph Weekly* as climaxing with a 'well-timed and satisfying round-up of chisellers'. 25 November 1943, p. 34.

63 BFI Microfiche Collection: Press Book – *Gert and Daisy Clean Up*.

64 *Daily Film Renter*, 17 June 1942, p. 9.

65 BFI Special Collections: *British Board of Film Censors Scenario Notes, 1941–42–43*, File 44a, 21 August 1942: *Old Mother Riley, Detective*.

66 *Spectator*, 28 December 1945, p. 617.

67 See, for example, TNA RG 23/9a: Wagner, 'Food During the War', p. 4.

68 TNA MAF 75/67: 'General Account of the Work of Public Relations Division, 1939–50', p. 10.

69 See Smithies, *Crime in Wartime*, p. 73.

70 See, for example, Murphy, *Realism and Tinsel*, p. 149.

71 See *Spectator*, 28 December 1945, p. 617, in which it is claimed that the wartime black market dealt almost entirely in whisky.

72 Edie Rutherford, diary entry, 8 January 1943, in Sandra Koa Wing (ed.), *Our Longest Days: A People's History of the Second World War* (London: Profile, 2008), p. 151.

73 Bodleian Library, Oxford: MS Woolton 12: Broadcast talk on the Home Service by the Minister of Food, 13 June 1941.

74 *Spectator*, 28 December 1945, p. 617.

75 William Mabane, Parliamentary Secretary to the Ministry of Food, 13 May 1943. *Parliamentary Debates: Commons*, 5th Series, vol. 389, col. 824.

5

The Honourable Company of Tea Drinkers: using food to position Britain, her allies and her enemies

Two men stand atop a hill that overlooks Canterbury Cathedral. One, an American, confesses that he is surprised by how much he likes Britain, but qualifies his admiration by admitting that he cannot understand why the British 'from sunrise to sunset, and at odd hours throughout the night, have to drink tea'. His companion, a British soldier, replies:

After Pearl Harbor you Americans joined the Honourable Company of Tea Drinkers. Don't forget that the Nazis and Japs have knocked down every country they've tried to except the tea drinkers: China, Russia and England. So long live drinking tea!

Tea is used here explicitly, and ironically, as the repository of the anti-fascist fighting spirit, the fuel which powers resistance to tyranny. Additionally, the drink is used to differentiate Britain from its enemies and link it with its allies. By locating some of the essence of the nation in gastronomic and cultural habits, *A Canterbury Tale* (1944), in which this exchange features, acknowledges the link that exists between food and nation, between consumption and identity. The film succinctly demonstrates the way in which many wartime films used food in general, and tea in particular, as a site of dialogue concerning notions of 'self' and 'other' and to investigate the nature of the relationships between individuals, groups and nations.

Consumption was just one of the themes used by British wartime filmmakers to explore ideas concerning the national and the international. Such a strategy was made possible by food's associations with both specific ideas of cultural and geographical place and individual and group identity, associations foregrounded within the 'food-based community' by rationing policy and Ministry of Food (MoF) publicity. Food has been described as a landmark on the 'imaginative geographies' that are essential to the construction of a national identity,[1] and one author has gone so far as to ask 'What is patriotism but the love of the good things we ate in our childhood?'[2]

As Claude Fischler has argued, 'Food not only nourishes, it also signifies.'[3] This is as true in cinema as in culture more generally. To take a single example, in *Secret Mission* (1942), the Frenchness of Raoul de Carnot (James Mason) is initially established by both his ability to cook and his mocking attitude towards British food, with his name, his uniform and his accent all serving to further accentuate the foreignness to which his gastronomic attitudes have already alerted the viewer. The link between food and communal identity is strong: 'To eat is to distinguish and discriminate, include and exclude. Food choices establish borders and boundaries.'[4] It is these borders and boundaries that this chapter investigates.

It is surely not coincidental that tea, so often regarded as the apotheosis of British cuisine, appeared so regularly at significant narrative moments in wartime cinema.[5] For instance, in a remarkable and powerful sequence in *This Happy Breed* (1944), the news that Phyllis Gibbons (Betty Fleetwood) has been killed in a car crash is delivered just as her family are about to take afternoon tea. The disruption caused to this most comforting of rituals focuses attention on the emotional dislocation that the news has on Phyllis's parents Frank (Robert Newton) and Ethel (Celia Johnson). Frank and Ethel are informed of Phyllis's death off-screen, and for a few seconds the shot of the family's living room, with the tea service laid out on a table, is shown entirely empty, devoid of human life. When the family enters the room, they sit in silence, unable to consume the drink that should have brought them together, attempting to come to terms with the event that has shattered the domestic ideal.

Cinematic narratives which featured tea mobilised a totemic foodstuff and utilised its national associations to position Britain in relation to its own citizens and its international allies, just as other films used food to encourage cinema-goers to reject criminality or celebrate community. The ritual of making and consuming tea became the focus of a dialogue about identity, a site of discourse concerning the nature of Britishness in a changing world. Filmmakers portrayed tea as being fundamentally important to British life and identity, a thirst-quenching synecdoche of the nation. Tea was, however, not the only product capable of playing this role, and other foods were also used to perform a similar function.

Tea became strongly enough associated with Britain and the British for a pre-war film like *The Lady Vanishes* (1938) to use it as a national signifier, while wartime films such as *San Demetrio, London* (1943) used tea's symbolic power to help define British characteristics and present an image of Britain to itself. Tea was such an established gastronomic stereotype that it could be used to explore the nature of Britain's wartime alliance with both the United States of America (in films such as *A Welcome to Britain,* 1943, and *The Way to the Stars,* 1945) and the Soviet Union (in *The Demi-Paradise,* 1943). Such films were intended to create workable alliances with two very different countries, and used food to demonstrate the continued appeal of British culture and customs in the face of American consumerism and Soviet communism. By focusing on how foreign nationals came to embrace British gastronomy, standing here for Britishness more generally, such films can be seen as attempts to bolster pride and interest in British traditions, so presenting audiences with a vision of the world in which their own customs are shown to be so laudable as to be worthy of emulation by citizens of the world's nascent superpowers. Just as food was used to build alliances by fostering a spirit of inclusivity, it was also used to exclude, to differentiate between self and other, ally and enemy. Films such as *Two Thousand Women* (1944) and *Went the Day Well?* (1942) use food to distinguish between British and 'foreign' characters, suggesting that gastronomy was so integral to the wartime nation's sense of self that failure to conform to culinary norms could be used as a demonstration of otherness.

When tea came off the ration in 1952 after more than twelve years of government control, *The Times* wrote of 'the liberation of [the] tea caddy' with almost the same zeal with which it had reported the liberation of Paris. Describing it as 'undoubtedly … the national drink', the paper, with tongue only half in cheek, suggested that Britain would only become whole again when consumers could unrestrictedly indulge themselves in the 'mystery and the passion' of tea.[6] The paper clearly understood the importance of specific foodstuffs in the formation of national identity, and this understanding was shared by British filmmakers, who encouraged consumers to recognise the importance of food as a crucial munition not only on the home front, but also in foreign theatres of war.

'Teatime! All the English will be there': food and nation

In 1947, Lord Woolton wrote the introduction to a book that discussed tea's importance to the British during the Second World War. Explaining his decision not to 'pool' tea into a single national brand, as in the Great War, Woolton stated that, 'If we had given up during the war the blending of tea, the use of brands, if we had decided on this dull level of equality, we should have lost something of our national life.'[7] Woolton thus clearly identified tea with Britain and Britishness, however vaguely defined. Woolton also suggests that the government was well aware of tea's symbolic value, and its importance in debates surrounding conceptions of what Britain was, what it stood and fought for. Indeed, by rationing tea, by guaranteeing its continued presence in British homes, the state demonstrated its conviction that it was an essential staple of the British diet.

The MoF's decision to ration tea was a courageous one, and led a friend to warn Woolton that, 'You are finished ... The person who touches tea in this country is politically a dead letter.'[8] Coming in July 1940, the decision was made public just three months into Woolton's tenure as Minister of Food and, if poorly handled, might have severely compromised his ability to build a relationship with the people of Britain. Further, tea rationing was introduced during a testing time: morale was sapped by the retreat from Dunkirk and the fall of France, the Battle of Britain was being fought daily over southern England and the prospect of a German invasion loomed large. Such events might have been expected to prompt an increase in tea consumption as millions of Britons looked to calm their nerves with a soothing cuppa.[9] Indeed, Professor Frederick Lindemann, head of Winston Churchill's Statistical Section, advised against the implementation of tea rationing, warning that restricting consumption might jeopardise morale, especially among working-class women.[10]

Despite the two-ounce weekly ration being lower than many had hoped for – it represented a 25 per cent decrease in average consumption – most Britons appear to have accepted the MoF's actions as essentially fair; rationing permitted equitable and continued distribution, even if it did force almost one third of consumers to reduce the amount of tea they drank.[11] Many employees, cinema staff among them, were able to augment their private ration by taking tea at work, providing that managers were prepared to apply to their local Food Office for additional supplies. Consequently, a Mass-Observation diarist could note that, 'One or two people described the ration as "a bit of a blow" but nobody grumbled about it.'[12]

The MoF's publicity machine, however, did not take any chances, and made sure to point out that the Ministry understood public anxiety about possible tea shortages and was fully aware of the symbolic importance of the drink. On 9 July, the day on which tea rationing came into effect, S. P. B. Mais began his *Kitchen Front* broadcast with the line 'I know what you're all thinking: "Oh, my tea, my tea!"', before proceeding to explain the reasoning behind the surprise decision.[13] The suddenness of Woolton's announcement – the shock news was brandished in front of an unsuspecting public 'like a knife' – was intended to prevent hoarding, especially by wealthier consumers.[14] A few weeks later, the very first Food Facts advertisement offered helpful tips on how to make the tea ration 'go further'.[15] Stories were soon circulating that the scheme might only be a temporary inconvenience, and while it is tempting to see such reports as the MoF's attempt to prevent disquiet, it seems more likely that this was a genuine hope for both the press and the Prime Minister, even if Woolton and his Ministry remained more cautious.[16]

As summer moved into autumn and winter, and with the ration still very much in place, shortages began to have more of an effect. In mid-November, a Glasgow woman noted that her colleagues were taking an increased interest in cocoa as their private stockpiles of tea ran low. This new cocoa-consciousness was not entirely coincidental. The MoF pushed for increased consumption via *Kitchen Front* broadcasts and Food Facts columns: 'Most people are comforted at a time of strain by sipping a hot drink. Cocoa is an excellent thing to serve in the air-raid shelter ... Add a tin to your emergency store.'[17] It is notable that, in this instance, tea is not advanced as performing a similar function. That said, despite the issues arising out of tea control, the drink continued to be enjoyed as a symbol of Britain.

Released less than a year before the start of the war, and seemingly anticipating it, *The Lady Vanishes* used tea to distinguish British from 'foreign' passengers on a train journey through the fictional European country of Bandrika, serving to bind together a motley group of exiles who had previously regarded their individual concerns as being more pressing than those of the nation. While helping British spy Miss Froy (May Whitty) avoid capture, Iris Henderson (Margaret Lockwood) and Gilbert Redman (Michael Redgrave) find themselves isolated and in need of assistance. Not knowing who they can trust, the pair prepare to stand alone against the authoritarian forces that surround them. However, a quick glance at Iris's watch reveals that it is teatime, meaning that the dining car will be full of potential allies: 'All the English will be there!'

In the mysterious, transient diegesis of *The Lady Vanishes*, Iris and Gilbert inhabit a chaotic and uncertain world where the senses are not always to be trusted and perception is often faulty. The tea ceremony is welcomed as a ritualistic expression of a more concrete and knowable reality, an experience that realigns Iris and Gilbert with their compatriots.[18] The Britons gathered in the dining car represent fixed reference points for the bemused sleuths, allowing them to exert a degree of control over an alien environment.

The British passengers are brought together by the predictability of their eating habits. However, tea is used in *The Lady Vanishes* to sketch the boundaries of the group, but not its nature; tea helps distinguish the British *as* British, but fails to offer any definition of what 'Britishness' might be. Indeed, if anything, *The Lady Vanishes* proposes that it is futile to suggest that there is any single definition of Britishness, implying that the identity of the national group is best understood as an uneasy and shifting alliance of bloody-minded and frequently eccentric individuals. Indeed, when assembled, the British passengers violently disagree as to the best course of action, bickering among themselves while the Bandrikan authorities surround the train. Although some favour surrender and others advocate fighting, all insist on being heard; their dogmatic adherence to the protocols of a sub-committee seems more suited to the niceties of the council chamber than what will soon become the venue of a shoot-out. Within this potentially violent space, little unites this disparate group beyond the nationality of its members, defined, initially at least, almost exclusively in terms of their shared diet.

Indeed, so secure are many of the Britons within this gastronomically-defined microcosm of home that they have to be reminded of their current unfamiliar environment. The comforting presence of tea has anaesthetised them to the extent that Miss Froy feels moved to exclaim, 'We're not in England now!' This statement makes the Britons aware of their isolation, but also of the possibility that, divorced from the feelings of cosy domesticity that their common meal instils, anything might happen. So mobilised, the group puts down its collective teapot and arms itself, prepared to fight to defend this corner of a foreign dining car that will be forever England.

While the use of tea in *The Lady Vanishes* might be regarded as lazy stereotyping, it neatly illustrates the visibility of the product in British culture. In films such as this and, indeed, in British culture more generally, tea came to be associated with Britain. Tea's relationship with Britishness can therefore be regarded as part of what food historians Ian Cook and Philip Crang see as a

> long history of constructed associations between foods, places and peoples, associations epitomised [by] the use of foods as emblems and markers of national, regional and local identities.[19]

Such an attitude is visible in George Orwell's description of tea as 'one of the mainstays of British civilisation'. However, the synthetic nature of this conception of Britishness was conceded by Orwell, who admitted that 'the best manner of making [tea] is the subject of violent disputes'.[20] Orwell points humorously to the ambiguity at the heart of tea's relationship with British identity and acknowledges the multiplicity of meanings that tea carried. Indeed, it might be safely assumed that any product which could provoke such passion more than three hundred years after first being introduced to Britain might be considered to have a complex relationship with the country and its inhabitants. It is important to understand, though, that tea had (and still has) no clearly defined meaning within British culture. Rather, it is a product loosely tied to British identity, a blank canvas with a Union flag watermark, which has frequently been mobilised to comment on or act as the site for dialogue about Britishness.

This is the case in *San Demetrio, London*. Inspired by actual events, the film tells the story of the journey made by a Merchant Navy petrol tanker from America to Britain in the winter of 1940. When the *San Demetrio* is shelled by a German ship, she is abandoned by her crew, some of whom, after drifting for three days in a lifeboat, reboard and guide her to Scotland. The film's unemotional style and underplayed heroics were praised by many critics, one of whom wrote that, 'No more stirring chapter has been written in our island story than this factual account of Merchant Navy heroism.'[21] In the *Observer*, C. A. Lejeune hoped that *San Demetrio* was an augury for British films to come.[22]

This vision of Britain afloat was careful to contain a number of Scottish and Welsh characters, and the ship's compliment was recognised by contemporary reviewers 'as coming from all parts of our country'.[23] The consensus and robust good humour demonstrated by the crew in the most trying of circumstances makes it possible to view the *San Demetrio* as a representation of the British nation at war – as, in Charles Barr's phrase, 'the ship of state'.[24] Indeed, so powerfully inclusive is the ship that it allows Preston (Robert Beatty), an American working his passage from his (still neutral) homeland to Britain in order to join the RAF, to confront and overcome his prejudices about Britain and gain honorary British status, as represented by his award at the film's conclusion of the *San Demetrio*'s red ensign.

Of the events that demonstrate the crew's collective identity, one of the most important is the first time that they take tea together. Reboarding the *San Demetrio*, the British sailors are cold and hungry, but are forced to eat uncooked food because the vapours escaping from the tanker's ruptured fuel tanks makes it too dangerous to use the stove. Chief Engineer Pollard (Walter Fitzgerald) admonishes messboy John 'Jock' Jamieson (Gordon Jackson) when he finds him preparing to light the range: 'Don't you realise that the ship's full of petrol fumes? Never heard about the man who looked for a gas leak with a lighted match? Never mind son, it was a good idea all the same.'

However, the film suggests that tea is of such importance to the crew, both physically and psychologically, that lighting the stove eventually becomes a risk worth taking. Understanding that in order to survive, the men need hot food, Pollard returns to the galley, carefully battens down the hatches, turns on the gas hob and gingerly strikes a match. At the moment the match is struck, there is a cut from the inside of the vapour-filled galley to an exterior shot of other characters going about their duties in the bitter cold of a North Atlantic winter. This cut acts not only to link the production of the tea to those that will eventually consume it, it also suggests the danger inherent in the making of the drink in these conditions: so perfectly timed is the transition from one shot to the next that the viewer almost expects to hear and witness an explosion as the match ignites the fumes. When the explosion does not come, the viewer is made to feel something of a sense of anticlimax. This feeling does not last for long. The absence of the explosion elevates the viewer to an enjoyable position of omniscience and allows them to derive pleasure in anticipating the arrival of the tea and the beneficial effect that it might have on the crew.

The script demanded that the tea be presented with a flourish 'like a conjurer bringing off his best trick' and the drink here is invested with such mystical significance that its arrival is described as 'magic' by Second Officer Hawkins (Ralph Michael). Pollard's arrival on deck with the steaming pot generates 'great excitement', which suggests the hold that tea has on the sailors' imaginations.[25] The power of the tea is magnified because the crew is so obviously cold and tired: as the wind whistles on the soundtrack, the crew, repeatedly soaked by waves whipped up by winter storms, are unable to take shelter for fear of losing the ship.

As might be expected, then, the arrival of the tea has an immediate physical impact on the crew. It also has something of a transformative effect on the viewer, for so evocative is the film's presentation of the icy conditions that they are communicated to and experienced by the audience. The *Manchester Guardian* insisted that the 'trials of the merchantmen cannot be understood through the medium of the written word' and suggested that only the cinematic art was capable of creating an almost physically real diegesis in which 'the voyage of the tanker has a maritime reality that sends out puffs of ozone and oil from the celluloid'.[26] *Kinematograph Weekly* concurred, suggesting that *San Demetrio, London* 'so effectively stimulates the imagination that all who see it are compelled to share the grim hazards' of life at sea.[27] By extension, the warmth and comfort afforded the crew by the arrival of the tea can also be enjoyed and experienced by the audience. The arrival of a mobile canteen offering tea and respite to exhausted firemen in *Fires Were Started* (1943) functions in a similar way and has a similar effect, permitting the viewer to draw breath and reflect on the dangers to which they have been party.

Tea becomes an ingestible icon symbolising the crew's increased likelihood of survival, offering comfort to men stranded in what had previously appeared to be a hopeless situation. It also strengthens the crew's collective identity and offers a point of reference on an otherwise featureless ocean. The hot drinks are greeted with a cry of 'All hands to tea!' and the communality of the tea ceremony, in which mugs are passed from man to man, reasserts the democratic nature of this isolated pocket of Britishness and anticipates – indeed, is mirrored by – a subsequent scene in which a vote is taken regarding the direction in which the *San Demetrio* is to be steered. Having taken tea, the drink of the mother country, there is only ever going to be one decision: the crew decides to take the tanker back to Britain.

The tea scene, however, is only one of several sequences in *San Demetrio, London* in which diet becomes a cultural touchstone and food is used to locate characters. When adrift in the lifeboat, two members of the crew fantasise about home:

Porter (John Coyle):	What wouldn't I give to be having a pint in the old Elephant right now!
Cottes (Charles Victor):	If it's still there…
Porter:	Of course it's still there.

To the sailors, the pub is a concrete expression of an exclusively British reality, a physical manifestation of British culture which is more immediate and real to them than intangible ideas of liberty or democracy. By believing so adamantly in the Elephant's continued survival, Porter refuses to concede that the war could have any lasting impact on his way of life and so denies the possibility that Britain might be defeated. To Porter, the pub *is* Britain, and every pint drunk there is a symbol of Britain's successful resistance of fascism; and a precursor of those to be enjoyed on VE Day.

Food is also used to establish Preston's difference early in the film. Before the *San Demetrio* leaves America, some of the crew visit a local bar. There they find Preston, enjoying a last night on the tiles before beginning his voyage. Speaking to bosun Fletcher (Frederick Piper), Preston brags that:

You find the best beer in Texas in Galveston, and you find the best beer in Galveston right here in this saloon. Moreover, Texan beer is the best beer in the United States, and American beer is the best beer in the world!

Fletcher is not impressed with this boast, nor with the standard of American beer, and counters 'If ever you come to England I'll take you to the Ship at Faversham and stand you a pint of "Four X". You don't know what beer is!' The scenes in the saloon are less grimly realistic than the rest of the film, a fact which highlights the fantasy world that American consumers – unlike their blitzed and rationed British counterparts – could still enjoy in 1940.

Although Preston's argument with Fletcher centres on the parochial tastes of the two men, it also serves to make visible the cultural differences that exist between them, differences that will ultimately be resolved through shared sacrifice and the development of mutual respect. The American Preston is loud and boastful and certain of his nation's superiority. Fletcher is no less sure of British brewing expertise, standing here for more general British prowess and worth, but presses his claim in a more modest style. Indeed, when the *San Demetrio* arrives in Scotland, Fletcher repeats his promise to buy Preston a pint of Kentish beer. Preston, now integrated into the crew and British culture more generally, suggests that Fletcher should 'make it a barrel'. The safe arrival in Britain of Preston, an individual American volunteer, anticipated the coming of huge numbers of GIs, a mass migration which required British filmmakers to adopt different strategies of integration.

'They don't warm the pot, you know': tea, beer and the Anglo-American alliance

When the United States entered the Second World War after the attack on Pearl Harbor on 7 December 1941, it became clear that for Britain's alliance with America to function smoothly the cultural differences that existed between the two nations would need to be addressed and, where possible, overcome. This was especially true for the legions of American personnel stationed in Britain.[28] Such differences have commonly been discussed in terms of linguistics, and Bertrand Russell observed in 1944 that, 'it is a misfortune for Anglo-American friendship that the two countries are supposed to have a common language'.[29] The same might be said of diet, where the differences were equally significant, and were used to explore the complexities of the Anglo-American relationship.

A Welcome to Britain was made by the Strand Film Company for the Ministry of Information and exhibited by the United States War Office to American troops arriving in the United Kingdom. Directed by a Briton, Anthony Asquith, the film is described in an address to camera by General Sir Ronald Adam as 'a gift from us ['the entire British army'] to you [U. S.

Servicemen]', and is intended to shine light on what GIs might consider to be peculiar British habits, thus defusing any tension that might arise from cultural misunderstandings. In an introductory speech, General Jacob L. Devers, U. S. Army, talks about some of the problems that American soldiers might face: 'Now you take the way coffee is made over here! We are apt to gripe. Some of us may have pretty set ideas about food, and people and behaviour.' Adam replies, archly, 'You're not alone in that, General.'

Money, sex, transport and geography are all discussed in *A Welcome to Britain*, but food is, I would argue, the most significant, and the only recurring, concern. Scenes dealing with food and drink account for more than a quarter of the film's 55-minute running time, and tea is offered to American soldiers on five separate occasions, its multiple appearances becoming something of a running joke. The first such offer comes even before the generals introduce the film, when a shot from the point of view of an American infantryman fresh off the boat focuses on a Women's Voluntary Service van, which stands in readiness to distribute tea. Indeed, the van is bedecked with a banner proclaiming 'Welcome to Britain' suggesting that only after drinking a cup of tea will the GI have actually arrived in the country. The soldier's gaze is unsure, however, and his uncertainty about whether he is allowed to approach the van, and whether he is prepared to risk exposing himself to British cuisine, effectively provides the starting point for the film. Later, narrator Burgess Meredith informs the audience that 'The English drink tea two or three times a day … like we drink Coke back in the States.'

However, for all the tea-centredness of this vision of Britain, it is to a country pub that Meredith repairs when he is ordered by the generals to make a film about life in the United Kingdom. Despite his inability to explain the difference between bitter and mild, Meredith celebrates the quiet, ancient rhythms of the pub and is insistent that his American audience should respect the reserved, unostentatious nature of British drinking habits. In taking the pub as a starting point for Anglo-American dialogue, Meredith anticipates the observations made by 'An American Soldier' in *Tribune* in January 1944:

> although the Yank may object to the quality of British beer … he enjoys the fact that he can go to a pub and carry on a friendly conversation with the circle gathered there. In fact, it might almost be said that the local pub is doing more to foster British-American friendship than many mightier institutions.[30]

When another GI enters the pub, he threatens the very foundations of Meredith's fragile relationship with the regulars by throwing his money around, flirting with the local women ('Say, you're really a hep tomato!') and insulting the other patrons. Meredith is so appalled by these actions that he causes this soldier to disappear in a puff of smoke.[31] The locals, who see the brash American dematerialise, do not comment on his mysterious exit, adding to the otherworldliness of a studio-bound country pub supposedly within walking distance of bombed-out central London. It is obvious that verisimilitude is not the prime concern of this scene, or the film more generally. Rather, its fantastical (and ironic) representation of the most sacred of British social institutions serves to prepare American viewers for a trip through the looking glass to a Carrollian land of dreamlike tea parties and mystical drinking spaces. The confounding of expectations is intentional, for if something as simple and fundamental as food and drink could potentially be the cause of misunderstanding, then all of the GIs' preconceived ideas concerning the nature of British culture and society must surely also be re-examined.

The film is knowing and humorously self-reflexive, and in its final, breathless moments it descends into an anarchic list of 'dos and don'ts' as Meredith tries to impart wisdom before the film ends. Consequently, it is not difficult to conclude that *A Welcome to Britain* is more concerned with making American troops acknowledge that they will be living among people who are different from them rather than in giving them precise instructions on how to behave in Britain. The primacy of the pub and of tea in particular, and of eating more generally, in the MoI film's representation of British illustrates the significance of food in international relations and the ways in which it can be used to demonstrate and explore cultural difference.

Tom Ryall sees *A Welcome to Britain* as 'a kind of prelude to *The Way to the Stars*', another film directed by Asquith which concerned the alliance between the United Kingdom and the United States.[32] One area of similarity between the two films is their repetitive use of food to initiate dialogue regarding the occasionally awkward reality of transatlantic relations. The British Board of Film Censors considered *The Way to the Stars* to be an investigation of 'the different manners, idioms, accents, etc. of American and English officers', but believed that despite the frankness with which such differences were addressed they were handled sensitively: 'not in any way disparaging or likely to give offence to either service'.[33] Yet whereas *A Welcome to Britain* illuminates British idiosyncrasies for the benefit of US servicemen, *The Way to the Stars* celebrates Britishness, in order to present British cinema audiences with an alternative to the glamorous clichés and Americanisms of many Hollywood films.

Historian Keith Robbins has written that by the mid-twentieth century America:

was not simply a fading aspect of the British past. Indeed, its present was so vibrant and dynamic that it threatened to become a more significant element in the twentieth-century British present than the British past itself.[34]

Robbins here directs attention to the fear felt by some members of the British cultural establishment that American cultural products – particularly films – were so integral to the lives of many Britons that they looked to California for their entertainment. The popularity of American cinema had of course exercised British commentators for some time. Writing in 1927, *Daily Express* cinema critic G. A. Atkinson had complained that the prominence of Hollywood films had produced 'several million [British] people, mostly women, who, to all intent and purpose, are temporary American citizens'.[35]

Despite the success of a number of British films in Britain, Hollywood products still tended to draw the largest crowds, and few British films moved into the cinematic and commercial mainstream in the United States. It is therefore possible to discern a certain defensiveness regarding the prominence that American films enjoyed in the UK and the difficulties that British filmmakers faced in getting their pictures exhibited in America. American censorship of British films during the war often centred on language, and, as in the case of *In Which We Serve* (1942), particularly on the issue of swearing.

In Which We Serve has been described as 'one of the most controversial British films in the history of the Production Code',[36] and arguments surrounding its American release focused on what was perceived as robust naval language: British writers felt such language could add realism and authenticity to the actions of servicemen, US censors believed it had the potential to corrupt.[37] Questions were asked in Parliament, and Minister of Information Brendan Bracken reported that 'these expressions are seamanlike and appropriate' before criticising the 'squeamishness and old-maiden-aunt-like apprehensions of the Hollywood censors'. Sensing that national pride was at stake, Sir Archibald Southby demanded that Bracken ensure 'a film which has pleased the British people is shown to the American people just as it is'.[38] Bracken refused to intervene, and failed to mention that the film had already been amended by British censors, a fact that many who criticised the American censors conveniently forgot either to ascertain or discuss.[39]

For all the hot air (and publicity) generated by this spat, *In Which We Serve* eventually succumbed to American censorship. But what this episode demonstrates is not only the pride that some critics were beginning to take in British films, but also the concern that was felt in some quarters about the way in which American culture was perceived to be dominating that of Britain. In

1945, *Picturegoer* published a letter from a correspondent who insisted: 'We want *British* films. Why should America decide what *Britons* are to see, or Americans infiltrate Hollywood into *British* films?'[40]

What we see in *The Way to the Stars*, and perhaps one of the reasons why it was voted the best film of the war years by readers of the *Daily Mail*,[41] is American culture being subsumed into British culture, with the appealing aspects of Britishness seducing and humbling American characters. The film tells the story of Halfpenny Field airbase and its personnel, first RAF, then the United States Army Air Force (USAAF), and the civilians who interact with them. Although three significant characters are killed in action, their deaths occur away from the camera, suggesting that *The Way to the Stars* is more interested in the social, cultural and emotional changes brought about by the war than the war itself.

The film is notable for its attitudes towards its American characters, for although it presents them positively, it has them adopt British habits and characteristics in order to reaffirm the legitimacy, superiority even, of British culture. The film shows that while there is much to admire in American culture and martial prowess, British cinema-goers should not be blind to the value of their own heritage and ways of doing things. In *The Way to the Stars*, some of the most notable sites of cultural resistance concern food. The British take pride in preserving (and sharing) their own gastronomic rituals, but this exchange is almost entirely one way, for the Americans adopt British eating habits while the British remain dismissive of American ones.

The initial American arrival at the airbase is presented as a form of invasion. Forced to vacate his room, Station Commander 'Tiny' Williams (Basil Radford) claims that 'The Yanks have taken over "E" Block', and watches as the RAF roundel is lowered and replaced with the Stars and Stripes in a ceremony which foreshadows the independence that would be granted to British colonies and imperial holdings in the decades following the war. Indeed, the USAAF effectively rename the airbase, pronouncing it as Halfpenny, rather than Ha'penny as the RAF do. Given the symbolic synonymy of land and soil with heritage and tradition (witness the romanticised pastoral imagery in, for example, *This England*, 1941, or *A Canterbury Tale*) this is a significant, almost hostile, act. Further, Williams and Flight Controller Peter Penrose (John Mills) watch as a game of baseball is played on the airfield's grassy expanses. The pair's incomprehension at the Americans' interest in the sport is reminiscent of a scene in *The Lady Vanishes* when Brits abroad Charters (Radford, again) and Caldicott (Naunton Wayne) discuss a baseball report in an American newspaper: 'We used to call it rounders. Children play it with a rubber ball and a stick. Not a word about cricket. The Americans have got no sense of proportion.' Williams's description of a successful hit in the baseball game as 'a bit of a cow shot' is a reference to an unorthodox and inelegant cricket stroke, and acts as a wistful lament for the trampling of the old culture under the stampeding, home-running feet of the new.

Standing in a crowd of cheering American baseball fans, the bewildered British officers resist and regroup by means of a caffeinated catechism: 'Tea?' 'Tea.' However, the pair soon discover that American influence is not limited to the sports field. They join 'Tinker' Bell (Hugh Dempster) in the mess, where he has just finished lecturing the newly-arrived American staff on tea etiquette: 'Not hot [milk], cold! Hot in coffee, cold in tea.' Bell, having been joined by his countrymen, launches into an incredulous tirade against the Americans, believing that their failure to understand the tea ritual marks them as uncivilised. 'They don't warm the pot, you know,' he rails, before proudly letting his companions know that tea only remains available because of his own good offices. For all the comic bluster demonstrated by the stereotypically British characters, the scene concludes with a withering dissection of American braggadocio. As the quiet, experienced British airmen drink their tea, they praise the keenness demonstrated by the American aircrews while gently mocking them as arrogant and as yet untested. Bell tells his colleagues that the Americans claim they can 'drop a bomb into a barrel from 30,000 feet', concluding his story with a click of his fingers and an Americanism, 'Zonk!', learned from a USAAF bombardier. Williams chooses this moment to drop a sugar cube into his cup of tea, an action that wordlessly demonstrates his contempt for American boastfulness.

Tensions between American personnel and their British counterparts continue off base, in the local town of Shepley. A resident at the Golden Lion Hotel orders whisky only to find that the hotel has been emptied of Scotch by thirsty, wealthy Americans: 'What a war!' is his anguished response. That same evening, USAAF bombardier Joseph Frizelli (Bonar Colleano, Jr) makes a scene in a restaurant, protesting about both British service and coffee, a drink, when considered alongside his willingness to complain, that neatly demonstrates his otherness. Johnny Hollis (Douglass Montgomery), Frizelli's commanding officer, is clearly embarrassed and, displaying a nascent Britishness that will become increasingly evident as the film progresses, reprimands his bombardier and advises him that talking in whispers in restaurants is a custom in Britain. Indeed, the disrespectful Americans are sent home to bed by Penrose, ostensibly because their first mission is scheduled for the next day, but partly, it could be suggested, as punishment for their boorish behaviour.

It is not until after the Americans return from this initial raid that relations between the two groups of airmen become more cordial. Having now become active participants in a war that the British have been fighting for almost three years, the Americans can finally understand and appreciate something of their hosts' mentality and culture, and join several RAF airmen in the public bar of the Golden Lion. Frizelli, the most outspoken of the USAAF airmen, apologises to Penrose for his previously dismissive attitude, while another concedes that the Americans had failed to heed British warnings about the dangers and difficulties of aerial conflict. Apologies accepted, first Penrose and then Williams insist on buying drinks for the Americans. That the British airmen are the senior partners in this alliance is confirmed by Penrose's insistence on buying 'pints of dark' for the Americans, rejecting as 'a bit ladylike' the half-pints of light ale that they had ordered for themselves.

Having shown the Americans and the British as being engaged in the same struggle, *The Way to the Stars* uses drinking and singing to demonstrate the warm, mutually respectful nature of the alliance. Representative of the Americans' new Britishness is Hollis's death at the end of the film. Rather than risk

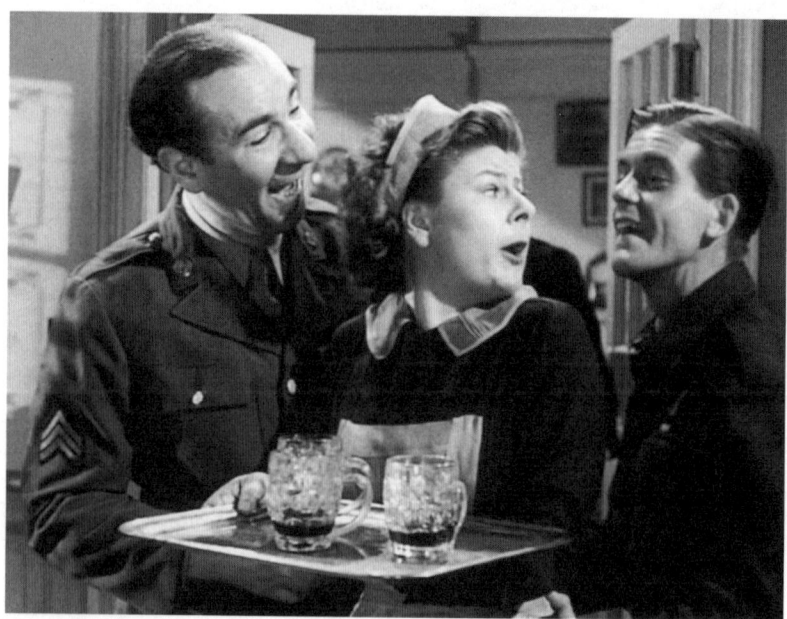

22   'You Americans, and you RAF, there's nothing to choose between you!'
Cementing friendship in the Golden Lion in *The Way to the Stars* (1945).

injuring the inhabitants of Shepley by baling out of his still bomb-laden plane, Hollis attempts to land even though he knows that this action will probably result in his own death. Hollis's sacrifice, clearly linked to those earlier in the film of Britons Carter (Trevor Howard) and Archdale (Michael Redgrave), is shown as having been made for Britain by a man who has come to understand and love the country, whose attitudes he has adopted as his own. Soon after Hollis's death, the film returns to the Golden Lion to witness a repeat of the drunken bonding of the two sets of airmen. Having been pestered by men from both air forces, Elsie (Vida Hope), the barmaid, claims with some justi-fication that 'You Americans, and you RAF, there's nothing to choose between you!' That she is holding a tray of empty beer glasses, evidence of the airmen's communal drinking, serves to emphasise the importance of consumption in the strengthening of the alliance (see figure 22). That this beer was drunk in the very British setting of the pub confirms an American commitment to British culture, and suggests that the film's American characters have become willing participants in it.

The film, produced during the last months of the European war and not released until after VE Day, can also be understood as using the experiences of the immediate past to prepare British viewers for the future. For while the USAAF airmen are shown to make a common cause with the British, and to fight and die for this cause, the film is keen to show that Britain need not prostrate itself before the increasingly confident American colossus. British culture, which was often shown in *The Way to Stars* in terms of gastronomy, was still viable and vibrant, and could be used as a touchstone for Britain as it looked to negotiate a position for itself in the post-war world.

'At once a beverage and a poem': *The Demi-Paradise* and Britain's alliance with the Soviet Union

On 29 June 1941, following the German invasion of the Soviet Union, Lieutenant-General Henry Pownall, Vice Chief of the Imperial General Staff, wrote of the USSR:

> I avoid using the expression 'Allies' for the Russians are a dirty lot of murdering thieves … *and* double crossers of the deepest dye. It is good to see the two biggest murderers in Europe, Hitler and Stalin, going for each other. I only hope that Stalin will make a deep gash in Hitler's throat.[42]

Pownall's private thoughts demonstrate the problematic nature of Britain's wartime alliance with the USSR, for although hostility to Soviet communism was (temporarily) outweighed by hostility to German fascism, residual concerns about forging an alliance with an ideologically suspect nation remained. For the duration of the war, Britain and the USSR would be uneasy bedfellows; allies but not friends, as the *Manchester Guardian*'s foreign correspondent had previously observed.[43]

Yet in December 1943 a feature film was released which presented the alliance, in reality a marriage of convenience, as a true romance. The fact that *The Demi-Paradise* was the only feature film that attempted to do so hints at the problems that the alliance with the USSR caused British filmmakers, not least of which was the sensitivity of the Soviet mission in London to the way their country and its inhabitants were portrayed. Indeed, concerns that the Soviet ambassador was planning an official protest against *The Demi-Paradise* led to the excision of a sequence in which the Russian protagonist gets drunk.[44]

The delicacy of the situation led the MoI to establish a policy of exhibiting Russian films to educate the British about Stalin, communism and the Eastern Front, believing that such films would 'announce themselves as Soviet propaganda'.[45] Claiming that 'the more Russian stuff that gets on our screens the better',[46] such films were welcomed by *Documentary News Letter*:

> If we are to fight and work together for a common good, it is essential for the peoples of every land to know and appreciate one another's way of life. [Soviet films released in Britain] are opening up the eyes of this country to the Russian way of life and the Russian war effort.[47]

It seems probable that *Documentary News Letter* would have found little to praise in *The Demi-Paradise*, a light comedy which, aside from a brief prologue and postscript at a snowy Soviet port, is set entirely in Britain.

In the film, Soviet engineer Ivan Kouznetsoff (Laurence Olivier) travels twice to Britain to oversee the manufacture at a British factory of a new ice-breaking propeller, the radical design of which is the one revolutionary idea that Ivan brings with him from the USSR. When he first arrives in 1939, Ivan is isolated and ridiculed, and leaves for Russia having been informed that his propeller design is fundamentally flawed. On his return in mid-1941, he discovers that the British are much changed, energised by the war and, following the German invasion of the USSR, happy to befriend the lone Russian in their midst. Welcomed into the British fold, Ivan finds the inspiration he needs to redesign his propeller in a cup of tea – a drink described by his British mentor, Mr Runalow (Felix Aylmer), as being 'at once a beverage and a poem'.

Olivier claimed that the purpose of *The Demi-Paradise* was to 'win the British public over to the idea of loving the Russians', but the film is less a tribute to Russia than a paean to Britain.[48] This is evident in a speech Ivan makes to his allies shortly before his second departure:

> When I came to your country I was filled with misconceptions and prejudices. But now that I have got to know you, I know that you are a grand, a great people. No, don't blush now, don't look embarrassed.

Although delivered to the workers who had built the propeller, Ivan's words seem primarily intended for British cinema audiences. Indeed, a contemporary review recognised that the objective of *The Demi-Paradise* was 'to show us ourselves through Russian eyes and … [show] us that on the whole we're very nice'.[49] The concentration on British themes and the British experience led the *Observer* to describe the film as 'a private, inexportable joke'.[50] The relationship between Britain and the USSR is legitimised, and made viable, by Ivan's discovery of the innate Britishness which the film suggests is present within all decent people, simultaneously demonstrating that the British could maintain their own identity while entering into an alliance with a geographically, politically and culturally foreign nation.

By working to negate the appeal of alien political and cultural systems, *The Demi-Paradise* adopts a similar strategy to *This Happy Breed*. In the latter film, the General Strike of 1926 is shown to be an intrusion into the Gibbonses' secure home environment. Just as the beginning of the strike is announced by a shot of a newspaper headline, so is its conclusion signalled in a similar manner. A crudely printed paper is shown in close-up on a kitchen table, with the shot maintained just long enough for the viewer to read the headline – 'Strike Over' – before it is covered by a teapot (see figures 23 and 24). The teapot obscures not so much the news of the strike's cessation as the memory of the strike itself, crushing attempted radical political and social change beneath a potent symbol of domestic stability and national identity. *This Happy Breed* thus uses tea to

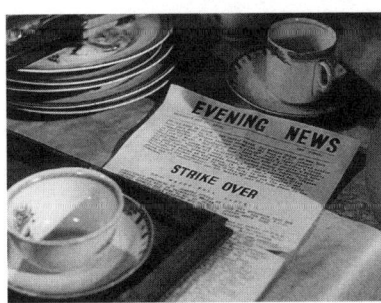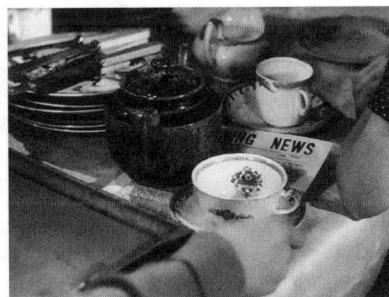

Reasserting Britishness in the face of the General Strike. *This Happy Breed*   **23–24**
(1944).

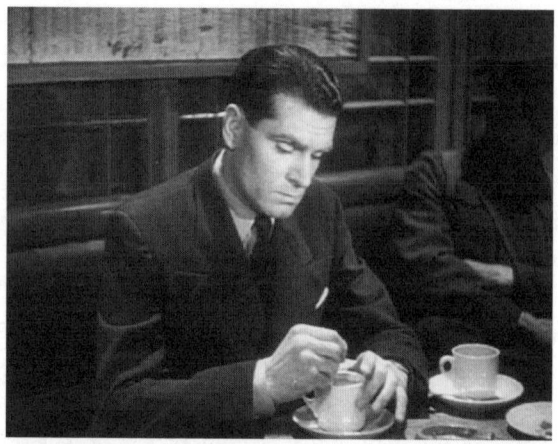

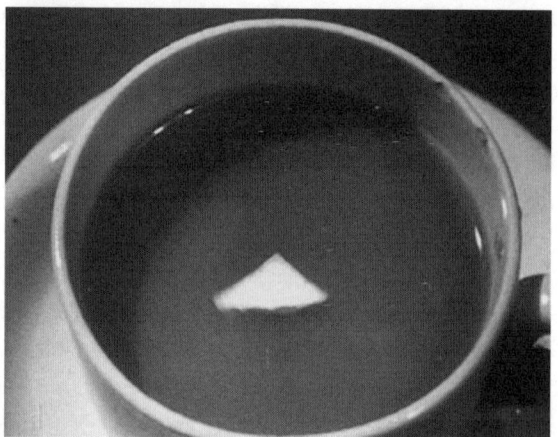

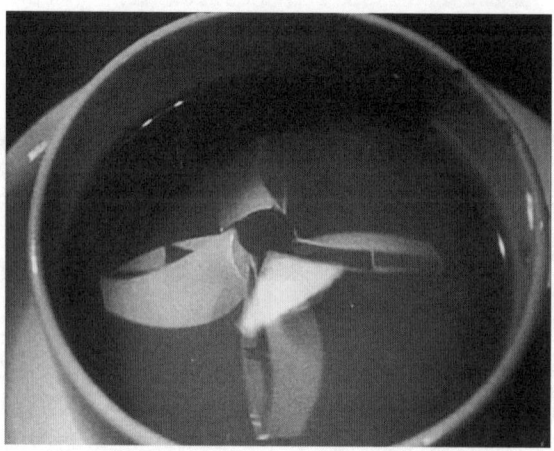

25–27   Tea and inspiration in *The Demi-Paradise* (1943).

defeat what the film presents as un-British political extremism, presenting the challenge of organised labour (with its very clear links to socialism and communism) as a best-forgotten moment in British history. The film also uses tea in its rejection of radical right-wing politics. Frank and Ethel Gibbons have their progress to the Lyon's Corner House at Marble Arch disrupted by a rally organised by the Fascist Party of Great Britain. The Gibbonses are disgusted by the speaker's diatribe, turn their backs on his proposed 'day of reckoning' and dismiss his ideas as nothing more than an abhorrent and unnecessary interruption in their quest for the comfort offered by a nice cup of tea.

By systematically showing radical foreign political systems and cultural ideas to be less attractive than their British equivalents, *The Demi-Paradise* demonstrates the powerful appeal of British customs and heritage to domicile and visitor alike. This appeal is not immediately evident to Ivan, however, and it is not until his second trip, when he revisits many of the experiences and locations of the first, that he comes to fully appreciate Britain and its inhabitants and is thus able to draw strength and inspiration from its traditions and culture.

The successful manufacture of the propeller, an object which will both literally and metaphorically break the ice between Britain and the Soviet Union, is found to be dependent upon Ivan's acceptance of British cuisine (see figures 25–7). Having seen several prototype propellers fail, Ivan sits alone in a tearoom and stares gloomily into a cup of tea, stirring it distractedly. There is a cut to a close-up of the cup, observed from the Russian engineer's point of view. Suddenly, the music changes, becoming more insistent and energetic: a fanfare pinpoints Ivan's moment of inspiration. Ivan drops a small piece of paper into the tea and his imagination super-imposes a propeller over the liquid as it circles in the cup. Ivan, like Mr Venus in Dickens's *Our Mutual Friend*, has been able to 'float his powerful mind in tea',[51] but finds that the national drink of Britain offers such buoyancy that it can support not only his intellect, but also the Russian merchant marine and Britain's alliance with the Soviet Union. The journey into Ivan's consciousness, begun a few moments earlier when a series of aural flashbacks cajole him into action, creates a bond between viewer and engineer, suggesting the similarity of his travails and their own. Further, the subjectivity communicated by the point-of-view shot of the cup insists that all who have ever observed such a sight could be similarly inspired; that Britain, symbolised here by a cup of tea, could provide its citizens with the passion, energy and inspiration needed to win the war.

The fact that Ivan finds the answer to his engineering problem in a cup of tea serves to underline the British origin of his inspiration, but also draws attention away from his Stakhanovite dedication to his work at the shipyard and its overtones of Soviet industry and economics. Runalow's shipyard is located in the ancient town of Barchester – a name redolent of Trollope's Wessex novels – where the senses are better catered for than the mind. Ivan is encouraged to *feel* Britain rather than analyse it, to succumb to its arcane traditions, to enjoy its humour, its food, and its tea.

The propeller-in-a-teacup incident is the most explicit example of how Ivan has been seduced into appreciating the manifold delights of Britain, but other scenes serve a similar function. Locations, events and products of which he was suspicious on his first trip are revisited more successfully during his second. Indeed, the tearoom scene that introduces his eventual triumph is made more meaningful by a similar scene at the end of his first stay in Britain. Ivan's initial failure to get his propeller manufactured is compounded by his unsuccessful courting of Runalow's granddaughter, Ann (Penelope Ward). As they take tea in a station waiting room, Ivan and Ann are listless and awkward, the Russian engineer's failure to overcome his otherness preventing him from reaching a rapprochement with his would-be partner.

Further, during the course of the film Ivan and Ann spend two evenings in London, visiting on both occasions the same locations and interacting with the same people: Leslie Henson, a comic pianist, performs exactly the same piece at a theatre, while service at a nightclub is provided by the same waiter. These obvious similarities make evident Ivan's changed nature: jokes which previously left him cold are now heartily enjoyed, while the beer drunk in the nightclub now makes Ivan's declaration of love for Ann loquacious rather than clumsy, and allows Ann to reciprocate rather than reject his feelings.

Two meals taken with Ann's family in Barchester show how Ivan, having jettisoned his ideological baggage, can now appreciate Britain's warm embrace. The first, more formal meal is unable to erase either the hostility that Ivan feels towards his hosts or their own concerns about him (witness, for instance, the delightful avian performance by Edie Martin as the elderly Aunt Winnie, who hands Ann a copy of *Crime and Punishment* and synopsis that 'it's all about a young Russian who splits open an old woman's skull with a hatchet'). Seated at the dining table, conversation revolves around geopolitical issues of empire and economics and noone looks as if they are enjoying themselves. Ivan's second visit to Barchester in 1941 is marked by a light meal eaten in the garden with Ann's family. Reconnected with the soil, the representatives of both nations seem more inclined to be cordial, drinking tea and discussing the ways in which the war has affected Britain. Aunt Winnie, still a little unsure as to the wisdom of being seated so close to a Russian, even permits Ivan to shake her hand. Although there is talk of rationing, mostly by the two evacuated children that Ann has taken in, the scene is notable for its tranquillity. As an aerial battle rages overhead, the family calmly carries on, unperturbed by the proximity of the war. The family's resolute cheerfulness is evidently contagious, for Ivan accepts their phlegmatic approach as a sign of determination, not effeteness. Ivan's tea room epiphany is in many ways a continuation of this lush repast, and the lessons that he learns about Britain in the bosom of Ann's family are applied to his own career, allowing for the successful conclusion of Ivan's second period in the United Kingdom.

Ivan's love of Britain, and thus the alliance which has brought him to Barchester, is shown to be predicated on the shunning of ideology and the embracing of those things – diet, leisure, nature, humour – which speak (although unconvincingly and myopically) of an apolitical, pre-industrial past. Tea is deemed a crucial aspect of this vision of Britain, the liquid embodiment of more mystical and complex themes.

'A funny sort of way to spell chocolate!': food and German difference

Just as food could be used to integrate foreign characters into British society, so too could it be used to demonstrate the differences between cultures, to communicate the otherness of Nazi Germany. In *The Day Will Dawn* (1942), for example, alcohol is used to distinguish between 'good' Norwegians and 'bad' Germans, with the drink and toast of each group operating in an easily recognisable schema of differentiation:

	Norwegian	**German**
Drink:	Aquavit	Schnapps
Toast:	*Skol!*	*Prost!*

A drunken brawl between German and Norwegian drinkers further reinforces the notion that gastronomic differences are significant indicators of cultural and political differences.

More pertinent to the current discussion, however, are films which use food to distinguish Briton from German. Based on a short story by Graham Greene,[52] *Went the Day Well?* sees Nazi paratroops, disguised as British soldiers, take control of Bramley End, a small rural village, in anticipation of a full-scale German invasion. Of the villagers, only Oliver Wilsford (Leslie Banks), who the viewer soon discovers to be a German agent, knows the soldiers' secret.

The soldiers imprison the residents, who eventually fight back and regain the village. A brief prologue makes clear the Germans' real identities, and although this robs *Went the Day Well?* of some of its suspense, this knowledge provides audiences with an omniscience which encourages them to acknowledge that appearances can be deceptive.

This is especially true with regard to food. The exaggerated way in which the Germans embrace British foodstuffs and culinary rituals, and the enthusiasm they demonstrate in their desire to embody British gastronomic stereotypes, is intentionally and sardonically placed in the spotlight. For while the villagers remain unaware of the danger they face, lulled into a false sense of security by the soldiers' ersatz Britishness, the viewer, knowing the true identity of the Germans, is allowed to read these scenes of consumption very differently.

When the soldiers first arrive, their commander, Major Hammond (Basil Sydney), a. k. a. Commandant Ortler, takes afternoon tea with the ancient vicar of Bramley End's ancient church. The ease with which Hammond participates in this British ritual acts as a warning about the often illusory nature of identity and, as it immediately precedes Wilsford's introduction, makes viewers acknowledge the feasibility of Wilsford's own more lengthy masquerade. Later, eating at the manor house with the self-appointed village elite, Hammond and Wilsford discuss 'the Hun' with such overblown theatricality that their shameless representation of the phlegmatic Briton is undeniably enjoyable. This frisson of voyeuristic pleasure arises from the viewer's knowledge that they are being let in on a private joke at the expense of the other members of this self-satisfied clique. Further, when Wilsford and Hammond take coffee after dinner they sip from their cups as 'There'll Always be an England' is heard on the radio. The slight hesitation evident as the pair acknowledge the obvious irony of the situation is subtly reinforced by their choice of drink.

So aware is Wilsford of the importance of keeping up gastronomic appearances that he encourages Hammond to send some of his troops to the local pub as a way of demonstrating their Britishness.[53] Three soldiers successfully order a round of light ale and bitter, and are joined by Mrs Collins (Muriel George), who proposes a toast: 'Your very good health. And down with Hitler!' Unseen by the villagers, but unmissable to anyone watching the film, the toast causes the three Nazis to exchange nervous glances, their evident distaste ignored by the oblivious Mrs Collins and therefore entertaining for the viewer.

Given the significance that the early scenes of the film place on food, it is fitting that gastronomic difference provides the clue which finally informs the village of the soldiers' true identities. Evacuee George Truscott (Harry Fowler),

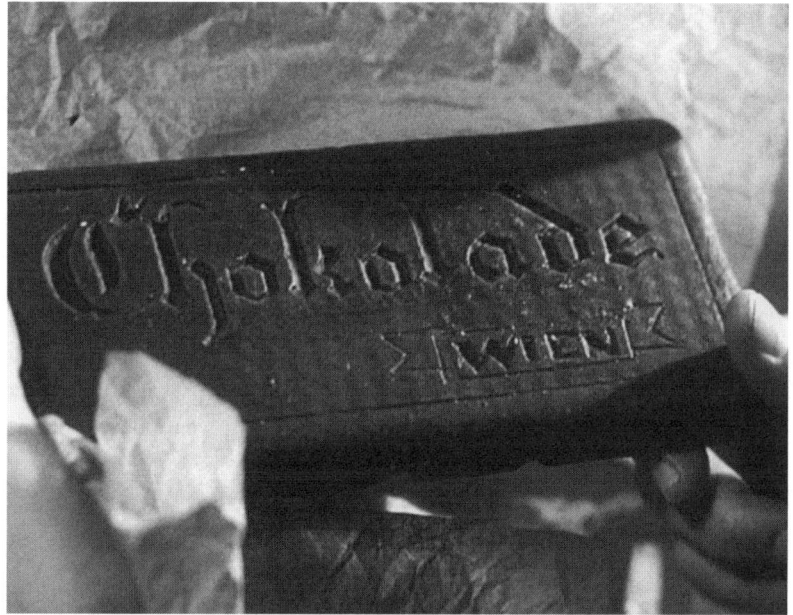

'A funny sort of way to spell chocolate.' *Went the Day Well?* (1942).   **28**

rooting around in Hammond's belongings, discovers a bar of confectionery and notes of the words imprinted on it, 'That's a funny sort of way to spell chocolate.' Nora Ashton (Valerie Taylor), distractedly tidying Hammond's room, replies, '"Chokolade" is the German for chocolate' before adding 'and "Wien" is the German for Vienna' (see figure 28). Nora, whose previous suspicions about the soldiers were dismissed, realises the implications of the spelling as a slow zoom concludes with a close-up of her horrified face. The filmmakers opt for silence during the zoom, and even George's stream-of-consciousness monologue pauses for long enough for the full meaning of Nora's discovery to be driven home.

When confronted with evidence of his Germanness, Hammond's imitative Britishness ceases immediately: 'Ach so!' he mutters as he angrily slams the chocolate down on a table, before delivering the remainder of his lines, in English, with a not entirely convincing German accent. The other German soldiers revert to type almost as quickly, shedding what the film suggests are the synonymous pretences of decency and Britishness.[54] Following this transformation, the Germans' consumption habits are similarly modified. No longer obliged to mimic their hosts, they gorge themselves animalistically on any food they are offered and revert to what the film proposes to be their native gastronomic habits, further demonstrating their dissimilarity to the villagers. One soldier demands coffee, only to be informed by a villager he is holding hostage that Mrs Collins, whose house he is in and whom he has killed, only has tea; her ability to defy the soldier from beyond the grave epitomising her resistance and her bloody-mindedness.

What's more, the gluttony demonstrated by the recently unmasked Germans deflects attention away from the awkward fact that these examples of Nazi vice carry around blocks of chocolate large enough to arouse longing in British viewers still smarting from the introduction of sweets rationing in July 1942. Rather than falling upon it themselves (and their restraint might be justified by the film being set *before* confectionery was rationed), George and Nora use the chocolate to liberate Bramley End. True Brits, it seems, demonstrated their commitment to their food-based community by observing restraint and controlling their selfish impulses, seeing the fight against Germany, which could only be joined once the chocolate becomes evidence rather than just food, as more important than their own base desires.

Once the soldiers' deceit has been revealed, the villagers express dismay at the fact that they have shared food with the enemy. Wilsford, yet to be revealed as Bramley End's resident spy and still acting as Britishness personi-fied, expresses distaste at the thought of eating with Germans: 'I should hate to think that we were sharing our dinner last night with a couple of Nazis.' Similarly, land-girl Ivy (Thora Hird) speaks for the entire community when she castigates the invaders for 'guzzling our rations'. But the hostility directed at the Germans arises from more than just anger at being duped into succouring the enemy or unknowingly wasting precious, edible munitions of war on enemy troops. By feeding them and by welcoming them into their homes, the villagers had formed a bond of companionship with the soldiers, and the resentfulness that emerges in the wake of this revelation arises from an abuse of trust and a violation of property and propriety. Food is so important a factor in both life and identity that mis-feeding can undermine an individual's (or, in the case of Bramley End, a community's) sense of self.

Food is also a communal and national signifier in *Two Thousand Women*, a film which tells the story of the British women interned at the Grand Hotel, Marneville. Setting aside their class and regional differences, the prisoners create what one of them describes as 'a British colony' in the heart of German-occupied France. When three RAF crewmen inadvertently bail out into the camp's grounds, the women have to hide them not only from the guards but also from a German agent in their midst.

The revelation of the agent's identity comes as little shock to viewers, for they have been given multiple hints as to her otherness. Teresa King (Betty Jardine), real name Teresa Resinger, dresses like a *Bund Deutscher Mädel* PE instructor, complete with regulation armband, and shuns the British concerns of the other interns. This is most notable in her rejection of tea, a drink of which she complains, 'There's more time wasted here drinking it, making it and talking about it than on anything else.' Further, she happily admits that she will be 'very glad when there's no more tea left', a blasphemous statement given the other women's obsession with the drink.

The film's other outsider is Bridie Johnson (Jean Kent), an internee who uses her sexuality to obtain supplies from the German guards. Bridie willingly positions herself outside the mainstream of the British community, procuring tea from her German 'boyfriend' but refusing to share this bounty with the rest of the imprisoned women. Such selfishness anticipates her eventual betrayal of the RAF airmen, one of whom has rejected her advances.

Teresa's claim about the interns' single-minded tea obsession is amended by Maud Wright (Renee Houston), who states that men are equally sought after. The linking of tea and sex suggests the importance of both to the propagation of the British nation and way of life, and while Teresa displaces her sexual energy into near-continual exercise classes, the British women seem more inclined to find satisfaction in continual cups of tea, thinking of home, meanwhile.

Tea is clearly marked as a symbol of Britain, and Teresa's hostility towards it establishes her difference. Newly arrived prisoners, some of whom have been confined for months, are welcomed into the fold with the offer of a cup. Meeting Freda Thompson (Phyllis Calvert) and Rosemary Brown (Patricia Roc) for the first time, Mrs Eleanor Hadfield (Kathleen Boutall) offers them tea – 'You must be dying for a cup' – and confesses that she can only afford to be so generous because she has recently traded 'a pair of corsets for a quarter of a pound'. This exchange neatly summarises the priorities of the women: in the confined space of the prison camp psychological comfort is considered more important than physical appearance.

There is, though, a degree of poignancy arising from the women's inability to live up to the grandeur of their surroundings; divorced from the 200-franc per night luxuries of the pre-war world, the women have to barter underwear for simple foodstuffs. For the British prisoners, tea is at once a placebo and opiate, a drink which allows them to indulge in illusions of stability and normality while simultaneously facilitating their fantastical mental journey beyond the camp's barbed wire fences to rejoin the unconfined spaces and unrestricted freedoms of the British national community.

Although there are some complaints about its quality – there's no milk, no sugar and it's not strong enough – the ritualistic taking of tea establishes the women as a bona fide community. Teresa, who is present yet does not participate, is excluded from this recreation of Britain, her outsider status communicated both through her defensive body language (crossed arms, her back turned to the other women) and her dismissive attitude: 'Tea! That's all they ever think about in this place.' The tea is drunk as the newly arrived prisoners bathe, and we might regard this scene as the women's reassertion and celebration of their Britishness: their ritual cleansing is accompanied by the ceremonial taking of tea. Their camaraderie thus demonstrated, the women are established as a community linked by nationality and diet.

'A grand gesture to throw in the face of Hitler'

While it should not be claimed that tea, or any food for that matter, can single-handedly define or determine Britishness, it is possible to assert that in many instances tea was, and indeed still is, used as a signifier of the British national community. Tea's imperial origin reminded consumers of their nation's global reach, while the communal nature of the tea ceremony, in which the drink was prepared and consumed alongside family members, colleagues or compatriots, helped Britons realise their shared cultural heritage and co-dependency. As a product strongly associated with the national experience, tea also helped the British to understand their position on the international stage, delineating the boundaries of the food-based community and, on occasion, incorporating other nationalities into the British fold by redefining them according to British social norms.

Thus the 'Honourable Company of Tea Drinkers' constructed by British filmmakers was at once exclusive and inclusive. Based upon the shared, mundane ritual of, as Swift wrote, 'water bewitched',[55] this group was defiantly and determinedly British, who also welcomed those prepared to allow the spirit of Britain to infuse them. And just as a few leaves could transform water into tea, so 'the cup that cheers' could transform foreigners into (temporary) Britons, or at least provide them with a surer understanding of the British character.

It was not only Britons who understood the powerful symbolism that tea enjoyed in relation to the British experience. German propagandists evidently believed that they could use tea to undermine British morale by forcing consumers to acknowledge their nation's international isolation and domestic stratification. On 4 October 1939, a month after the start of the war, the German radio station Zeesen informed British listeners that:

> The high priests and priestesses of the cult of five o'clock tea in Britain are clamouring for an early peace. Their tea supplies from Java and China are running short. These high-class victims have been compelled to fall back on the coarser brand from India. The British people are slowly being convinced that Mr. Chamberlain's war is something worse than a temporary inconvenience. It is a damn nuisance.

The next day, the *Daily Express* responded with a slightly defensive article, the strained politeness of which is telling:

> Sorry, Zeesen, but you've got it wrong. FOUR o'clock, not five, is tea-time. And few of us in England drink China tea. And for those of us who do there are still tons and tons of Chinese tea here.[56]

Interesting here is the extent to which tea's central role in the British diet is taken as read by Briton and German alike, a fact which both recognises and reinforces a particular gastronomic stereotype for political and ideological ends. Further, with its pedantic reference to timekeeping, its acceptance that tea drinking in Britain is a diverse practice which aids in the creation of a coherent national whole and its insistence that the British alone fully understand their relationship with tea, the *Express* attempts to define the drink's position within national life.

When, less than a year later, these 'tons and tons' of tea were exhausted and rationing was finally introduced, the MoF attempted to put a positive spin on what S. P. B. Mais called 'this tea business': 'It's only a reduction by a quarter of what we used to drink and it's a grand gesture to throw in the face of Hitler. What? The Englishman prepared to go short in *tea*? He must be on his toes.'[57]

Of course, the mobilisation of gastronomic stereotypes also allowed British films, especially comedies, to mock foreign customs and discuss the impact that Nazi rule was having on the German diet: celebration of the British food-based community was matched by a denigration of the German. In *The Goose Steps Out* (1942), inept British spy William Potts (Will Hay) travels to Germany. Once there, he discusses the food situation with the bibulous local academic Professor Hoffman (Frank Pettingell):

> Hoffman: I'm afraid you'll find that things have changed greatly in Germany. Only four ration tickets a month for alcohol…
> Potts: You mean you've got to have ration tickets for drinks now?
> Hoffman: Just one small glass of lager a week.

Despite such a restriction being placed on the consumption of this typically German drink, Potts and Hoffman beg, borrow and steal enough tickets to get outrageously – and therefore illegally – drunk. While the discussion of beer rationing is clearly intended to show the severity of the impact of the war on Germany and therefore remind British consumers that they were lucky not to be subject to such laws – and the day after tea rationing was announced the *Express* noted that consumers 'get much less in Germany' – the ease with which the pair circumvent Nazi restrictions serves other purposes.[58] For not only does Potts's drunkenness afford the film the opportunity for an extended comic routine, it also suggests that the German population's acceptance of food control was strictly limited. Given the restrictions associated with the MoF's own control of British eating and drinking practices, such a tactic might have raised a few eyebrows, especially as Potts and Hoffman take great pleasure in their excess. However, what seems more important is the way in which this film, like many others, used food to establish and define the British as a distinct and special group, and thus encouraged cinema-goers to understand the privileged nature of their own food-based community and its position alongside, and its relationship with, the cuisines, cultures and politics of other nations.

Notes

1 Ian Cook and Philip Crang, 'The world on a plate: culinary culture, displacement and geographical knowledge', in David B. Clark, Marcus A. Doel and Kate M. L. Housiaux (eds), *The Consumption Reader* (London: Routledge, 2003), p. 115.

2 Lin Yutang quoted in Gary Alan Fine, *Kitchen: The Culture of Restaurant Work* (Berkeley: University of California Press, 1996), p. 1.

3 Claude Fischler, 'Food, self and identity', *Social Science Information*, 27:2 (1988), p. 276.

4 Warren Belasco, 'Food matters: perspectives on an emerging field', in Warren Belasco and Philip Scranton (eds), *Food Nations: Selling Taste in Consumer Societies* (New York and London: Routledge, 2002), p. 2.

5 This tendency had become clichéd enough by the start of the 1960s to be satirised in the *Beyond the Fringe* sketch, 'The Aftermyth of War'. See Ronald Bergen, *Beyond the Fringe … and Beyond* (London: Virgin Books, 1989), pp. 10–11.

6 *The Times*, 3 October 1952, p. 7.

7 Lord Woolton, 'Introduction', in The Tea Centre, *Tea on Service* (London: Graham Watson, 1947), pp. 75–6.

8 Quoted in *The Times*, 17 October 1940, p. 2.

9 A Home Intelligence Report produced on 12 July 1940 suggested that the introduction of tea rationing had affected people's ability to take tea after an air raid. Paul Addison and Jeremy A. Crang (eds), *Listening to Britain: Home Intelligence Reports on Britain's Finest Hour, May to September 1940* (London: Bodley Head, 2010), p. 222.

10 Memo from Lindemann to Churchill. Martin Gilbert (ed.), *The Churchill War Papers: Vol. 2 – Never Surrender, May 1940–December 1940* (London: Heinemann, 1994), p. 537, n. 1.

11 *Daily Express*, 9 July 1940, p. 1; Gallup opinion poll, October 1940. *The Gallup International Public Opinion Poll: Great Britain 1937–1975: Vol. 1 – 1937–1964* (New York: Random House, 1976), p. 36.

12 Frank Edwards, diary entry, 9 July 1940, in Sandra Koa Wing (ed.), *Our Longest Days: A People's History of the Second World War* (London: Profile, 2008), pp. 37–8.

13 The National Archives (TNA) MAF 102/2: *Kitchen Front*, 9 July 1940.

14 *Daily Mirror*, 9 July 1940, p. 3.

15 See Food Facts No. 1, week of 29 July 1940.

16 *Manchester Guardian*, 10 July 1940, p. 8; *Daily Express*, 10 July 1940, p. 2.

17 Pam Ashford, diary entry, 16 November 1940, in Simon Garfield (ed.), *Private Battles: How the War Almost Defeated Us* (London: Ebury Press, 2006), p. 20; Food Facts No. 15, week of 4 November 1940.

18 Jeffrey Richards advances a similar argument in *Films and British National Identity from Dickens to* Dad's Army (Manchester: Manchester University Press, 1997), p. 86.

19 Cook and Crang, 'The world on a plate', p. 113.

20 *Evening Standard*, 12 January 1946, p. 6.

21 *Today's Cinema*, 10 December 1943, p. 23.

22 *Observer*, 9 January 1944, p. 2.

23 *Today's Cinema*, 10 December 1943, p. 23.

24 Charles Barr, *Ealing Studios* (London: University of California Press, 3rd edn, 1998), p. 36.

25 BFI Script Collection: S15094, 'Amended Final Shooting Script' for *San Demetrio, London*, 20 January 1943.

26 *Manchester Guardian*, 7 January 1944, p. 6.

27 *Kinematograph Weekly*, 16 December 1943, p. 18.

28 As many as three million Americans were stationed in Britain during the war. Keith Robbins, *Great Britain: Identities, Institutions and the Idea of Britishness* (London: Longman, 1998), p. 311.

29 *Saturday Evening Post*, 3 June 1944, pp. 14–15, 57–9.

30 *Tribune*, 7 January 1944, p. 10.

31 'There is one question which beats [Meredith]. The difference between mild and bitter. Well, here is one answer. In the country pub he leaves an atmosphere of mild friendliness behind him. The locals like him because he has approached them with tact and courtesy. But the other US private, bumptious, back-slapping, called up to give an exhibition of how not to behave in an English pub, rouses only bitter hostility.' Winifred Holmes, 'Mild or bitter?', *Sight and Sound*, 12:48 (1944), p. 82.

32 Tom Ryall, *Anthony Asquith* (Manchester: University of Manchester Press, 2005), p. 14.

33 BFI Special Collections: *British Board of Film Censors Scenario Notes, 1944–1945*, File 106, 16 February 1945: *Rendezvous. Rendezvous* was the working title of the film.

34 Robbins, *Great Britain*, p. 216.

35 *Daily Express*, 18 March 1927, p. 6.

36 Anthony Slide, *'Banned in the USA': British Films in the United States and Their Censorship, 1933–1960* (London: I. B. Tauris, 1998), p. 82.

37 *The Times*, 10 December 1942, p. 3. *The Times* adopted a dismissive tone towards the American censors: 'words uttered in the heat of naval action ... gave no offence in this country'. *The Times*, 9 December 1942, p. 6.

38 9 December 1942. *Parliamentary Debates: House of Commons*, 5th Series, vol. 385, cols. 1552–3. Not all who participated in the debate took it seriously. One MP provoked laughter by asking Bracken to list the offensive words.

39 On the British censorship of *In Which We Serve*, see Tom Dewe Mathews, *Censored. What They Didn't Allow You To See and Why: The Story of Film Censorship in Britain* (London: Chatto & Windus, 1994), p. 111.

40 Letter from O. J. Wilkins, Portsmouth. *Picturegoer*, 29 September 1945, p. 14.

41 *Daily Mail*, 24 April 1946, pp. 1, 2.

42 Diary entry, in Brian Bond (ed.), *Chief of Staff: The Diaries of Sir Henry Pownall: Vol. 2 – 1940–1944* (London: Leo Cooper, 1974), p. 29.

43 Frederick Voigt in a letter to his editor, 21 March 1939. Quoted in P. M. H. Bell, *John Bull and the Bear: British Public Opinion, Foreign Policy and the Soviet Union, 1941–1945* (London: Edward Arnold, 1990), p. 30.

44 *Daily Express*: 19 April 1943, p. 3; 20 November 1943, p. 2.

45 Frances Thorpe and Nicholas Pronay, *British Official Films in the Second World War: A Descriptive Catalogue* (Oxford: Clio Press, 1980), pp. 42–3.

46 *Documentary News Letter*, 2:9, September 1941, p. 168.

47 *Documentary News Letter*, 3:2, February 1942, p. 19.

48 Laurence Olivier, *Confessions of an Actor* (London: Weidenfeld & Nicolson, 1982), p. 97.

49 *Picture Show*, 15 January 1944, p. 12.

50 *Observer*, 21 November 1943, p. 2.

51 Charles Dickens, *Our Mutual Friend* (London: Penguin, 1997), p. 300.

52 'The Lieutenant Died Last' was originally published in *Collier's Magazine*, 29 June 1940. Republished in Graham Greene, *The Last Word and Other Stories* (London: Reinhardt Books, 1990).

53 Ironically, given the nationwide warning for an invasion, the pub is called the Ring of Bells. In Greene's story, the pub was called the Black Boar.

54 For more on this transformative process, see S. P. MacKenzie, 'Nazis into Germans: Went the Day Well? (1942) and The Eagle Has Landed (1976)', *Journal of Popular Film and Television*, 31:2 (2003).

55 Quoted in *Manchester Guardian*, 25 June 1940, p. 4.

56 Broadcast transcript and response both in *Daily Express*, 5 October 1939, p. 7. English-language broadcasts by German radio stations made multiple mentions of the food and rationing situation in Britain.

57 TNA MAF 102/2: *Kitchen Front*, 9 July 1940. Emphasis in original.

58 *Daily Express*, 9 July 1940, p. 1.

Conclusion

Four years after the end of the Second World War, Britain experienced an acute constitutional crisis. Clement Attlee and Winston Churchill temporarily set aside their political differences in an attempt to resolve the situation. Eyeing with suspicion a country nestled behind a 'self-imposed iron curtain', the British government was forced to come to an accommodation with one of Europe's oldest, and by now smallest, nations. Following a bomb blast in central London, Burgundy forced its way onto Britain's political agenda. Such is the plot of *Passport to Pimlico* (1949), an Ealing comedy that details what happens after the residents of Miramont Place, London, find an ancient yet still legally binding charter which establishes their street as an independent nation – Burgundy – within Britain's borders. This 'newest brother of the world's democracies' is within sight of the Houses of Parliament, and much of the film is spent exploring Burgundian living conditions in order to debate Britain's own post-war experience.

In 1945, Michael Balcon, the film's producer, had expressed a desire to explore and project British national identity for the benefit of both British and international cinema audiences, and hoped that his films would mirror 'the post-war aspirations not of governments or parties, but of individuals'.[1] And what these individuals were interested in, if *Passport to Pimlico* is to be believed, was the nature of the relationship between the citizen and the state, and, in particular, how this relationship played out in terms of consumption.

Food's explicit association with a particular set of wartime experiences had led British consumers to equate the coming of peace with the return of those goods, services and activities that they had been asked, and forced, to do without during the conflict. Rationing was understood parenthetically; the consensual and unified vision of Britain that food control helped to communicate was but a temporary construct. This was recognised by Mass-Observation diarist Pam Ashford:

> During the day in the office conversation turned on what we will do after the war. We heard about gorging ices, chocolates and cakes, about orgies of spending on clothes, about dancing till the small hours. All the wishes were of a pleasurable nature; all presumed victorious conclusion; all presumed a reversion to pre-war conditions.[2]

This diary entry, penned during the autumn of 1941, yearns for the return of *ante bellum* norms that had been transformed into wartime luxuries: food, clothes, leisure. Striking, though, is the lack of bitterness about the loss of these things in wartime. They are missed – and they are certainly longed for – but their absence is registered as a short-term sacrifice made as part of the war effort.

The anticipated return of specific luxuries, and the resumption of consumer culture more generally, was therefore important for two reasons. First, the enjoyment that could be taken from these products and activities in and of themselves: sensual gratification and individual indulgence had not, of course, been entirely absent during the war, but they were often fleeting and enjoyed as a counterpoint to the daily grind.

Second, they would serve to demonstrate that the war was finally over. Although the surrender of Germany and then Japan brought great relief, on the Home Front, many of the mundane inconveniences of wartime life continued unabated, making it difficult to discern an absolute boundary between wartime and post-war life. In addition, during the years immediately following the war, British troops were sent to conflict zones such as Palestine and Greece, making something of a mockery of the phrase 'post-war' for the soldiers themselves and also for their families, who were forced to endure the continued absence of loved ones as well as the continued privations of the rationing system.

Thus it was that while the actual celebrations attending the end of the war were enjoyed by most Britons, the shadow cast by the war loomed large and long. Nella Last's experiences might be understood as speaking for many. In July 1945 the presence of a bracken-fringed display at a fishmongers led her to declare that she felt, finally, 'as if the war *was* over'. The following summer, she noted of a trip into the centre of Barrow-in-Furness that 'the women who hurried from shop to shop looked so harassed, all speaking of "more difficult to get things now than in the war when U-boats were sinking our ships". Not one word about V celebrations.'[3] Here, the transition from war to peace is understood in terms associated not with the construction of a New Jerusalem, but instead with the easing of the hundreds of petty restrictions that had come to define the British wartime experience.

It is not difficult to understand why the post-war Age of Austerity came to be so bitterly resented. By having to continue to eat a rationed diet and, in the words of a famous wartime slogan, 'make do and mend', most Britons had to continue living as they had done while they were at war – after almost six years, this was enough to break the spirit of many. The maintenance of draconian sumptuary laws denied the psychological release offered by victory. In a total war where civilian society had been corralled and mobilised as never before, the return to peace could only come with the return to pre-war dietary and consumptional norms.

Delaying the end of government control of food risked prompting what the *Observer* had in 1944 called 'gastric despondency among the war-bread-weary' who regarded '"freedom from vitamins" (as well as from officials and form-filling) as a chief pleasure of peace'.[4] Such comments speak not only of the rejection of bureaucratic food control, but also of the rejection of some of the cultural constructs which underpinned the food-based community – vitamins were a key element of the Ministry of Food's (MoF) publicity campaigns, just as the words 'freedom from' echoed the main provisions of the Beveridge Report. The tensions generated by the sidelining of the individual in favour of the communal had been managed during the war by the demonisation of the enemy, something that was now clearly no longer possible.

In *Passport to Pimlico*, the inhabitants of Burgundy are no longer subject to the policies of the MoF or the Board of Trade and so are freed from the shackles of regulation, shortages and queues. Simultaneously British and alien, and caught between the unloved realities and the unfulfilled but still anticipated dreams of the post-war world, the residents of Miramont Place are established as, and asked to choose between, being both self and other: 'Blimey! I'm a foreigner!' The Burgundians' immediate preference is made very clear. Drunk on their newfound freedoms, and also on the beer served at a pub that can now choose its own opening hours, the Burgundian citizenry engage in what one reviewer described as 'a wild orgy of foreign liberty and licence'.[5] They also tear up their ration books, an act with enough emotional and symbolic significance to be mentioned in almost every contemporary review of the film. Entrepreneurial businessmen arrive and take advantage of the very specific trading conditions, selling hard-to-come-by goods without fear of prosecution. Shooting on location, the filmmakers found that the open trade in controlled goods attracted attention, with Philip Stainton, who played PC Spiller, 'harangued one day by an irate shopper, who complained that coupon-free Nylons and black market eggs were being dispensed to a queue *which she was not allowed to join!*'[6]

The localised 'bonfire of controls' that transformed Miramont Place into a post-war consumerist utopia had clear echoes of the national move towards the deregulation of everyday life promised by the Labour government. However, while Miramont Place's position as a fantasy state allowed it to cast yard upon yard of red tape upon the pyre with minimal thought of the consequences, the task facing Attlee's administration was not so easy. The acute economic crisis that accompanied the end of the war meant that many restrictions were not simply maintained, but were actually extended. Food was a case in point. Bread rationing, introduced in 1946, was another cross to bear, while the temporary control of potatoes, a foodstuff which the MoF's constant promotion had established as the wartime staple par excellence, suggested just how desperate Britain's struggle to win the peace had become.

The maintenance of rationing, increasingly associated with widespread shortages rather than common sacrifice, created ambivalence towards government control in general, and also towards the bureaucrats that administered the systems. While the Labour party placed much faith in experts, increasing numbers were coming to view 'the gentlemen in Whitehall' with a degree of scepticism, especially in regard to their dedication to central planning. In *Passport to Pimlico*, established ideas of personal liberty and the rights of the individual are appealed to when the Burgundians come to construct their new identity: 'We always were English and we'll always be English, and it's just because we are English that we're sticking up for our right to be Burgundian!' The butt of this joke is not so much the woman who delivers it, twisted and enjoyable though her (il)logic might be, but rather a bureaucratic machine that establishes a diegesis in which it needs to be told. The film 'laughs at Government, at officialdom, bureaucracy, bumbledom', the *Daily Herald* cheerfully observed.[7] It is out of this landscape that Straker (Naunton Wayne) and Gregg (Basil Radford) saunter. These two civil servants, who spend much of the film reminiscing about foreign junkets and passing the buck, are sent to the Pimlico-Burgundy border in an attempt to resolve the crisis. They bring with them, though, the bluster and buffoonery of the two characters on which they are so obviously based, Charters and Caldicott. This baggage ensures that although the bureaucrats are presented as neither actively unpleasant nor incompetent, they are associated with inefficiency and unworldliness. Anachronisms even before the war, their presence acts as an indictment of the role played by government in determining the fate of the individual.

Labour politicians, though, seemed unable or unwilling to accept that for many Britons individual choice was one of the basic rights for which they believed themselves to have been fighting. While many were happy to maintain the supposed egalitarianism of wartime, what they envisioned was not a dull and uniform period of enforced austerity, but rather a democratic meritocracy where freedom to consume was enshrined as a fundamental right.

During the general election campaign of 1950, Douglas Jay's observation that 'the gentleman in Whitehall really does know better what is good for the people than the people know for themselves' was seized on by the Conservative party as an indication of Labour's commitment to state regulation of the minutiae of people's lives. The words with which Jay introduced this idea – 'housewives as a whole cannot be trusted to buy all the right things where nutrition and health are concerned' – were unlikely to have won him many new friends among those who spent a significant proportion of their lives shopping and cooking.[8]

The resumption of party politics did little to calm nerves, and food became a key electoral battleground. Post-war Labour Ministers of Food found notably less favour than their wartime predecessors, Lord Woolton in particular. Opinion polls suggested that John Strachey, Minister of Food between May 1946 and February 1950, was less popular than Woolton had been even at the height of the fuss that attended the introduction of egg control.[9] And just as Woolton's name had once been evoked to assuage concerns about rationing, Strachey's would soon become integral to a popular slogan that seemed to epitomise the problems, not all of their own making, of Britain's first post-war government: 'Shiver with [Emanuel] Shinwell [Minister of Fuel and Power] and starve with Strachey.'

The weather did not help the government, or the national mood. The 'broad, sunlit uplands', promised by Churchill as a reward for wartime toil were subjected in the early months of 1947 to a period of such sustained 'climactic malevolence' that eventually Big Ben froze and stopped working.[10] In such circumstances, it was hard to believe that Britain was making progress. The damage to domestic food production was notable, and the psychological damage caused by the possibility of hunger was exacerbated by the imposition of strict controls on fuel consumption. Two years later, Burgundy was to enjoy meteorological as well as political and gastronomic independence; secession was accompanied by a prolonged period of hot, dry weather conjured in the main by the cinematic arts: production was hampered by wet, overcast and generally unpleasant weather.[11] At the end of the film, as Miramont Place rejoins Britain, it begins to rain with such intensity that the streets are soon deluged; the diluvian imagery reminiscent of newsreel images of the floods produced by melting snow in spring 1947.

And yet, for all the population's desperation to throw off the shackles of government control, also visible within the film is nostalgia for wartime consensus and community. Burgundy, free from food control, becomes a lawless space, a 'spiv's paradise' where the supposedly cherished British ideas of fair play and equality are cast aside by consumers looking to indulge their previously suppressed desire for unrestricted access to bacon, butter and coupon-free clothing.

Thus the retreat from state control that the film initially appears to celebrate is shown as coming at the cost of the egalitarian communalism that the propaganda of the war years had done so much to promote. Although rationing had further restricted the flavours available to an already unadventurous British palate, food control was understood as a necessary evil and contributed to a sense of unity and social cohesiveness. The makers of *Passport to Pimlico* were not willing to throw the baby out with the wartime bathwater, and instead tapped into ideas established during the war to justify the film's rose-tinted attempt to find a place for rationing in post-war Britain.

Rationing had been the product of a distinct set of circumstances that allowed for public acceptance of direct state interference in British consumer culture. After January 1940, when the state took control of food importation and distribution, the MoF helped shape the national experience and played an essential role in maintaining the strength and morale of the British people. The wartime food-based community was not some naturally occurring, atavistic phenomenon, but rather sprang from the state, which was responsible for its formation and its maintenance.

Like all identities, the gastronomically delineated wartime British persona was a fluid construct (although not necessarily less powerful for that), and was consequently capable, and perhaps in need, of continual refinement, redefinition and reaffirmation. Food was so central an element of the war as experienced by the people of Britain that it could not help but became culturally prominent. This process was helped in no small measure by the MoF's willingness to publicise its work. *Kitchen Front* radio broadcasts, Food Facts newspaper advertisements and *Food Flash* films all sought to establish understanding of, sympathy for, and belief in rationing. The MoF's success in publicising not only its practical achievements but also its social and cultural functions established food as a key component of wartime British life and as an important feature of a shared experience and identity.

While changes to the national diet helped to promote an image of Britain as distinct from other nations, such changes also redefined popular ideas of what it meant to be British. By promoting an alimentary *esprit de corps*, rationing temporarily papered over some of the cracks between the different strata of British society and advanced the concepts of community and equality in an attempt to realise the society of 'food companions' envisioned in 1940 by Robert Boothby.[12] Contemporary commentators were confident that the abstract communal ideal advanced by the rationing system had in some instances been made real. *The Times* might have wistfully described the unrestricted consumption of pre-war Britain as 'a temporarily vanished civilisation', yet it still felt obliged to warn its post-war readers that if a gastronomic free for all, of the type seen in *Passport to Pimlico*, accompanied the end of rationing, 'the rough justice of [regulated] consumption, which has unquestionably been a triumph of British democracy, would be upset.'[13]

The powerful sense of community established by MoF and other government propaganda meant that ideas of consensus and social unity remained culturally significant well into the post-war period, assisted, no doubt, by the debates that presaged the formation of the welfare state. When the residents of Miramont Place find themselves cut off from their erstwhile compatriots, they decide to construct their own nation, choosing to project a *vision* of the motherland onto their freshly minted state, recreating from memory a version of Britain not so much *as it is* (full of war-bread-weary consumers grasping for illicit goods) but as they remember it *as having been* (consensual and democratic). Despite its temporary otherness, Burgundy showed an idealised image of Britain to itself: as Britain in miniature, Miramont Place is a distillation of a particularly romantic, bloody-minded and communal form of specifically wartime Britishness. Indeed, the spirit of Churchill is itself evoked when one resident, with a suitably parochial rhetorical flourish, promises that in order to protect the community's ideals 'We'll fight them in the tramlines and we'll fight them in the local.'

In response to secession, Britain imposes an economic blockade, cutting off Miramont Place from the outside world and strengthening the wartime parallels: Burgundy is at bay in 1949 in much the same way Britain was in 1940. The microstate reintroduces rationing, pooling food in order to preserve and equitably distribute stocks. In such a small community, those in charge of food policy are more knowable, and therefore the system is more personal, than even the MoF had been during the war. As a newsreel commentator puts it: 'Now that all food is stored in one place and meal times can be standardised, communal feeding has been introduced under the supervision of the Duke [of Burgundy, played by Paul Dupuis].' The community is shown dining en masse and *en fête*, coming together to celebrate its cohesiveness through reference to its shared diet.

Despite rationing, food stocks are soon exhausted. Such is the familiarity of the Burgundian social and political experiment, however, that it serves to remind British citizens of the values that allowed the nation to successfully endure, and triumph over, wartime hardships. In scenes which ape the Berlin airlift – coming to a conclusion just as *Passport to Pimlico* was released – food is delivered by ordinary Britons to Burgundians isolated by barricades and barbed wire, sustaining them and allowing them to continue their valiant resistance. Again, though, we might discern a faint whiff of anti-authoritarianism, for it is individual donations, made in spite of the government's blockade, that assist Burgundy: personal agency trumps adherence to government strictures.

Secure and well-fed, Burgundy is able to negotiate a peaceful settlement. When the day comes for Miramont Place to be reintegrated into Britain, new ration books are distributed to replace those destroyed during the independence celebrations. The return of the ration books is accompanied by a conversation between PC Spiller and Connie Pemberton (Betty Warren):

> Spiller: I never thought anybody would be pleased to see these things again.
> Connie: You never know when you're well-off 'til you aren't.

In a draft of the script, Connie's eyes are said to 'dwell affectionately' on the new ration books, and it was in the act of returning to the rationed national fold that *The Times* found the film's 'comforting and characteristic moral', for as printed representations of stability, certainty and social cohesion, the ration book had become an icon in a distinctly British communion.[14]

Rationing had required Britons to share simultaneously in an experience that was at once personal and communal, and to participate in an act of both consumption and production, for a common diet helped to construct a sense of collective identity. As such, the ration book became the membership card of a society that was at the same time inclusive (in that all Britons were encouraged to join and feel a part of this community) and exclusive (the community established, and was protective of, its boundaries). Food was used to distinguish between the national 'self' and the international 'other' in a manner which concretised in an explicitly political way pre-existing gastronomic boundaries and distinctions.

What we see, then, in *Passport to Pimlico* are two visions of Britain. On the one hand we have the spiv's paradise, with its promise of unfettered consumption and its celebration of the end of government interference in the life of the individual. The release offered by this vision is tempered by cut-throat competition and the prospect of the anarchy that might attend the end of regulation. On the other, we have the cosy community in which all were equal and order was maintained but dull and frequently unsatisfying uniformity was imposed at the expense of personal liberty.

It is difficult to know which Burgundy would have been more appealing to post-war cinema audiences, and the film seems unwilling to side defini-tively with either, instead choosing to play with the instability of meaning that attended rationing and the food-based community in the age of austerity. Although food control, re-established at the end of the film, is shown to be a 'Good Thing', the reintroduction of rationing is unable to fully eliminate memories of the population's initial, vital desire to reject it. The film speaks of the benefits of rationing, but also of the frustrations associated with having to endure it; of the shared sense of purpose that might arise from a common diet, but also of the continued desire for individualistic self-expression; of gratitude to and resentment of the state.

Such divisions were evident at one of the first screenings of the film:

> The preview audience clapped when they saw Hermione Baddeley [who played a local dressmaker] ... obtaining and selling gowns on the 'export only' tag ... And shouts of 'encore' greeted the spectacular finale showing how sympathetic Londoners helped the besieged 'foreigners' in their midst – dropping 'Bundles for Burgundy' by helicopter and throwing food parcels from an electric train as it skirted the 'alien' frontier.[15]

Those watching the film were, it seems, capable of enjoying not only the powerful feelings of community that accompanied the end of the film, but also the ways in which the early sequences of *Passport to Pimlico* encourage the viewer to associate with characters who take pleasure from contesting the ideological constructs from which such feelings emerged.

This, of course, is unsurprising. British consumers were able to maintain contradictory positions on the same subject. It does not necessarily follow that an individual's recognition of the need for sacrifice made them immune from the siren song of the black market, or prevented them from grumbling about shortages: many Britons were staunch supporters of rationing *and* capable of exempting themselves from its more onerous regulations just long enough to buy a joint of lamb from 'under the counter'. Films that contested the absolutism of 'comradeship in matters of food' demonstrated the limited appeal of rationing and operated in a liminal space that offered cinema-goers the possibly guilty pleasure of a brief respite from the relentless optimism and asceticism of both the MoF's advertisements and feature films advocating a communal gustatory ideal.[16]

The uneasiness to be found at the heart of *Passport to Pimlico* is inextricably linked to the film's status as the product of a post-war culture, for attitudes to food control and government regulation were temporally very sensitive. Reviewing the film, the *Daily Express* explored this idea: 'The little people of Pimlico suddenly realise they are Burgundians – and therefore aliens. And being 1949, what do they do? They tear up their ration books and start buying everything in their shops.' In short, 'Everybody goes crazy.'[17] The specific mention of the year operates to both explain and justify the consumerist rampage that dominates the early sequences of the film. However, implicit within the review is the recognition that it is only because it is 1949 that such actions are not immediately censured; post-war Britain was subject to a different set of moral and social imperatives from those that had existed between 1939 and 1945.

Passport to Pimlico thus adopts a Janus-like stance, using post-war frustrations to look forward to a future free from restrictions and back to a period of supposed egalitarianism. With this in mind, the image that opens the film, a funeral wreath dedicated to the memory of clothes coupons and sweets rationing, becomes deeply ambiguous (see figure 29).[18] For the film positions

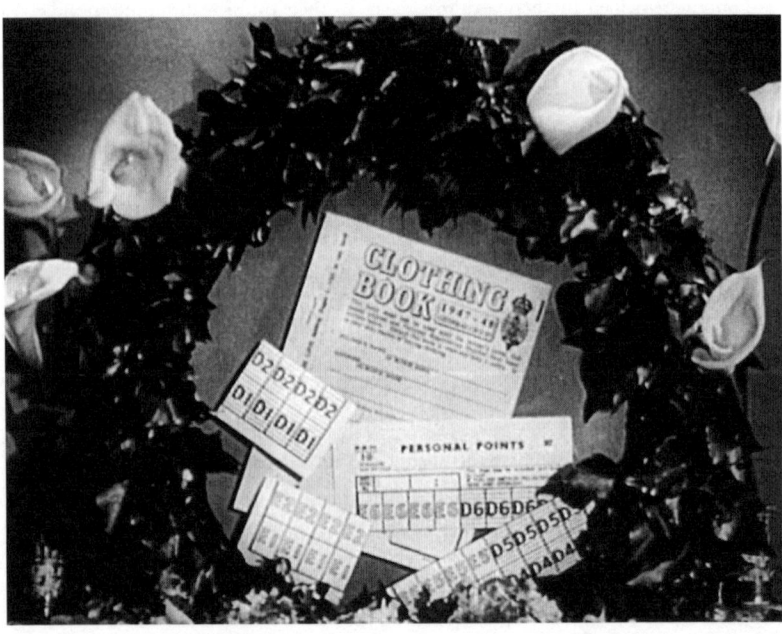

29   In memoriam... *Passport to Pimlico* (1949).

government control of consumption in such as way as to make this lament, at first glance seemingly so ironic, a more sincere tribute to a system that it was hopefully, if mistakenly, assumed would soon be retired. Grieving not so much the cessation of rationing as the end of the corporate identity established by a society of food companions, the dedication mourns the passing of a distinct period during which, the film suggests, the strength of the nation was founded on political and social consensus and unity. Be it playful or serious, the shot demonstrates that crucial role that food and consumption played in defining both individual and national identity.

The nostalgia evident in *Passport to Pimlico* speaks of the powerful appeal of the ideas of consensus and community evident in so much British wartime culture. While the film might be considered the last hurrah of the food-based community, it is also part of an established tradition of films from the 1940s that addressed and constructed viewers through appeals to their gastronomic experiences. Images of food and eating in wartime British cinema and other media helped shape how the national community was imagined, and offered a vision of Britain that encouraged consumers to define themselves in very particular terms.

This was made possible by the fact that the rationing system operated at both a physical and a psychological level; food was at once a reality and an idea. The goods distributed by the MoF were tangible and ingestible, and therefore acted as concrete evidence of the continued functioning of the state and also of the more abstract notion of the food-based community. The propaganda that accompanied the introduction of a supposedly common diet also had a significant emotional appeal, and accepting and partaking in rationing were promoted as essential elements of what it meant to be British.

The comprehensive nature of the wartime rationing system meant that food and consumption – already concerns of universal interest – became proportionately more important, and this increased significance found expression in a large number of films made in widely varying styles. The rapidly changing reality of the real-world food situation created a complex tangle of meanings for filmmakers to explore, with the result that consumption could be used in numerous ways to investigate the nature of the British wartime experience. Be they state-sponsored or commercially made, short or feature length, critically acclaimed, lambasted or ignored, comedies, costume dramas, thrillers, and documentary realist features all found time to discuss the role that food played in shaping the experiences of British wartime society. Although it would be wrong to suggest that British wartime cinema should be categorised solely as a series of films about food, it is possible to assert that the MoF was so insistent in its attempts to persuade British consumers of the importance of the subject that it became a pervasive cultural and social element of wartime life.

The dialogue between the picturegoer-as-consumer, the filmmaker and the government was not always harmonious, but the numerous food images contained in wartime films and propaganda suggest that consumption was critical to the morale and the physical health of the nation and to the discursive construction of what that nation might look like. The ways in which people respond to films is, of course, not static, and the potential meanings contained in particular films were shaped by the individual experiences of cinema-goers as consumers of both film and food. Food was the subject of a constant process of negotiation that permitted it to unite, define and sustain Britain at a time of national crisis; it was an essential element of the British war effort, a crucial munition of war.

Notes

1 *Kinematograph Weekly*, 11 January 1945, p. 163.
2 Diary entry, 21 October 1941, in Simon Garfield (ed.), *Private Battles: How the War Almost Defeated Us* (London: Ebury Press, 2006), p. 174.
3 Diary entry, 14 July 1945, in Richard Broad and Suzie Fleming (eds), *Nella Last's War: The Second World War Diaries of Housewife, 49* (London: Profile, 2006), p. 285; diary entry, 5 June 1946, in Patricia and Robert Malcolmson (eds), *Nella Last's Peace: The Post-War Diaries of Housewife, 49* (London: Profile, 2008), p. 98.
4 *Observer*, 7 May 1944, p. 3.
5 *The Times*, 2 May 1949, p. 7.
6 *Daily Mirror*, 29 April 1949, p. 4. Emphasis added.
7 *Daily Herald*, 29 April 1949, p. 4.
8 Douglas Jay, *The Socialist Case* (London: Faber & Faber, 1947), p. 258.
9 In April 1947, 49 per cent of people questioned for a Gallup poll stated the opinion that Strachey was doing a 'bad job'. Although by September 1949 this figure had fallen to 45 per cent, it was still greater than those who felt he was doing a good job. *The Gallup International Public Opinion Poll: Great Britain 1937–1975: Vol. 1 – 1937–1964* (New York: Random House, 1976), pp. 155–6, 208.
10 18 June 1940. *Parliamentary Debates: House of Commons*, 5th Series, vol. 362, col. 60; Alex J. Robertson, *The Bleak Midwinter: 1947* (Manchester: Manchester University Press, 1987), pp. 10, 21.
11 *Daily Mirror*, 29 April 1949, p. 4.
12 *Manchester Guardian*, 21 September 1940, p. 9.
13 *The Times*: 3 May 1944, p. 5; 22 February 1949, p. 5.
14 BFI Script Collection: S202 – 'Second Shooting Script' for *Passport to Pimlico*, 9 July 1948; *The Times*: 2 May 1949, p. 7.

15 *Daily Mirror*, 29 April 1949, p. 4.

16 Robert Boothby in *Manchester Guardian*, 21 September 1940, p. 9.

17 *Daily Express*, 29 April 1949, p. 4.

18 The shot of the wreath must have been inserted very shortly before the film's initial release in late April 1949, for the first announcements concerning the repeal of clothes rationing were made in February 1949, with full de-rationing coming into effect on 14 March. Further, the decision to take sweets off the ration was announced on 21 February 1949 and was implemented on 24 April, just days before the first public screenings of *Passport to Pimlico*. Such serendipitous timing may have pleased the film's producers, but the wreath also proved to be somewhat premature: sweets rationing was reintroduced in August 1949 and only finally ended in February 1953.

Appendix

List of *Food Flash* films

Dates and film titles are taken from the National Archives file MAF 75/67: Public Relations and Food Advice, Section IV, Appendix P. Supplementary information is taken from Denis Gifford, *The British Film Catalogue: Vol. 2 – Non-Fiction Film, 1888–1994* (London: Fitzroy Dearborn, 2001), pp. 320, 331, 339–40, 348, 358.

A number of films were reissued, and in instances where it is not clear if *Flashes* with the same title are separate films, I have followed the MoF's lead, only describing as reissues films designated as such by the Ministry. Because many films were given similar or, on occasion, identical titles, it is not always possible to state categorically exactly which film was re-released: for instance two 'Waste Bread' films had been produced and screened before a *Food Flash* with this name was reissued in the week of 4 October 1943. In these cases I have referred to all previous films with the same title.

Abbreviations used in film titles

BU	Bread Unit
CLO	Cod Liver Oil
Namco	National Milk Cocoa

Release Date	Title	Notes
2 March 1942	Baker's Deliveries	
9 March 1942	Points Ration	
16 March 1942	Fruit Juices, Vitamins	
23 March 1942	Shopping Baskets	
30 March 1942	Prunes and Dates	
6 April 1942	Waste Bread	
13 April 1942	Sugar for Jam	
20 April 1942	Soap for Babies	
27 April 1942	MoF Booklet	
4 May 1942	Recipe of the Week	
11 May 1942	Ration Book	

18 May 1942	Ration Book 'B'	
25 May 1942	Ration Book 'C'	
1 June 1942	Shopping List	
8 June 1942	Ration Book 'D'	
15 June 1942	Ration Book 'E'	
22 June 1942	Ration Book 'F'	
29 June 1942	Egg Dishes	
6 July 1942	Cheese Ration	
13 July 1942	*No Film*	
20 July 1942	New Ration Period	
27 July 1942	Personal Ration Book	
3 August 1942	Sour Milk	
10 August 1942	Potatoes	
17 August 1942	Dried Eggs	
24 August 1942	Clean Milk Bottles	
31 August 1942	Dried Eggs No. 2	
7 September 1942	Potato Pete	
14 September 1942	Carrots	
21 September 1942	Points Reduction	
28 September 1942	Milk Bottle Tops	
5 October 1942	Milk Coupons	
12 October 1942	Milk Registration	
19 October 1942	Personal Ration 2	
26 October 1942	Dried Milk and Eggs	
2 November 1942	Chicken	
9 November 1942	Lay of the Land	
16 November 1942	Cod Liver Oil and Orange Juice	
23 November 1942	Waste Bread	
30 November 1942	Milk and Water	
7 December 1942	*No Film*	
14 December 1942	Dried Eggs No. 3	
21 December 1942	Potato Pete Fair	London only
21 December 1942	Food Information	Outside London
28 December 1942	Potato Resolution	
4 January 1943	Milk Bottles and Farthings	
11 January 1943	Dried Milk and Eggs	
18 January 1943	Bread Costs Lives No. 1	
25 January 1943	Bread Costs Lives No. 2	
1 February 1943	Bread Costs Lives No. 3	
8 February 1943	Covent Garden	
15 February 1943	Fish	
22 February 1943	Potatoes Dishes	
1 March 1943	Pool Delivery	
8 March 1943	Vitamin Greens	
15 March 1943	Eat More Potatoes	
22 March 1943	*No Film*	

29 March 1943	Victory Dish	
5 April 1943	Help the Grocer	
12 April 1943	Canned Jam	
19 April 1943	Identity Card	
26 April 1943	Dried Milk	
3 May 1943	Waste	
10 May 1943	Swedes	
17 May 1943	New Ration Book	
24 May 1943	New Ration Book No. 2	
31 May 1943	Newspaper	
7 June 1943	Food Queues	
14 June 1943	Breath and Bread	
21 June 1943	Potato Plan	
28 June 1943	Dried Eggs 1/3d	
5 July 1943	New Potatoes	
12 July 1943	New Ration Book No. 3	
19 July 1943	Sugar for Jam	
26 July 1943	Price of Dried Eggs	
2 August 1943	*Reissue: Sour Milk (see 3 Aug. 1942)*	
9 August 1943	Changing Retailers	
16 August 1943	Crumpled Ration Book	
23 August 1943	Luxury Dish	
30 August 1943	Milk Bottle Tops	
6 September 1943	Eggs – Egg Powder	
13 September 1943	*Reissue: Clean Milk Bottles (see 24 Aug. 1942)*	
20 September 1943	Points	
27 September 1943	Kitchen Front	
4 October 1943	Rats	London only
4 October 1943	*Reissue: Waste Bread*	
	(see 6 Apr. 1942 or 23 Nov. 1942)	Outside London
11 October 1943	Vitamin 'C'	
18 October 1943	Milk Powder	
25 October 1943	Rats No. 2	
1 November 1943	Rats No. 3	
8 November 1943	Milk Priorities	
15 November 1943	Oranges	
22 November 1943	Jam for Sugar	
29 November 1943	Salt Fish	
6 December 1943	Baby's Vitamin D	
13 December 1943	Double Dried Eggs	
20 December 1943	Milk – Babies Only	
27 December 1943	Dried Milk and Eggs	
3 January 1944	Orange Juice and CLO Coupons	
10 January 1944	National Milk Cocoa	
17 January 1944	Biscuits	
24 January 1944	Leeks	

31 January 1944	*No Film*	
7 February 1944	Dried Milk	
14 February 1944	*Reissue: Salt Cod (see Salt Fish, 29 Nov. 1943?)*	
21 February 1944	Smoking Chimney and Vitamin Waste	
28 February 1944	Marmalade	
6 March 1944	*Reissue: Leeks (see 24 Jan. 1944)*	*London only*
6 March 1944	*Reissue: Rats (see 4 Oct. 1943)*	*Outside London*
13 March 1944	Soup	
20 March 1944	*Reissue: Rats No. 3 (see 1 Nov. 1943)*	
27 March 1944	Family Milk	
3 April 1944	Broken Glass	
10 April 1944	Kitchen Front News	
17 April 1944	Small Potatoes	
24 April 1944	Jam or Sugar	
1 May 1944	Read Food Facts	
8 May 1944	Green Ration Book	
15 May 1944	Ration Book Advertisement	
22 May 1944	Clean Milk Bottles	
29 May 1944	Ration Book Poster	
5 June 1944	Sour Milk	
12 June 1944	Ration Book Pages 31 & 32	
19 June 1944	Cutting Ration Books	
26 June 1944	Re-registration	
3 July 1944	Pork	
10 July 1944	Rush Egg Dishes	
17 July 1944	Ration Book Care	
24 July 1944	Shredded Greens	
31 July 1944	Hen's Days Work	
7 August 1944	Wheels and Keels	
14 August 1944	Dried Eggs	
21 August 1944	Children's Milk	
28 August 1944	Namco No. 2	
4 September 1944	No Dried Eggs	
11 September 1944	5th Birthday	
18 September 1944	Namco No. 3	
25 September 1944	Rain and Cold	
2 October 1944	Rickets	
9 October 1944	Retailers Addresses	
16 October 1944	Milk – Babies Only	
23 October 1944	Household Milk	
30 October 1944	*No Film*	
6 November 1944	Double Egg Ration	
13 November 1944	Dates and Figs	
20 November 1944	In a Hurry (Dried Eggs)	

27 November 1944	Children's Rations
4 December 1944	*Reissue: Namco No. 3 (see 18 Sep. 1944)*
11 December 1944	Christmas Fare
18 December 1944	Broken Milk Bottles
25 December 1944	*No Film*
1 January 1945	Vitamins A, C, D
8 January 1945	Priority Vitamins
15 January 1945	Your Empties Wanted
22 January 1945	Oranges
29 January 1945	Winter Hen
5 February 1945	Potato Peeling
12 February 1945	Personal Points
19 February 1945	Clean Milk Bottles
26 February 1945	Children's Milk
5 March 1945	Small Potatoes
12 March 1945	Dried Milk
19 March 1945	Spring
26 March 1945	New Distribution – Vitamins A, C, D
2 April 1945	Marmalade
9 April 1945	Bottle Battle
16 April 1945	Bottle Battle No. 2
23 April 1945	Cyril Fletcher No. 1
30 April 1945	Cyril Fletcher No. 2
7 May 1945	Cyril Fletcher No. 3
14 May 1945	Ration Books
21 May 1945	Ration Books No. 2
28 May 1945	Ration Books No. 3
4 June 1945	Ration Books No. 4
11 June 1945	Ration Books No. 5
18 June 1945	Ration Books No. 6
25 June 1945	*No Film*
2 July 1945	*No Film*
9 July 1945	Picnics
16 July 1945	Fats Reduced
23 July 1945	Tea Ration
30 July 1945	Sugar
6 August 1945	Orange Juice
13 August 1945	*Reissue: Bottle Battle (see 9 Apr. 1945)*
20 August 1945	*Reissue: Bottle Battle 2 (see 16 Apr. 1945)*
27 August 1945	*No Film*
3 September 1945	Fresh and Green
10 September 1945	Your Empties Wanted
17 September 1945	Waste Bread
24 September 1945	Bread
1 October 1945	*No Film*
8 October 1945	Kids in Winter

15 October 1945	*Reissue: Rickets (see 2 Oct. 1944)*
22 October 1945	New Dried Milk
29 October 1945	*Reissue: Clean Milk Bottles (see 24 Aug. 1942,*
	22 May 1944 or 19 Feb. 1945)
5 November 1945	Kiddies Milk
12 November 1945	National Milk Cocoa
19 November 1945	Dried Milk
25 November 1945	Dried Fruit – Dates
3 December 1945	Bread and Money
10 December 1945	Waste Not
17 December 1945	Radio Doctor No. 1
24 December 1945	Canned Jam
31 December 1945	*No Film*
7 January 1946	Radio Doctor No. 2
14 January 1946	*No Film*
21 January 1946	Food Facts Recipes
28 January 1946	Radio Doctor No. 3
4 February 1946	*No Film*
11 February 1946	ABC Cookery Book
18 February 1946	Cutting Bread
25 February 1946	*No Film*
4 March 1946	Keeping Bread
11 March 1946	Welfare Foods
18 March 1946	Keeping Bread
25 March 1946	Bread and Money
1 April 1946	Cutting Bread
8 April 1946	Bread and Crusts
15 April 1946	Rain and Waste
22 April 1946	Save Bread
29 April 1946	*No Film*
6 May 1946	*No Film*
13 May 1946	Ration Book No. 1
20 May 1946	Ration Book No. 2
27 May 1946	Milk Registration
3 June 1946	Wrap Bread
10 June 1946	Babies only
17 June 1946	Dried eggs again
24 June 1946	Milk Registration
1 July 1946	Kiddies' Bread-Bus
8 July 1946	BUs – Food Facts
15 July 1946	Keeping Bread
22 July 1946	Issue of BUs
29 July 1946	Keeping Milk
5 August 1946	L. BU Coupons
12 August 1946	Milk 1½d or Free
19 August 1946	Orange Juice

26 August 1946	Don't Take Children's Milk
2 September 1946	Extra Sugar
9 September 1946	*No Film*
16 September 1946	*No Film*
23 September 1946	Clean Ration Book
30 September 1946	Tinned Jam
7 October 1946	Charlie Chester No. 1
14 October 1946	Charlie Chester No. 2
21 October 1946	Charlie Chester No. 3
28 October 1946	Charlie Chester No. 4
4 November 1946	Charlie Chester No. 5

Filmography

Title; year; production company; *Producer*, *Director*, *Commentator* (where applicable); *Cast* – principles only; running time (in minutes). Films are British unless otherwise stated.

49th Parallel: 1941; Ortus Films; *Producer* – John Sutro; *Producer, Director* – Michael Powell; *Cast* – Eric Portman, Laurence Olivier, Anton Walbrook, Leslie Howard; 123 mins.

Babette's Feast (Denmark): 1987; Panorama Films; *Producers* – Just Betzer, Bo Christensen; *Director* – Gabriel Axel; *Cast* – Stephane Audran, Bodil Kjer; 102 mins.

Back Room Boy: 1942; Gainsborough; *Producer* – Edward Black; *Director* – Herbert Mason; *Cast* – Arthur Askey, Moore Marriot, Graham Moffatt; 82 mins.

The Balloon Goes Up: 1942; New Realm; *Producer* – Edwin J. Fancey; *Director* – Redd Davis; *Cast* – Ethel Revnell, Gracie West; 58 mins.

Band Waggon: 1940; Gainsborough; *Producer* – Edward Black; *Director* – Marcel Varnel; *Cast* – Arthur Askey, Richard Murdoch; 85 mins.

Battle for Music: 1943; Strand; *Producer, Director* – Donald Taylor; *Cast* – Hay Petrie, Joss Ambler, Clifford Buckton; 74 mins.

The Bells Go Down: 1943; Ealing; *Producer* – Michael Balcon; *Director* – Basil Dearden; *Cast* – Tommy Trinder, James Mason, Mervyn Johns; 90 mins.

Big Night (USA): 1996; Rysher Entertainment; *Producer* – Jonathan Filley; *Directors* – Campbell Scott, Stanley Tucci; *Cast* – Stanley Tucci, Tony Shalhoub; 107 mins.

Brief Encounter: 1945; Cineguild for Independent Producers; *Producers* – Noel Coward, Anthony Havelock-Allan, Ronald Neame; *Director* – David Lean; *Cast* – Celia Johnson, Trevor Howard; 86 mins.

A Canterbury Tale: 1944; Archers for Independent Producers; *Producers, Directors* – Michael Powell and Emeric Pressburger; *Cast* – Eric Portman, Dennis Price, Sheila Sim, Sgt John Sweet; 124 mins.

Champagne Charlie: 1944; Ealing; *Producer* – Michael Balcon; *Director* – Alberto Cavalcanti; *Cast* – Tommy Trinder, Stanley Holloway; 105 mins.

The Common Touch: 1941; British National; *Producer, Director* – John Baxter; *Cast* – Geoffrey Hibbert, Edward Rigby, Greta Gynt; 104 mins.

Cookery Hints (series, 6 episodes): 1940; Verity for Ministry of Food; *Producer* – Sydney Box; *Director* – Jay Gardner Lewis; 5–9 mins.

The Cook, the Thief, his Wife and her Lover: 1989; Allarts Cook; *Producer* – Kees Kasander; *Director* – Peter Greenaway; *Cast* – Michael Gambon, Richard Bohringer, Helen Mirren; 124 mins.

Cottage to Let: 1940; Gainsborough; *Producer* – Edward Black; *Director* – Anthony Asquith; *Cast* – Leslie Banks, Alistair Sim, John Mills; 90 mins.

Dancing on a Dime (USA): 1940; Paramount; *Producer* – A. M. Botsford; *Director* – Joseph Santley; *Cast* – Robert Paige, Grace MacDonald, Peter Hayes; 74 mins.

The Day Will Dawn: 1942; Paul Soskin Productions; *Producer* – Paul Soskin; *Director* – Harold French; *Cast* – Hugh Williams, Finlay Currie, Deborah Kerr; 99 mins.

The Demi-Paradise: 1943; Two Cities; *Producer* – Anatole de Grunwald; *Director* – Anthony Asquith; *Cast* – Laurence Olivier, Penelope Dudley Ward, Felix Aylmer; 114 mins.

Desert Victory: 1943; Army Film and Photographic Unit; *Producer* – David Macdonald; *Director* – Roy Boulting; *Commentator* – J. L. Hodson; 60 mins.

Down at the Local: 1945; Public Relationship Films for Army Welfare Film Unit; *Director* – Richard Massingham; 18 mins.

Eat Drink Man Woman (Taiwan): 1994; Ang Lee Productions; *Producers* – Kong Hsu, Li-Kong Hsu; *Director* – Ang Lee; *Cast* – Sihung Lung, Yu-Wen Wang, Chien-Lien Wu; 124 mins.

Eating at Work: 1941; Strand for Gas Council; *Producer* – Edgar Anstey; *Director* – Ralph Bond; 12 mins.

Eating Out with Tommy Trinder: 1941; Strand for Ministry of Information; *Producer* – Donald Taylor; *Director* – Desmond Dickinson; *Cast* – Tommy Trinder, Marjorie Fielding; 6 mins.

Fanny by Gaslight: 1944; Gainsborough; *Producer* – Edward Black; *Director* – Anthony Asquith; *Cast* – James Mason, Stewart Granger, Phyllis Calvert; 108 mins.

Fiddlers Three: 1944; Ealing; *Producer* – Michael Balcon; *Director* – Harry Watt; *Cast* – Tommy Trinder, Sonnie Hale, Francis L. Sullivan; 88 mins.

Fires Were Started: 1943; Crown Film Unit; *Producer* – Ian Dalrymple; *Director* – Humphrey Jennings; *Cast* – George Gravett, Philip Wilson-Dickson, Fred Griffiths; 63 mins.

Food Flash (series, 218 episodes, 1942–46): NSS for Ministry of Food; for full list of titles and release dates see Appendix.

Food for Thought: 1940; Ealing for MoF; *Producer* – Michael Balcon; *Director* – Adrian Brunel; *Cast* – Mabel Constanduros, Muriel George; 5 mins.

Germany Calling: 1941; Spectator; *Director* – Charles Ridley; 3 mins.

Gert and Daisy Clean Up: 1942; Butcher's; *Producer* – F. W. Baker; *Director* – Maclean Rogers; *Cast* – Elsie Waters, Doris Waters; 85 mins.

Gert and Daisy's Weekend: 1941; Butcher's; *Producer* – F. W. Baker; *Director* – Maclean Rogers; *Cast* – Elsie Waters, Doris Waters; 79 mins.

Go to Blazes!: 1942; Ealing for Ministry of Information; *Producer* – Michael Balcon; *Director* – Walter Forde; *Cast* – Will Hay, Thora Hird; 8 mins.

The Good Companions: 1933; Gaumont British; *Producer* – T. A. Welsh, George Pearson; *Director* – Victor Saville; *Cast* – Jessie Matthews, John Gielgud; 113 mins.

Goodbye, Mr Chips: 1939; MGM British; *Producer* – Victor Saville; *Director* – Sam Wood; *Cast* – Robert Donat, Greer Garson; 113 mins.

The Goose Steps Out: 1942; Ealing; *Producer* – Michael Balcon; *Directors* – Basil Dearden, Will Hay; *Cast* – Will Hay, Frank Pettingell; 79 mins.

Great Day: 1945; RKO; *Producer* – Victor Hanbury; *Director* – Lance Comfort; *Cast* – Eric Portman, Flora Robson, Sheila Sim; 79 mins.

The Halfway House: 1944; Ealing; *Producer* – Michael Balcon; *Director* – Basil Dearden; *Cast* – Mervyn Johns, Glynis Johns; 95 mins.

Hatter's Castle: 1941; Paramount British; *Producer* – Isadore Goldsmith; *Director* – Lance Comfort; *Cast* – Robert Newton, Beatrice Varley, Deborah Kerr; 102 mins.

The Hundred Pound Window: 1943; WB-First National; *Director* – Brian Desmond Hurst; *Cast* – Anne Crawford, Frederick Leister, Richard Attenborough; 84 mins.

I Thank You: 1941; Gainsborough; *Producer* – Edward Black; *Director* – Marcel Varnel; *Cast* – Arthur Askey, Richard Murdoch, Moore Marriot; 83 mins.

In Which We Serve: 1942; Two Cities; *Producer, Director* – Noel Coward; *Director* – David Lean; *Cast* – Noel Coward, John Mills, Bernard Miles; 115 mins.

Johnny Frenchman: 1945; Ealing; *Producer* – Michael Balcon; *Director* – Charles Frend; *Cast* – Tom Walls, Françoise Rosay, Patricia Roc; 105 mins.

The Lady Vanishes: 1938; Gainsborough; *Producer* – Edward Black; *Director* – Alfred Hitchcock; *Cast* – Michael Redgrave, Margaret Lockwood, May Whitty; 97 mins.

The Lamp Still Burns: 1943; Two Cities; *Producer* – Leslie Howard; *Director* – Maurice Elvey; *Cast* – Rosamund John, Stewart Granger; 87 mins.

Let the People Sing: 1942; British National; *Producer, Director* – John Baxter; *Cast* – Alistair Sim, Patricia Roc, Fred Emney; 105 mins.

The Life and Death of Colonel Blimp: 1943; Archers for Independent Producers; *Producers, Directors* – Michael Powell, Emeric Pressburger; *Cast* – Roger Livesey, Anton Walbrook, Deborah Kerr; 163 mins.

Like Water for Chocolate (Mexico): 1992; Arau Films; *Producer, Director* – Alfonso Arau; *Cast* – Marco Leonardi, Lumi Regina Torné; 105 mins.

The Lion Has Wings: 1939; London Films; *Producer* – Alexander Korda; *Directors* – Michael Powell, Adrian Brunel, Brian Desmond Hurst; *Commentator* – E. V. H. Emmett; *Cast* – Ralph Richardson, Merle Oberon; 76 mins.

Listen to Britain: 1942; Crown Film Unit; *Producer* – Ian Dalrymple; *Directors* – Humphrey Jennings, Stewart McAllister; 19 mins.

London Can Take It!: 1940; GPO Film Unit for Ministry of Information; *Director* – Harry Watt, Humphrey Jennings; *Commentator* – Quentin Reynolds; 10 mins.

Madonna of the Seven Moons: 1944; Gainsborough; *Producer* – R. J. Minney; *Director* – Arthur Crabtree; *Cast* – Phyllis Calvert, Stewart Granger, Patricia Roc; 110 mins.

The Man in Grey: 1943; Gainsborough; *Producer* – Edward Black; *Director* – Leslie Arliss; *Cast* – Margaret Lockwood, Phyllis Calvert, James Mason, Stewart Granger; 116 mins.

Men of Two Worlds: 1946; Two Cities; *Producer* – John Sutro; *Director* – Thorold Dickinson; *Cast* – Eric Portman, Phyllis Calvert; 109 mins.

Millions Like Us: 1943; Gainsborough; *Producer* – Edward Black; *Directors* – Frank

Launder, Sidney Gilliat; *Cast* – Patricia Roc, Eric Portman, Gordon Jackson; 103 mins.

Mrs T. and her Cabbage Patch: 1941; Gaumont-British Instructional with cooperation of Board of Education; *Director* – Mary Field; *Commentator* – William Ashley; 13 mins.

My Learned Friend: 1943; Ealing; *Producer* – Michael Balcon; *Director* – Basil Dearden, Will Hay; *Cast* – Will Hay, Claude Hulbert; 76 mins.

The Next of Kin: 1942; Ealing; *Producer* – Michael Balcon; *Director* – Thorold Dickinson; *Cast* – Mervyn Johns, John Chandos; 102 mins.

The 1940s House (television series, 5 episodes): 2001; Wall to Wall Television for Channel 4 Television.

Ninotchka (USA): 1939; MGM; *Producer* – Sidney Franklin; *Producer, Director* – Ernst Lubitsch; *Cast* – Greta Barbo, Melvyn Douglas, Bela Lugosi; 110 mins.

Noose: 1948; Edward Dryhurst Productions for ABPC; *Producer* – Edward Dryhurst; *Director* – Edmund T. Greville; *Cast* – Joseph Calleia, Nigel Patrick, Derek Farr; 95 mins.

The Nose Has It: 1942; Gainsborough for Ministry of Information; *Producer* – Edward Black; *Director* – Val Guest; *Cast* – Arthur Askey; 7 mins.

Old Mother Riley, Detective: 1943; British National; *Producer* – John Baxter; *Director* – Lance Comfort; *Cast* – Arthur Lucan, Kitty McShane, Ivan Brandt; 80 mins.

Old Mother Riley in Society: 1940; British National; *Producer* – John Corfield; *Director* – John Baxter; *Cast* – Arthur Lucan, Kitty McShane; 81 mins.

Old Mother Riley Joins Up: 1939; British National; *Producer* – John Corfield; *Director* – Maclean Rogers; *Cast* – Arthur Lucan, Kitty McShane; 75 mins.

Old Mother Riley MP: 1939; Butcher's; *Producer* – F. W. Baker; *Director* – Oswald Mitchell; *Cast* – Arthur Lucan, Kitty McShane, Henry Longhurst; 77 mins.

Old Mother Riley's Circus: 1941; British National; *Producer* – Wallace Orton; *Director* – Thomas Bentley; *Cast* – Arthur Lucan, Kitty McShane; 80 mins.

Partners in Crime: 1942; Gainsborough for Ministry of Information; *Producer* – Edward Black; *Directors* – Frank Launder, Sidney Gilliat; *Cast* – Robert Morley, Irene Handl; 8 mins.

Passport to Pimlico: 1949; Ealing; *Producer* – Michael Balcon; *Director* – Henry Cornelius; *Cast* – Stanley Holloway, Paul Dupuis, Margaret Rutherford; 84 mins.

Perfect Strangers: 1945; London Films; *Producer, Director* – Alexander Korda; *Cast* – Robert Donat, Deborah Kerr; 102 mins.

The Peterville Diamond: 1942; WB-First National; *Producer* – A. H. Salomon; *Director* – Walter Forde; *Cast* – Anne Crawford, Donald Stewart; 85 mins.

Playtime for Workers: 1943; Federated Film Corporation; *Producer* – M. Swift; *Director* – Harold Baim; *Cast* – Gerry Wilmot, The Cavendish Three; 51 minutes.

Queen's Messengers: 1941; Strand for Ministry of Information; *Producer, Director* – Jay Gardner Lewis; 5 mins.

Sailors Three: 1940; Ealing; *Producer* – Michael Balcon; *Director* – Walter Forde; *Cast* – Tommy Trinder, Claude Hulbert, Michael Wilding; 86 mins.

Saloon Bar: 1940; Ealing; *Producer* – Michael Balcon; *Director* – Walter Forde; *Cast* –

Gordon Harker, Mervyn Johns; 76 mins.

San Demetrio, London: 1943; Ealing; *Producer* – Michael Balcon; *Director* – Charles Frend; *Cast* – Walter Fitzgerald, Ralph Michael, Gordon Jackson; 104 mins.

Secret Mission: 1942; Excelsior for Independent Producers; *Producer* – Marcel Hellman; *Director* – Harold French; *Cast* – Hugh Williams, Michael Wilding, Roland Culver, James Mason; 94 mins.

Spare a Copper: 1940; Ealing/Associated Talking Pictures; *Producer* – Michael Balcon; *Director* – John Paddy Carstairs; *Cast* – George Formby, Dorothy Hyson; 77 mins.

Sport at the Local: 1940; Cameo; *Director* – Mr Carr; *Commentator* – A. P. Herbert; 20 mins.

Tawny Pipit: 1944; Two Cities; *Producers* – Bernard Miles, William Sistrom; *Directors* – Bernard Miles, Charles Saunders; *Cast* – Bernard Miles, Rosamund John, Niall MacGinnis; 81 mins.

Theatre Royal: 1943; British National; *Producer, Director* – John Baxter; *Cast* – Bud Flanagan, Chesney Allen; 92 mins.

They Made Me a Fugitive: 1947; Gloria Films for Warner Bros. ; *Producers* – N. A. Bronsten, James Carter; *Director* – Alberto Cavalcanti; *Cast* – Trevor Howard, Sally Gray, Griffith Jones; 103 mins.

This England (Scotland: *Our Heritage*): 1941; British National; *Producer* – John Corfield; *Director* – David Macdonald; *Cast* – John Clements, Emlyn Williams, Constance Cummings; 84 mins.

This Happy Breed:
1944; Cineguild for Two Cities; *Producers* – Noel Coward. Anthony Havelock-Allan; *Director* – David Lean; *Cast* – Celia Johnson, Robert Newton, John Mills, Kay Walsh; 111 mins.

Thunder Birds (USA): 1942; Twentieth Century-Fox; *Producer* – Lamar Trotti; *Director* – William Wellman; *Cast* – Gene Tierney, Preston Foster, John Sutton; 78 mins.

Two Cooks and a Cabbage: 1941; A & D Productions for Ministry of Information; *Director* – Alex Bryce; *Cast* – Mrs Inglestone; 6 mins.

Two Thousand Women: 1944; Gainsborough; *Producer* – Edward Black; *Director* – Frank Launder; *Cast* – Phyllis Calvert, Flora Robson, Patricia Roc, Renee Houston; 97 mins.

Unpublished Story: 1942; Two Cities; *Producer* – Anthony Havelock-Allen; *Director* – Harold French; *Cast* – Richard Greene, Valerie Hobson; 92 mins.

Up With the Lark: 1943; New Realm; *Producer* – E. J. Fancey; *Director* – Phil Brandon; *Cast* – Ethel Revnell, Gracie West, Anthony Hulme; 83 mins.

Warwork News (series, 81 episodes, 1942–45): British Paramount News for Ministry of Supply.

Waterloo Road: 1945; Gainsborough; *Producer* – Edward Black; *Director* – Sidney Gilliat; *Cast* – Alistair Sim, John Mills, Stewart Granger; 76 mins.

The Way Ahead: 1944; Two Cities; *Producers* – John Sutro, Norman Walker; *Director* – Carol Reed; *Cast* – David Niven, Stanley Holloway, John Laurie; 115 mins.

The Way to His Heart: 1942; Strand for Ministry of Food; *Director* – Donald Taylor; *Cast* – The Aspidistras; 2 mins.

The Way to the Stars: 1945; Two Cities; *Producer* – Anatole de Grunwald; *Director* – Anthony Asquith; *Cast* – Michael Redgrave, John Mills, Rosamund John, Douglass Montgomery; 109 mins.

We Dive at Dawn: 1943; Gainsborough; *Producer* – Edward Black; *Director* – Anthony Asquith; *Cast* – John Mills, Eric Portman; 98 mins.

A Welcome to Britain: 1943; Strand for Ministry of Information (for US Army); *Producer* – Arthur Elton; *Director* – Anthony Asquith; *Cast* – Burgess Meredith, Felix Aylmer, Bob Hope; 55 mins.

Went the Day Well?: 1942; Ealing; *Producer* – Michael Balcon; *Director* – Alberto Cavalcanti; *Cast* – Leslie Banks, Valerie Taylor, Basil Sydney; 92 mins.

The Wicked Lady: 1945; Gainsborough; *Producer* – R. J. Minney; *Director* – Leslie Arliss; *Cast* – Margaret Lockwood, James Mason, Patricia Roc, Griffith Jones; 104 mins.

World of Plenty: 1943; Paul Rotha Productions for Ministry of Information; *Producer, Director* – Paul Rotha; *Commentators* – Eric Knight, E. V. H. Emmett; *Cast* – Lord Woolton, Sir John Orr; 46 mins.

A Yank in the RAF (USA): 1941; Twentieth-Century Fox; *Producer* – Darryl F. Zanuck; *Director* – Henry King; *Cast* – Tyrone Power, Betty Grable; 98 mins.

The Young Mr Pitt: 1942; Gainsborough for Twentieth Century-Fox British Productions; *Producer* – Edward Black; *Director* – Carol Reed; *Cast* – Robert Donat, Robert Morley, John Mills; 118 mins.

Bibliography

Archival and unpublished sources

The National Archives, Kew, London

BT 64/4747: Wartime Social Survey: Ministry of Information inquiry into cinema audiences.

INF 1/214: *World of Plenty.*

INF 1/343: Publicity on Behalf of the Ministry of Food.

INF 6/1831: *The Way to His Heart.*

MAF 75/67: Public Relations and Food Advice (Including Finance).

MAF 102/2: *Kitchen Front* Broadcasts.

MAF 102/53: Queen's Hall Meeting: Publicity.

MAF 102/59: Minister's Public Relations: Correspondence.

MAF 102/65: Food Facts Pulls.

MAF 129/110: Treasury Letters: Publicity.

MAF 138/160: Public Accounts Committee Reports.

MAF 138/161: Public Accounts Committee Reports.

MAF 138/162: Public Accounts Committee Reports.

MAF 138/163: Public Accounts Committee Reports.

MAF 156/195: Public Relations Division: General Papers and Reports.

MAF 286/19: Prime Minister's Correspondence: Enforcement.

PREM 4/2/2: Policy; Ministry of Food.

RG 23/9a: Food During the War: A Summary of Studies.

RG 23/18: Short Reports on Food Publicity, Shopping and Shortages.

RG 23/46: Report on the 'Eat More Potatoes' campaign.

British Film Institute, London

BFI Microfiche Collection: Press Book – *Gert and Daisy Clean Up.*

BFI Microfiche Collection: Press Book – *Madonna of the Seven Moons.*

BFI Microfiche Collection: Press Book – *Old Mother Riley, Detective.*

BFI Microfiche Collection: Press Book – *Up With the Lark.*

BFI Microfiche Collection: Press Book – *The Young Mr Pitt.*

BFI Script Collection: S15094 – 'Amended Final Shooting Script' for *San Demetrio, London*, 20 January 1943.

BFI Script Collection: S202 – 'Second Shooting Script' for *Passport to Pimlico*, 9 July 1948.

BFI Special Collections: *British Board of Film Censors Scenario Notes*, 1941–1942–1943, 1944–1945.

BFI Special Collections: BECTU Oral History Project – Tape 465: Esther Harris.

History of Advertising Trust, Raveningham, Norfolk

'Official History of the Publicity Club of London' (4 volumes, unpublished, no date).

The Woolton Papers, Bodleian Library, Oxford

MS Woolton 2 – Diary: September 1940 to 1942.

MS Woolton 3 – Diary: September 1942 to 1960.

MS Woolton 11 – Correspondence and Papers as Minister of Food, March to December 1940.

MS Woolton 12 – Correspondence and Papers as Minister of Food, January 1941 to July 1942.

MS Woolton 13 – Correspondence and Papers as Minister of Food, August 1942 to November 1943.

Published government documents

Central Statistical Office, *Annual Abstract of Statistics, No. 84: 1935–1946* (London: HMSO, 1948).

Parliamentary Debates: House of Commons, 5th Series.

Parliamentary Debates: House of Lords, 5th Series.

Report from the Committee of Public Accounts, Session 1941–42 (London: HMSO, 1942).

Report from the Committee of Public Accounts, Session 1942–43 (London: HMSO, 1943).

Report from the Committee of Public Accounts, Session 1944–45 (London: HMSO, 1945).

Report of the Committee on the Cost of Home Information Services (London: HMSO, 1949).

Periodicals, newspapers and trade papers

Periodicals

Announcer

Documentary News Letter

The Economist

Ministry of Food Bulletin

Monthly Film Bulletin

Programme of the National Film Theatre

Picturegoer

Picture Post
Picture Show
Sight and Sound
Spectator
Time

Newspapers

Cambridge Daily News
Daily Express
Daily Herald
Daily Mail
Daily Mirror
Evening News
Evening Standard
Manchester Guardian
Observer
Saturday Evening Post
The Times
Tribune

Trade papers

Advertiser's Weekly
Daily Film Renter
Kinematograph Weekly
Today's Cinema

Books and journal articles

Addison, Paul and Jeremy A. Crang (eds), *Listening to Britain: Home Intelligence Reports on Britain's Finest Hour, May to September 1940* (London: Bodley Head, 2010).

Aldgate, Anthony and Jeffrey Richards, *Britain Can Take It: The British Cinema in the Second World War* (Edinburgh: Edinburgh University Press, 2nd edn, 1994).

Aspinall, Sue and Robert Murphy (eds), *BFI Dossier Number 18: Gainsborough Melodrama* (London: BFI, 1983).

Banks, Morwenna and Amanda Swift, *The Joke's On Us: Women in Comedy from Music Hall to the Present Day* (London: Pandora, 1987).

Barr, Charles, *Ealing Studios* (London: University of California Press, 3rd edn, 1998).

—— (ed.), *All Our Yesterdays: 90 Years of British Cinema* (London: BFI, 1986).

Barr, Terry, 'Eating kosher, staying closer: families and meals in contemporary Jewish American cinema', *Journal of Popular Film and Television*, 24:3 (1996).

BBC Handbook, 1941 (London: Hazell, Watson and Viney, 1941).

Belasco, Warren, 'Food matters: perspectives on an emerging field', in Warren Belasco and Philip Scranton (eds), *Food Nations: Selling Taste in Consumer Societies* (London: Routledge, 2002).

—— and Philip Scranton (eds), *Food Nations: Selling Taste in Consumer Societies* (London: Routledge, 2002).

Bell, Amy Helen, *London Was Ours: Diaries and Memoirs of the Blitz* (London: I. B. Tauris, 2008).

Bell, P. M. H., *John Bull and the Bear: British Public Opinion, Foreign Policy and the Soviet Union, 1941–1945* (London: Edward Arnold, 1990).

Bergen, Ronald, *Beyond the Fringe … and Beyond* (London: Virgin Books, 1989).

Bird, Peter, *The First Food Empire: A History of J Lyons & Co.* (Chichester: Phillimore, 2000).

Blishen, Edward, *A Cackhanded War* (London: Thames & Hudson, 1972).

Bond, Brian (ed.), *Chief of Staff: The Diaries of Sir Henry Pownall: Vol. 2 – 1940–1944* (London: Leo Cooper, 1974).

Bower, Anne L. (ed.), *Reel Food: Essays on Food and Film* (London: Routledge, 2004).

Briggs, Asa, *The History of Broadcasting in the United Kingdom: Vol. III – The War of Words* (Oxford: Oxford University Press, revised edn, 1995).

Broad, Richard and Suzie Fleming (eds), *Nella Last's War: The Second World War Diaries of Housewife, 49* (London: Profile, 2006).

Brown, Geoff, *Launder and Gilliat* (London: BFI, 1977).

Browning, H. E. and A. A. Sorrell, 'Cinemas and cinemagoing in Great Britain', *Journal of the Royal Statistical Society*, 117:2 (1954).

Burton, Elaine, *And Your Verdict?* (London: Frederick Muller, 1942).

Butler, Margaret, *Film and Community in Britain and France: From* La Regle du Jeu *to* Room at the Top (London: I. B. Tauris, 2004).

Calder, Angus, *The People's War: Britain, 1939–45* (London: Jonathan Cape, 1969).

——, *The Myth of the Blitz* (London: Jonathan Cape, 1991).

—— and Dorothy Sheridan (eds), *Speak for Yourself: A Mass-Observation Anthology, 1937–49* (London: Jonathan Cape, 1984).

Chapman, James, '*The Life and Death of Colonel Blimp* (1943) reconsidered', *Historical Journal of Film, Radio and Television*, 15:1 (1995).

——, *The British at War: Cinema, State and Propaganda, 1939–1945* (London: I. B. Tauris, 1998).

Chibnall, Steve and Robert Murphy (eds), *British Crime Cinema* (London: Routledge, 1999).

Chibnall, Steve, *Quota Quickies: The Birth of the British 'B' Film* (London: BFI, 2007).

Christie, Ian (ed.), *Powell, Pressburger and Others* (London: BFI, 1978).

Churchill, Winston, *The Second World War: Vol. III – The Grand Alliance* (London: Cassell, 1950).

Clark, David B. , Marcus A. Doel and Kate M. L. Housiaux (eds), *The Consumption Reader* (London: Routledge, 2003).

Cole, J. A., *Lord Haw-Haw – and William Joyce: The Full Story* (London: Faber & Faber, 1964).

Cook, Ian and Philip Crang, 'The world on a plate: culinary culture, displacement and geographical knowledge', in David B. Clark, Marcus A. Doel and Kate M. L. Housiaux (eds), *The Consumption Reader* (London: Routledge, 2003).

Cook, Pam, 'Neither here nor there: national identity in Gainsborough costume drama', in Andrew Higson (ed.), *Dissolving Views: Key Writings on British Cinema* (London: Cassell, 1996).

——, *Fashioning the Nation: Costume and Identity in British Cinema* (London: BFI, 1996).

Costello, John, *Love, Sex and War: Changing Values, 1939–45* (London: Collins, 1985).

Davies, Jennifer, *The Wartime Kitchen and Garden* (London: BBC Books, 1993).

Delafield, E. M., *Diary of a Provincial Lady* (London: Macmillan, 1930).

Dickens, Charles, *Our Mutual Friend* (London: Penguin, 1997).

Donnelly, Peter (ed.), *Mrs Milburn's Diaries: An Englishwoman's Day-to-Day Reflections, 1939–1945* (London: Abacus, 1995).

Douglas, Mary and Baron Isherwood, *The World of Goods: Towards an Anthropology of Consumption* (London: Allen Lane, 1979).

Drake, Barbara, *Community Feeding in Wartime* (London: The Fabian Society and Victor Gollancz, 1942).

Durgnat, Raymond, *A Mirror for England: British Movies from Austerity to Affluence* (London: Faber & Faber, 1970).

Ellis, John, 'The quality film adventure: British critics and the cinema, 1942–48', in Andrew Higson (ed.), *Dissolving Views: Key Writings on British Cinema* (London: Cassell, 1996).

Farmer, Richard, 'Exploiting a universal nostalgia for steak and onions: the Ministry of Information and the promotion of *World of Plenty* (1943)', *Historical Journal of Film, Radio and Television*, 30:2 (2010).

Ferry, Jane F., *Food in Film: A Culinary Performance of Communication* (London: Routledge, 2003).

Fine, Gary Alan, *Kitchen: The Culture of Restaurant Work* (Berkeley: University of California Press, 1996).

Finkelstein, Joanne, *Dining Out: A Sociology of Modern Manners* (Oxford: Polity Press, 1989).

Fischler, Claude, 'Food, self and identity', *Social Science Information*, 27:2 (1988).

Fleming, Kate, *Celia Johnson: A Biography* (London: Weidenfeld & Nicolson, 1991).

Fox, Jo, *Film Propaganda in Britain and Nazi Germany: World War II Cinema* (Oxford: Berg, 2007).

Fox, Kate, *Watching the English: The Hidden Rules of English Behaviour* (London: Hodder & Stoughton, 2004).

The Gallup International Public Opinion Poll: Great Britain 1937–1975: Vol. 1 – 1937–1964 (New York: Random House, 1976).

Garfield, Simon (ed.), *We are at War: The Remarkable Diaries of Five Ordinary People in Extraordinary Times* (London: Ebury Press, 2005).

—— (ed.), *Private Battles: How the War Almost Defeated Us* (London: Ebury Press, 2006).

Gifford, Denis, *The British Film Catalogue: Vol. 1 – Fiction Film, 1895–1994* (London: Fitzroy Dearborn, 2001).

——, *The British Film Catalogue: Vol. 2 – Non-Fiction Film, 1888–1994* (London: Fitzroy Dearborn, 2001).

Gilbert, Martin (ed.), *The Churchill War Papers: Vol. 2 – Never Surrender, May 1940–December 1940* (London: Heinemann, 1994).

——, *The Churchill War Papers: Vol. 3 – The Ever-Widening War, 1941* (London: Heinemann, 2000).

Gledhill, Christine (ed.), *Home Is Where The Heart Is: Studies in Melodrama and the Woman's Film* (London: BFI, 1987).

—— and Gillian Swanson (eds), *Nationalising Femininity: Culture, Sexuality and British Cinema in the Second World War* (Manchester: Manchester University Press, 1996).

Greene, Graham, *The Last Word and Other Stories* (London: Reinhardt Books, 1990).

Grisewood, Frederick, *The World Goes By* (London: Secker & Warburg, 1952).

Hammond, R. J. , *Food: Vol. I – The Growth of Policy* (London: HMSO, 1951).

——, *Food: Vol. II – Studies in Administration and Control* (London: HMSO, 1956).

——, *Food: Vol. III – Studies in Administration and Control* (London: HMSO, 1962).

Harper, Sue, 'Historical pleasures: Gainsborough costume melodramas', in Christine Gledhill (ed.), *Home Is Where The Heart Is: Studies in Melodrama and the Woman's Film* (London: BFI, 1987).

——, *Picturing the Past: The Rise and Fall of the British Costume Film* (London: BFI, 1994).

——, 'Fragmentation and crisis: 1940s admission figures at the Regent cinema, Portsmouth, UK', *Historical Journal of Film, Radio and Television*, 26:3 (2006).

Harvey, Frank, *Saloon Bar: A Play in Three Acts* (London: Year Book Press, 1942).

Haskell, Arnold L., Dilys Powell, Rollo Myers and Robin Ironside, *Since 1939: Ballet, Films, Music, Painting* (London: Phoenix House, 1948).

Hepworth, Cecil, *Came the Dawn: Memories of a Film Pioneer* (London: Phoenix House, 1951).

Higson, Andrew, *Waving the Flag: Constructing a National Cinema in Britain* (Oxford: Clarendon Press, 1995).

—— (ed.), *Dissolving Views: Key Writings on British Cinema* (London: Cassell, 1996).

Hill, Charles, *Both Sides of the Hill* (London: Heinemann, 1964).

——, *Behind the Screen: The Broadcasting Memoirs of Lord Hill of Luton* (London: Sidgwick & Jackson, 1974).

Hodgkinson, Anthony W., and Rodney E. Sheratsky, *Humphrey Jennings – More Than a Maker of Films* (Hanover and London: University Press of New England, 1982).

Hodgson, Vere, *Few Eggs and No Oranges: A Diary Showing How Unimportant People in London and Birmingham Lived Through the War Years, 1940–1945* (London: Dennis Dobson, 1976).

Holmes, Winifred, 'Mild or bitter?', *Sight and Sound*, 12:48 (1944).

Hurd, Geoff (ed.), *National Fictions: World War Two in British Films and Television* (London: BFI, 1984).

Jackson, Kevin (ed.), *The Humphrey Jennings Film Reader* (Manchester: Carcanet, 1993).

Jay, Douglas, *The Socialist Case* (London: Faber & Faber, 1947).

Jones, Thomas G., *The Unbroken Front: Ministry of Food, 1916–1944 – Personalities and Problems* (London: Everybody's Books, 1944).

King, Steve, *As Long As I Know, It'll Be Quite Alright: The Life Stories of Lucan and McShane* (Blackpool: Lancastrian Transport Publications, 1999).

King-Hall, Magdalen, *Life and Death of the Wicked Lady Skelton* (London: Peter Davies, 1974).

Kuhn, Annette, '*Desert Victory* and the People's War', *Screen*, 22:2 (1981).

——, *An Everyday Magic: Cinema and Cultural Memory* (London: I. B. Tauris, 2002).

Lant, Antonia, *Blackout: Reinventing Women for Wartime British Cinema* (Princeton, NJ: Princeton University Press, 1991).

Lawrence, Margery, *The Madonna of Seven Moons* (London: Hurst and Blackett, 1931).

Longmate, Norman, *How We Lived Then: A History of Everyday Life During the Second World War* (London: Hutchinson, 1971).

Mackay, Robert, *Half the Battle: Civilian Morale in Britain During the Second World War* (Manchester: Manchester University Press, 2002).

MacKenzie, S. P., 'Nazis into Germans: *Went the Day Well?* (1942) and *The Eagle Has Landed* (1976)', *Journal of Popular Film and Television*, 31:2 (2003).

Mais, S. P. B., *Calling Again: My* Kitchen Front *Talks with Some Results on the Listener* (London: John Crowther, 1941).

Malcolmson, Patricia and Robert Malcolmson (eds), *Nella Last's Peace: The Post-War Diaries of Housewife, 49* (London: Profile, 2008).

Malcolmson, Robert (ed.), *Love and War in London: A Woman's Diary, 1939–1942* (Stroud: History Press, 2008).

Manvell, Roger, *The Film and the Public* (Harmondsworth: Penguin, 1955).

Mass-Observation, *Home Propaganda* (*Bulletin of the Advertising Service Guild*, No. 2) (London: Curwen Press, 1941).

——, *People in Production: An Enquiry into British War Production, Part 1* (London: John Murray, 1942).

——, *The Pub and the People: A Worktown Study* (London: Victor Gollancz, 1943).

Mathews, Tom Dewe, *Censored. What They Didn't Allow You To See and Why: The Story of Film Censorship in Britain* (London: Chatto & Windus, 1994).

Mayer, J. P. , *British Cinemas and Their Audiences* (London: Dennis Dobson, 1948).

McLaine, Ian, *Ministry of Morale: Home Front Morale and the Ministry of Information in World War II* (London: George Allen and Unwin, 1979).

Medhurst, Andy, 'Music hall and British cinema', in Charles Barr (ed.), *All Our Yesterdays: 90 Years of British Cinema* (London: BFI, 1986).

Mencken, H. L., 'War words in England', *American Speech*, 19:1 (1944).

Mosley, Leonard, *Backs to the Wall: London Under Fire, 1939–45* (London: Weidenfeld & Nicolson, 1971).

Murphy, Robert, *Realism and Tinsel: Cinema and Society in Britain, 1939–49* (London: Routledge, 1989).

——, 'Riff-raff: British cinema and the underworld', in Charles Barr (ed.), *All Our Yesterdays: 90 Years of British Cinema* (London: BFI Publishing, 1986).

National Council of Social Service, *British Restaurants: An Inquiry* (London: Oxford University Press, 1946).

Nicholas, Siân, *The Echo of War: Home Front Propaganda and the Wartime BBC, 1939–45* (Manchester: Manchester University Press, 1996).

Olivier, Laurence, *Confessions of an Actor* (London: Weidenfeld & Nicolson, 1982).

Orwell, Sonia and Ian Angus (eds), *The Collected Essays, Journalism and Letters of George Orwell: Vol. 2 – As I Please* (London: Secker & Warburg, 1968).

Pimlott, Ben (ed.), *The Second World War Diary of Hugh Dalton, 1940–45* (London: Jonathan Cape, 1986).

Poole, Gaye, *Reel Meals, Set Meals: Food in Film and Theatre* (Sydney: Currency Press, 1999).

Poole, Julian, 'British cinema attendance in wartime: audience preference at the Majestic, Macclesfield, 1939–46', *Historical Journal of Film, Radio and Television*, 7:1 (1987).

Powell, Dilys, 'Films since 1939', in Arnold L. Haskell, Dilys Powell, Rollo Myers and Robin Ironside, *Since 1939: Ballet, Films, Music, Painting* (London: Phoenix House, 1948).

Priestley, J. B., *The Good Companions* (London: Heinemann, 1929).

——, *Britain Speaks* (New York: Harper and Brothers, 1940).

——, *Postscripts* (London: Heinemann, 1940).

——, *British Women Go to War* (London: Collins, 1943).

Pulleine, Tim, 'Spin a dark web', in Steve Chibnall and Robert Murphy (eds), *British Crime Cinema* (London: Routledge, 1999).

Ramsden, John, *The Age of Churchill and Eden, 1940–1957* (Harlow: Longman, 1995).

——, *An Appetite for Power: A History of the Conservative Party Since 1930* (London: HarperCollins, 1998).

Reynolds, Quentin, *The Wounded Don't Cry* (London: Cassell, 1941).

Richards, Jeffrey, *The Age of the Dream Palace: Cinema and Society in Britain, 1930–1939* (London: Routledge & Kegan Paul, 1984).

——, 'Wartime British cinema audiences and the class system: the case of *Ships With Wings* (1941)', *Historical Journal of Film, Radio and Television*, 7:2 (1987).

——, 'Cinemagoing in Worktown: regional film audiences in 1930s Britain', *Historical Journal of Film, Radio and Television*, 14:2 (1994).

——, *Films and British National Identity: From Dickens to* Dad's Army (Manchester: Manchester University Press, 1997).

Robbins, Keith, *Great Britain: Identities, Institutions and the Idea of Britishness* (London: Longman, 1998).

Robertson, Alex J., *The Bleak Midwinter: 1947* (Manchester: Manchester University Press, 1987).

Ryall, Tom, *Anthony Asquith* (Manchester: University of Manchester Press, 2005).

Sevareid, Eric, *Not So Wild a Dream* (New York: Alfred A. Knopf, 1946).

Shawn, William (ed.), *London War Notes, 1939–1945* (London: Longman, 1972).

Silvey, R. J. E., 'Listening in 1940', in *BBC Handbook, 1941* (London: Hazell, Watson and Viney, 1941).

Slide, Anthony, *'Banned in the USA': British Films in the United States and Their Censorship, 1933–1960* (London: I. B. Tauris, 1998).

Smithies, Edward, *Crime in Wartime: A Social History of Crime in World War II* (London: George Allen & Unwin, 1982).

——, *The Black Economy in England Since 1914* (Dublin: Gill & Macmillan, 1984).

Social Issues Research Centre, *Social and Cultural Aspects of Drinking: A Report to the Amsterdam Group* (A report presented to the European Commission on 29 November 2000).

Spicer, Andrew, *Typical Men: The Representation of Masculinity in Popular British Cinema* (London: I. B. Tauris, 2001).

Stacey, Jackie, *Star Gazing: Hollywood Cinema and Female Spectatorship* (London: Routledge, 1994).

Stokes, Lisa Odham and Michael Hoover, 'Food fight, food fight: culture and economy in *Chicken and Duck Talk*', *Asian Cinema*, 14:2 (2003).

St Pierre, Paul Matthew, *Song and Sketch Transcripts of British Music Hall Performers Elsie and Doris Waters* (Lewiston, NY: Edwin Mellen Press, 2003).

Sutton, David, *A Chorus of Raspberries: British Film Comedy 1929–39* (Exeter: University of Exeter Press, 2000).

Swann, Paul, *The British Documentary Film Movement, 1926–1946* (Cambridge: Cambridge University Press, 1989).

Swanson, Gillian, '"So much money and so little to spend it on": morale, consumption and sexuality', in Christine Gledhill and Gillian Swanson (eds), *Nationalising Femininity: Culture, Sexuality and British Cinema in the Second World War* (Manchester: Manchester University Press, 1996).

Taylor, A. J. P., *English History, 1914–1945* (Harmondsworth: Pelican, 1970).

The Tea Centre, *Tea on Service* (London: Graham Watson, 1947).

Thomas, Donald, *An Underworld at War: Spivs, Deserters, Racketeers and Civilians in the Second World War* (London: John Murray, 2003).

Thorpe, Frances and Nicholas Pronay, *British Official Films in the Second World War: A Descriptive Catalogue* (Oxford: Clio Press, 1980).

Tritton, Paul, A Canterbury Tale*: Memories of a Classic Wartime Movie* (Maidstone: Tritton Publications, 2000).

Turner, E. S., *The Phoney War on the Home Front* (London: Michael Joseph, 1961).

Waller, Jane and Michael Vaughan-Rees, *Women in Wartime: The Role of Women's Magazines, 1939–1945* (London: Optima, 1987).

Walton, John K., *Fish and Chips and the British Working Class, 1870–1940* (Leicester: Leicester University Press, 1992).

Weymouth, Anthony, *Plague Year, March 1940–February 1941* (London: George G. Harrap, 1942).

Wilt, Alan F., *Food for War: Agriculture and Rearmament in Britain Before the Second World War* (Oxford: Oxford University Press, 2001).

Wing, Sandra Koa (ed.), *Our Longest Days: A People's History of the Second World War* (London: Profile, 2008).

Wollen, Peter, 'Riff-raff realism', *Sight and Sound*, 8:4 (1998).

Wood, Linda (ed.), *British Films, 1927–1939* (London: BFI, 1986).

Woolton, Lord, 'Introduction', in The Tea Centre, *Tea on Service* (London: Graham Watson, 1947).

——, *The Memoirs of the Rt. Hon. The Earl of Woolton* (London: Cassell, 1959).

Ziegler, Philip, *London at War, 1939–1945* (London: Sinclair-Stevenson, 1995).

Zimmerman, Steve and Weiss, Ken, *Food in the Movies* (Jefferson, North Carolina: MacFarland, 2005).

Zweiniger-Bargielowska, Ina, 'Bread rationing in Britain, July 1946–July 1948', *Twentieth Century British History*, 4:1 (1993).

——, *Austerity in Britain: Rationing, Controls, and Consumption, 1939–1955* (Oxford: Oxford University Press, 2000).

Index

Notes: 'n.' after a page reference indicates the number of a note on that page. Numbers that appear in italics refer to an illustration on that page.